T0336479

Going Beyond The Waterfall

Managing Scope Effectively
Across the Project Life Cycle

Barbara Davis
Darren Radford

J.ROSS
PUBLISHING

Copyright © 2014 by Barbara A. Davis and Darren Radford

ISBN-13: 978-1-60427-090-7

Printed and bound in the U.S.A. Printed on acid-free paper.

10 9 8 7 6 5 4 3 2 1

Library of Congress Cataloging-in-Publication Data

Davis, Barbara, 1969-
  Going beyond the waterfall : managing scope effectively across the project life cycle / by Barbara Davis and Darren Radford.
     pages cm
  Includes bibliographical references and index.
  ISBN 978-1-60427-090-7 (hardcover : alk. paper)
  1. Project management. 2. Business planning. I. Radford, Darren, 1972-
II. Title.
  HD69.P75D384 2014
  658.4'04--dc23
                                  2014011202

This publication contains information obtained from authentic and highly regarded sources. Reprinted material is used with permission, and sources are indicated. Reasonable effort has been made to publish reliable data and information, but the author and the publisher cannot assume responsibility for the validity of all materials or for the consequences of their use.

All rights reserved. Neither this publication nor any part thereof may be reproduced, stored in a retrieval system, or transmitted in any form or by any means, electronic, mechanical, photocopying, recording or otherwise, without the prior written permission of the publisher.

PMI, PMP, OPM3, PgMP, PfMP, and PMBOK are registered marks of Project Management Institute, Inc. PMI does not endorse or otherwise sponsor this publication.

The copyright owner's consent does not extend to copying for general distribution for promotion, for creating new works, or for resale. Specific permission must be obtained from J. Ross Publishing for such purposes.

Direct all inquiries to J. Ross Publishing, Inc., 300 S. Pine Island Rd., Suite 305, Plantation, FL 33324.

Phone: (954) 727-9333
Fax: (561) 892-0700
Web: www.jrosspub.com

DEDICATION

On behalf of Barbara, this book is dedicated to:

My husband Robert, for bringing out the best in me and inspiring me to reach higher every single day.

Amy Ruddell, for bringing together great and passionate experts at conferences across North America and helping me to be a part of that.

On behalf of Darren, this book is dedicated to:

My wonderful wife Sunny, for her kindness, devotion, endless support, and proving that behind every great man is indeed a better woman! Here's to kicking up the Autumn leaves with the children...

TABLE OF CONTENTS

FOREWORD

"I'M WATER-GILE!"

I have been building software for over 15 years. I've been on the front line as a programmer, led teams as a Vice President, engaged clients as a business owner, and am currently creating best-of-class software for distributed workforces as an entrepreneur. Over the years, I have honed a process that helps ensure quality development and timely deliveries. A good portion of that process is the topic of this book.

Back in the days when I was a programmer, I had the privilege of working on a large, Vice Chairman-backed project that led to my eventual promotion to Vice President. The company was a start-up and needed to move fast. In those days the conventional wisdom was that Agile, practiced to the letter, was the most efficient way of delivering software. Waterfall was a bad word . . . and watch out if you even hinted at a waterfall method.

When the project started, I followed Agile methodically. I delivered in bi-weekly sprints, and demoed my progress to a team of stakeholders for feedback. Post feedback, I would prepare the next sprint. This was Agile, and I was good at "Agile." But something was bugging me. We knew where we wanted to go long term . . . we knew the long-term vision of the software. We knew where we were going short term . . . the bi-weekly sprints defined our short-term deliverables. But we didn't know what we wanted to do for the mid-term. In other words, we knew where we wanted to be one year from now and where we wanted to be two weeks from now, but nobody could say where we wanted to be six months from now.

I felt it was imperative that everyone on the team know the long-term vision, the short-term deliverable, and the mid-term goals. In other words, instead of "winging it" each sprint, let's plan out our next six months now. Then, after each bi-weekly demo and stakeholder feedback, we could plan our next sprints from two perspectives . . . the feedback from the last two weeks and the current, mid-term goals.

I suggested this new plan to my boss, the senior architect at the company. He cited that it smelled like waterfall and that the time needed to plan and revise requirement docs would be a waste of time. After all, Agile is meant to replace the stacks of upfront requirements because we don't really know what we want. Right?

I heard my boss' advice, but I decided to implement this new process anyway. At the next bi-weekly demo, I asked the stakeholders where they'd like to see the product six months from now. They were all eager to jump in and offer goals. After an hour or so of weeding the best goals, we came up with a six month plan. The regular demo followed, and guess what? As the stakeholders provided their end-of-sprint feedback, they frequently referred to six-month plan . . . instant success!

The next demo, two weeks later, began with a review of the mid-term goals. Some minor modifications were made that were precipitated by a change in market conditions. Those changes rippled into the next sprint. This is the process that was honed over two-and-a-half years. I eventually became VP of Product Development at the company and had a process I could call my own.

These days, when a client asks me if I follow the waterfall method or the Agile method, I respond, "I'm water-gile." I explain what that means and describe the development process that I honed. The process is especially useful for teams that are distributed, as I built the entire process into my latest business, Spotlight, a communication and task management platform for distributed teams.

Going Beyond the Waterfall is a masterful guide to creating and navigating changing requirements. I wish that I had this book ten years ago when I was honing my craft . . . it would have saved me a few years of trial and error. You now have the opportunity to leapfrog your skill set.

Good luck and much success!

Vincent Serpico
Founder, CEO Spotlight Software
http://GetSpotlight.com

PREFACE

THE PURPOSE OF THIS BOOK

A few months ago, I had the opportunity to sit down for lunch with Wing Lam, cofounder of Wahoo's Fish Tacos, at a business event. During that lunch, I asked him what the single-most important thing he has learned in surfing that he has been able to translate into his business. He told me that it was flexibility. He further explained that when you start to learn how to surf, there is only so much that you can rely on in theory. For the rest of it, you have to rely on your own ability to adapt to the conditions around you. He went on to say that while you are working the surfboard, you are also working with the waves and the weather. If you're not able to adapt your approach or be flexible, you will fall off.

In the past, the scope of a project was a clearly defined set of objectives, tangible goals, and high-level features designed to solve a particular problem or create some vehicle for enabling strategy. It was fixed and rigid, and considered immovable. The concept of scope as unchangeable is very much like staying on course even when a road gets washed away or a blizzard interferes with the trip.

Therefore, scope must also change as the business goals, drivers, and conditions change. The reality is that scope must also change as the project progresses, for the mere fact that the project starts with unclear information and a high lack of clarity and moves toward an increasing level of certainty and clarity. It is through project tasks and activities that analyze and decompose the information into greater and greater levels of detail that the project moves toward increasing clarity. The clarity itself will cause scope to evolve and fluctuate as the project moves forward.

The purpose of this book is to help project teams and business stakeholders dissect and gain a full understanding of the truth behind scope and how it changes across the project life cycle. This understanding will enable those same teams to focus their efforts where it counts and make better decisions about how, why, and when the scope of their project should actually change. It is this anticipation that enables more precise planning before the project starts and helps to establish more realistic expectations all around.

This book demonstrates that scope is not a rigid and fixed target as it was once perceived to be. It evolves and fluctuates as the project solution is developed and defined, and the unknown details become exposed. The three focal points that span this book are:

- How scope is impacted from both internal and external factors.
- What specific events and activities will impact scope across the project life cycle.
- How those events and activities can be better managed in order to mitigate the risks of watering down the solution.

The objective of this book is to enable business sponsors, chief information officers, project managers, and project teams understand that everything they say and do on a project is important. It will either add to successful outcomes or take away from them. By this understanding, it is hoped that resources and project teams will make better judgments and be better able to service their business counterparts by providing them with solutions that fully align to their needs and goals.

WHO WILL BENEFIT FROM THIS BOOK?

Many people will benefit from reading this book, including:

- *Chief information officers* looking to redefine project management within their organizations in order to achieve more productivity and increase quality results. This includes those who want to accomplish at least one of the following objectives: more accurately determine scope and control the fluctuations as it evolves; reduce operating costs; increase alignment between technology products and business needs; and, obtain peace of mind by establishing a functional framework for the evolution and management of scope that effectively reduces scope creep on projects and the frequent change requests rates that cause project holdups and headaches.

- *Project managers and leaders* who are looking to elevate their performance through due diligence in project scope changes and to utilize better techniques for ensuring complete alignment between the solution and the business need.
- *Consulting firms* that are interested in better managing scope across their projects so that they can deliver on their promises to clients; reduce operating costs; increase alignment between technology products and business needs; and, obtain a higher return on investment for their technology projects and solutions.
- *Business analysts, architects, and developers* who are interested in elevating their performance.

HOW THIS BOOK IS ORGANIZED

This book is organized in the same flow and logic as the average project. It explores the initiation as well as the full spectrum of the project life cycle in the same basic order in which the project itself would run, and thus, the information will be most useful. Of course, if you are working on an Agile project, you can read only Section 2 in multiple sprints so as to capture all of the information you require, as it becomes necessary.

Once the reader is exposed to the basic understanding of how to define scope, and then how it changes across the project life cycle, it becomes easier to see how seemingly minor incidents across the project could lead to catastrophic results and a change control nightmare. Next, the book explores the mandates of key strategies as contributing and detracting factors to project success. It becomes clear that everything, including the project environment, is responsible for contributing to scope and scope change. Finally, the book explores how implementation and the closing out of a project impacts scope and the success of the final product, once it is released and live within the environment.

In Section 1, the reader should gain an understanding of how to identify scope and develop the solution. Further, Chapter 1 discusses scope from the program and portfolio management perspectives and puts a big-picture spin on the definition of scope and its overall alignment to business objectives and positioning. This chapter also makes a pointed replacement of the *business case* with the *decision case,* as it is far more pertinent to establishing the foundations for making the critical decision which will guide the solution and the project. Further, the chapter discusses how discovery projects are leveraged as a source for developing more accurate scope up-front in order to better predict and estimate project outcomes.

Next, Chapter 2 breaks down scope into what it is and how it can be affected. It changes the viewpoint of scope as a single, hard-edged object, which is to be defined up-front, to a fluid concept for the development of the right solution. The difference will literally be in how the project team and the business view changes to the scope as it fluctuates across the project life cycle. This view will change the costs associated with both change control, and scrap and rework.

Chapter 3 describes the methods and means for engaging stakeholders at the outset of the project as the primary opportunity to establish expectations for subsequent management. A project is really the vehicle by which the business will build the solutions that enable its strategy and propel it forward. Therefore, it is imperative to consider all of the aspects of how to engage and involve stakeholders and user groups in meaningful and collaborative ways.

Chapter 4 closes the first section with a discussion about the implications of business architecture on scope. It is important to remember that architecture gives the solution context and puts it into the framework of the overall business landscape.

Section 2 is about how to change scope in the midst of the project without causing panic or wreaking havoc, and instead, drawing the deliverables closer into alignment with the overall business objectives. As such, this section describes the end-to-end requirements process as well as the mechanisms of governance.

In discussing requirements, Chapter 5 exposes how requirements have the greatest impact on scope, and as such, pose the most significant risk to its alignment with business objectives. It is by understanding the tasks and activities of requirements that project teams can effectively mitigate the risks associated with the poor quality of requirements and the frequent unnecessary changes that often accompany an inadequate process.

Next, Chapter 6 exposes the truth behind changes to scope as a means of better understanding how to establish more mature and comprehensive governance programs. This understanding creates a higher degree of success in the overall development of the solution due simply to a greater (and arguably more appropriate) level of due diligence. It is this due diligence and maturity in governance that will truly and effectively impact the quality of the end product. After all: quality is a process, not a destination.

In Section 3, the discussion expands to include the implications of the project methodology on the overall outcome of a project. This includes discussions about Agile, Waterfall, and even enterprise architecture. By exposing the strengths and weaknesses of Agile in Chapter 7, and Waterfall in Chapter 8, this book is able to identify subtleties that could mean the difference between success and failure in any project. This is also true for exposing the nuances of the enterprise architecture, which could dramatically shift the outcome of a project.

Finally, Section 4 carries the discussion about scope through implementation and the transition to business-as-usual or operations for usage, support, and maintenance of the final solution, once it has been put into place. Chapters 10, 11, and 12 outline some of the key areas where project planning tends to fall short: marketing and socializing the solution, handover, and decommissioning, respectively. These areas highlight the need for complete and comprehensive planning of the product life cycle as a full entity, instead of conducting planning in short bursts on an as-needed basis.

Combining Agile and Waterfall spells out success for any project team because it ensures that nearly every possible risk to scope can be mitigated in early planning. This increases the likelihood of a greater alignment to overall business objectives and driving factors.

THE KEY TAKEAWAYS

The strongest takeaways can be found in the answers to of each of these questions:

1. Are we doing the right things, and are we doing them right?
2. What tasks and activities impact scope at the microscopic level?
3. How can project teams, business stakeholders, and user groups ensure that everything they do will help them achieve targeted outcomes?

A Personal Message

Project scope is one of those areas that often perplex me. I'll admit the fact that the some of the same types of behaviors that we see in relationships (both personal and professional) are often present in how companies and project teams establish and manage scope.

There is the noncommittal approach to scope: "We really haven't made the decision about whether or not that will be included. It depends on…"

Then there is the power-trip approach to scope: "We're only going to include that in scope if we get to add this and that too."

And then there is the healthy approach: "We are going to include X, Y, and Z in scope because the business needs it to achieve its goals, and because we did our due diligence and discovered that now is the best time and that this project is the best place for it."

I like the last one because it is about doing what is best for the business to achieve its long-term strategies and goals. That is the best part of my job.

—Barbara Davis

ABOUT THE AUTHORS

BARBARA DAVIS

The author of *Managing Business Analysis Services: A Framework for Sustainable Projects and Corporate Strategy Success* (J. Ross Publishing, 2013), Barbara Davis has been a champion for technology standards and infrastructure for more than 13 years. Davis is an international speaker, who also works with Fortune 500 companies to realign business analysis services, aid critical and struggling projects, and establish operational infrastructure in order to ensure successful outcomes in the face of conflict and challenging circumstances. She has launched and grown numerous business analysis portfolios. During her career, she has grown other service portfolios to more than $51 million and enabled clients to reduce operational spending by salvaging struggling projects and driving operational changes for clients in excess of $220 million, while contributing to project estimates worth more than $114 million.

Davis's articles have been published in *Strategize Magazine*. She also created the world's first university-accredited Business Analyst diploma program, and has spoken at Project Summit/BA World conferences across Canada, the United States, and India.

Davis came into the technology field with more than 15 years of functional business experience in the areas of project management, community development, business ownership, change management, and conflict resolution. She has drawn on these experiences throughout the course of her career, and has become a business champion by defining the organizational capability through infrastructure (e.g., career paths, assessment tools, competencies, key performance indicators), training (e.g., educational programs and workshops), and creation of centers of excellence and management frameworks. She continuously audits and redefines operational management of key practice areas and methodologies.

Throughout her career, Davis has interviewed and assessed hundreds of resources and has held various titles and roles, including Business and IT Portfolio Management, IT Operational Management, Methodologist, Solutions Consultant, Project Manager, Business Analyst, and Professional Skills Trainer. Her experiences include operational management, organizational change management, document management, vendor management, configuration management, change control, practice management, business analysis, project management, and auditing PMO methodologies.

DARREN RADFORD

A goal-oriented leader accountable for the development of business and IT-enabled strategy and execution of major transformational change programs in North America and Europe, Darren Radford has a track record of driving "beyond the obvious" outcomes and motivating teams to succeed during complex, high-risk, high-visibility, must-win change initiatives.

Working extensively with organizations that are undergoing significant growth or requiring major cultural change, Radford believes in aspiring for excellence to bring about appropriate, feasible, and desirable change that creates a sustainable competitive advantage. The pursuit of excellence necessarily demands highly pragmatic solutions that are flexible to accommodate today's dynamic, uncertain, and fast-changing environment, while ensuring alignment to agreed organizational goals, operational parameters, and proven-practice tenets.

With regard to change, Radford's philosophy is that the capability to effect the right changes and create an adaptive organization is not only a distinctive competence for all organizations in the digital age, but a critical requirement to an enduring presence in the marketplace.

Radford's experience of organizational change and business value delivery is supplemented by international project management professional credentials (PMP, PRINCE2, and DSDM–Agile), an LL.B (Hons) Law Degree, a Master of Science in Management, and a Master of Business Administration from Henley Management College, Oxford, United Kingdom. He is currently the President and CEO of Aspire, Ltd., a management consulting firm located in Vancouver, Canada.

 Web
Added
Value™

This book has free material available for download from the
Web Added Value™ resource center at *www.jrosspub.com*

At J. Ross Publishing we are committed to providing today's professional with practical, hands-on tools that enhance the learning experience and give readers an opportunity to apply what they have learned. That is why we offer free ancillary materials available for download on this book and all participating Web Added Value™ publications. These online resources may include interactive versions of material that appears in the book or supplemental templates, worksheets, models, plans, case studies, proposals, spreadsheets and assessment tools, among other things. Whenever you see the WAV™ symbol in any of our publications, it means bonus materials accompany the book and are available from the Web Added Value Download Resource Center at www.jrosspub.com.

Downloads for *Going Beyond the Waterfall* include a decision case template; charter, scope, and benefits realization planning documents; project issue and risk tables; a deliverables and artifacts index; and a change control log.

SECTION 1: DISCOVERY, SCOPE, AND DEFINING BUSINESS SOLUTIONS

IDENTIFYING SCOPE AND SOLUTIONS: ARE WE DOING THE RIGHT THINGS?

In an information age, an on-demand era associated with a "have it now" culture, the natural, human condition is to gravitate toward consumption and use of a product or service (the "what"), typically with little concern for the complicated world of how those products or services came to be, or why. In the business world, when it comes to change, the last forty years have seen a heavy focus on "doing things right," with a view to satisfying ever demanding user expectations. From process improvement and reengineering to change management, product and project management, a focus on methodology, process compliance, a series of linear, almost mathematical "painting-by-numbers" steps is observed in identifying scope and solutions.

While doing things right is vital, it is not immediately clear in many organizations that the list and mix of the things they are doing and have planned to do over a given timeline are the "right" things: balancing the needs of the environment, capabilities, and assets of the organization with constraining factors such as risk, costs, dependencies, and resources to produce the optimal portfolio of investments (change initiatives), as aligned to the companies' missions, strategies, and objectives. It is suggested that doing the wrong things really well is not a good measure of success. Organizations need to demonstrate execution competence of the right things at the right time to maximize their chances of remaining relevant.

CHANGE: PORTFOLIO, PROGRAM, AND PROJECT MANAGEMENT

While the terms "portfolio, program, and project management" are commonplace in today's business vernacular, a clear, concise, and commonly accepted understanding of these concepts does not exist. Further, in the broader context, the distinctions between portfolio, program, and project management are blurred, at best. A major part of the difficulty in this respect is that these concepts are: a) broad, and b) complex. In a time where solutions are desired quickly and simply, selling complex disciplines that can enable the journey to this utopia presents challenges in terms of adopting a program management capability. For example, the "What's in it for me" factor is difficult to articulate in a 15-second elevator pitch.

A Focus on Program Management

Strictly speaking, portfolio management is about ensuring that enterprises are "doing the right things." This concept will be clarified and demonstrated in this chapter. Focus is given to the domain of program management; however, this is a critical enabler of the concepts of portfolio management and project delivery. It is also a key component of an enterprise-level change capability.

It is not easy to find a shared understanding of "what" program management is and of critical importance, "how" to do it. There are a number of (commonly accepted) interpretations as to what a "program" is. The three main definitions of a program are:

1. simply, a large project,
2. a group of interrelated projects, or
3. a composite of identifying and selecting major change initiatives, and seeing them manifest.

One thing is clear: the domain of program management is multifaceted and relatively complex. As such, it is difficult, and perhaps futile, to provide an isolated, meaningful definition of a clear, coherent understanding and definition of the differences between portfolio, program, and project management.

The Project Context: *Doing Things Right*

Projects exhibit a short-term focus, a "product-centric" perspective, and are tactical in nature. They have well-defined objectives and deliverables, and therefore, possess a certain degree of predictability. There may be high uncertainty at the beginning (high assumptions/facts ratio), such that the focus is to reduce uncertainty via work breakdown, planning, and risk analysis, followed by quality, time, and cost control. Projects focus on achieving "operational improvement," and the paradigm for projects is about "performance." Project management is a decision implementation process that seeks to keep change to a minimum. The measure of success is typically delivering the right output (scope), at the right time, within the right cost.

The Program Context: *Bridging Strategy and Execution*

As shown in Table 1.1, there are key differences between project, program, and portfolio management. Programs exhibit a medium-to-long term focus and a "benefit-centric" perspective. The organizational situation is complex, and there are multiple stakeholders. There is uncertainty (degree as to known, knowable, and unknown solutions) and ambiguity (expectations vs. defined requirements; conflicting aims; continuous readjustments). Programs reduce uncertainty and ambiguity through the elaboration of needs and expectations, as aligned to the strategic objectives being pursued (concept of "value management"), negotiation, and decision making. Programs focus on achieving "business change" and the paradigm is a "learning and performance" cycle. Program management is both a decision-making and decision-implementation process.

Programs comprise projects in addition to other key management capabilities of governance and decision management, benefits realization, stakeholder engagement, and dependency management. All of these enable the program to effectively deal with expected change, while bridging the domains of strategy and execution.

Portfolio Management: *Doing the Right Things*

As illustrated in Figure 1.1, there is a clear relationship between executive, portfolio, program, and project management. While the initiatives that comprise projects and programs are largely concerned with "doing things right," portfolio management focuses on ensuring that there is an appropriate, feasible, and desirable return on investment—that the organization is "doing the right things." To achieve this, portfolio management is concerned with ensuring that change initiatives contribute to the organization's strategic objectives, and the outcome represents value for money.

Table 1.1   Differences between project, program, and portfolio management

	Project	Program	Portfolio
Context	Tactical, predictable, reliable, performance-based methods, output focused	Strategic, complex, uncertain and ambiguous, requires responsiveness, learning-based methods, results focused	Manage needs and pressures to change, identify, select, prioritize, balance, and initiate the right mix of change
Scope	Set, limited scope with clearly defined deliverable	Broad scope with flexible boundaries. Multiple deliverables in alignment with strategic goals	Business scope that changes organizational structures
Change	To be avoided; processes to keep change managed and controlled	Expected from inside and outside the program and seen as an opportunity	Changes in the broader external environment continually assessed
Planning	Standard approach and detailed delivery plans created	Overall program plan to drive stakeholder, milestone sequence and pacing, and benefit realization planning	Create and maintain necessary practices and communication relative to the aggregate portfolio
Management	Transactional, authority-based directive style, conflict resolution, rational decision making	Transformational (provide vision and leadership), facilitating style, management of powerful stakeholders, intuitive decision making	Manage and coordinate the accounting of business benefit
Success	Measured by process compliance and product quality, timeliness, adherence to budget, customer satisfaction	Measured by the degree to which the program creates value and delivers benefits for the capability in focus	Measured in terms of aggregate performance of business road maps
Monitoring	Monitor and control the work of producing the products the project was undertaken to supply	Monitor the progress of program components to ensure overall goals, schedules, budget, and benefits of the program are met	Monitor aggregate benefit realization performance and cost-to-value indicators

While a project may deliver all the required features to the specified quality, deadline, and budget (therefore, traditionally declared "successful"), it would be difficult not to accept a reduced measure of success where, in the fullness of time, the project turned out to be the wrong initiative to commit time, money, and resources to in the first place. The outputs of the project

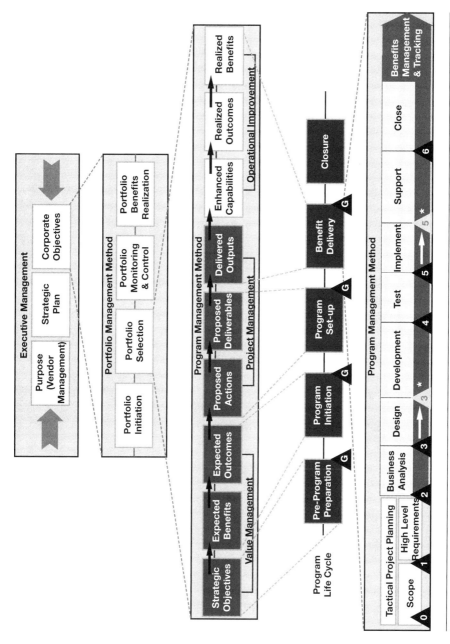

Figure 1.1 Relationship between executive, portfolio, program, and project management

perhaps were never being consumed and used by the business, and therefore, the targeted benefits were never realized.

Portfolio management addresses these issues by providing the mechanisms for translating strategic objectives into an appropriate, feasible, and desirable mix of change initiatives focused on optimizing the realization of targeted benefits and effectively balancing cost, resources (available capacity), risk (achievability), and dependencies at the enterprise level.

Program Management as a Key Capability

The ability to adapt and change at the organizational level is a key driver to maturing business capability and growing sustainable value. In addition to the classic business capabilities defined in the value chain (sales, operations, etc.), a modern, dynamic, and fast-paced environment requires that a core competence of any organization going forward must be the ability to identify, react, and adapt to change (in technology, attitudes, trends, and so on) to ensure continued relevancy and competitive viability. Program management provides a consistent approach to effect larger-scale organizational change in this environmental context.

As an integral part of a corporate change capability, programs provide the bridge between business strategy (manifested in portfolios) and tactical change initiatives (projects) to deliver results. As a structured approach to enterprise driven management of change, programs exist to make sense of complex, often ambiguous environments enabling a robust, business-led evaluation of options.

Management of programs is a distinctive business service of a change capability. As a service, it works within the construct of an enterprise architecture that incorporates organizational and systems design through a coordinated set of capability based planning services. Collectively, these services prepare business users in readiness for end-to-end change. Program management provides the vehicle to address pressures on, and the needs of, business, as expressed through its environmental factors, business strategies, and strategic working assumptions.

Key change behaviors support a consistent approach to business governance. The goal in utilizing program management practices, shown in Table 1.2, is to drive business thinking toward achieving the right coordinated outcomes within each business unit. Providing clarity on change value propositions enables effective governance and investment (portfolio) alignment, and empowers decision making at all levels of leadership in a timely manner.

Table 1.2 Enterprise change capability

Preparing for Change	Managing Change	
Enterprise Architecture (Unified Change Network)	Corporate Portfolio Management (Benefit Framework)	**Management of Operations**
Business Planning & Analysis (Organizational Coordination)	Business Program Management (Business Outcomes)	
Platform & Application Portfolio Management (Life Cycle Management)	Project Delivery (Solution Outputs)	
Communication		

Once expected outcomes are clearly defined, program management becomes a performance management practice that is intended to deliver outcomes with the highest possible efficiency (best scope/quality vs. lowest cost/time).

Another key benefit of managing programs versus projects is that the management of change occurs at the enterprise level. Instead of simply managing change, you have a broader concept, and thus, a broader reach. Finally, developing program management skills and practices offers a number of organizational benefits to effect sustainable change, i.e., the transformation as shown in Table 1.3.

With the above context in mind, a simple, pragmatic definition of a program is offered:

> A *program* is a group of related change actions (projects and operational activities), managed in a coordinated way, to obtain benefits and control not available from managing the actions independently.

Adopting Program Management

Program management is a complicated discipline. Therein lies a number of challenges to its adoption and successful application. Program management calls for a certain level of application to appropriately understand it. It involves many moving parts, and many management and leadership concepts, and needs to marry other professional disciplines and associated practices, such as change management, vendor management, and procurement practice. It requires intelligent knowledge of organizational operating models (ways of

Table 1.3 Benefits of a program management service

Area of Impact	Benefit
Delivery of change	More effective delivery of changes because the changes are planned and implemented in an integrated way to ensure current business operations are not adversely affected
Alignment between strategy and project level execution	Effective response to strategic initiatives by filling the gap between strategic value and project efficiencies
Management support	Keeping activities focused on business objectives by providing a framework for senior management to direct and manage change practices
Resource management	More efficient management of resources by providing a mechanism for benefit prioritization and project integration
Risk management	Better management of risk at all levels because the wider context is understood and explicitly acknowledged
Benefit realization	Help to achieve sustainable business benefits through a formal process of benefit identification, management, realization, and measurement
Management control	Improved control through a decision framework within which the costs of introducing new capability, standards, and quality regimes can be justified, measured, and assessed
Business practices	Clarification of how new business practices will deliver improved performance by defining the expected benefits and linking these to the achievement of new working behaviors
Management of business case	More effective management by building and maintaining a business case that clearly compares current business operations with the more beneficial future business operation
Coordination of dependencies	More efficient coordination and control of the often complex range of interrelated activities by clearly defining roles and responsibilities for managing and realizing the benefits delivered by the program
Transition management	Smooth transition from current to future business operational states through the clear recognition and responsibility for preparing the organization for migration to new ways of working
Communication consistency	Achieving a consistent system of new or amended policies, standards, and work practices through the integrated definition, planning, delivery, and assurance of the required changes

working) and experience at effecting enterprise-level change. It requires an understanding of how to assemble and calibrate the correct features and functions, in the appropriate sequence and pace, which is only possible by having experienced the journey previously—ideally, experienced several times. In the words of Lao Tzu, "A journey of a thousand miles begins with a single step,"[1] and the first step is often the hardest.

To undertake programs, organizations need to be comfortable with a number of conditions that traditional leadership approaches strived to reduce or stamp out, such as:

- Knowing what you want to achieve, but being comfortable with the fact that you do not yet have the answer as to how you're going to achieve the goal;
- Uncertainty, a turbulent, often volatile environment;
- Risk, and increased understanding and appetite for it; and
- Failure, and acceptance that some failure (albeit, not catastrophic) is part of the journey and should be embraced.

There are numerous indirect benefits of such a "learning experience," the ability (and willingness) to make decisions where the desired facts, information, and time to implement simply do not reside.

Organizations that are willing to at least consider that the classical management model practiced since the Industrial Revolution is perhaps an anachronism. Understand that embracing a new delivery paradigm will involve a certain amount of missteps, when it truly wants to (or must) implement larger-scale, more transformational change, and recognize that as part of the journey, more than 30% of the individuals that commence the journey will not finish it. Those organizations also understand that this is normal, and that the way we define success and reward/recognize it needs to change. Finally, those organizations understand that the concept of "ready, fire, aim" is more conducive to many modern day situations, and that overanalysis and decision procrastination kills creativity, innovation, growth, and the very essence of the human spirit. Only then are the conditions ripe to take on the challenge associated with leveraging the profound benefits a well-executed program framework can enable.

A simple test of readiness to adopt a program management capability is to ask if those accountable for delivering key change initiatives are prepared to stand in front of the senior management team or company board and support decisions, such as in the following scene:

Tom Watson, the founder of IBM, sent a meeting request to an employee who had recently lost over $10 million for his division in under three months. When the employee arrived at the meeting, apologizing and asking if he was going to be fired, Tom responded, "Fire you? Why would I fire you? I've just spent $10 million educating you!"[2]

To further assess the readiness to adopt programs, Table 1.4 shows some of the basic criteria for effective adoption strategies.

THE DECISION CASE

In the same way that projects have stages, programs have phases. As projects have business cases, a program revolves around a decision case. The term *decision case* is used for a number of reasons:

1. To simply distinguish a program-level process/document/output from a project.
2. Start the idea that the scale of change in scope requires a number of decisions to be made, both up-front and ongoing.
3. To emphasize the personal accountability that is associated with decisions (i.e., people make decisions).

The decision case supports the effective decision-making process by describing the solution and the reasons that it is necessary, as well as how the solution will exist within the environment. That means the decision case is composed of the following elements:

- Program justification/drivers
- Purpose/objectives

Table 1.4   Criteria for effective strategies and evaluating options

Appropriateness	Feasibility	Desirability
SWOT: What is the current strategic position?	What are the business readiness issues (change demands)?	Strategic needs: What is the planning gap?
What is the effect on the strategic perspective?	What is the availability of finance and other resources?	What levels of return are expected?
What skills and resources are available?	What is the capability to meet defined key success factors (KSF)?	How is the level of synergy?
What are the mission and objectives?	What is the competitive advantage?	Does it meet stakeholder needs and preferences?
What is the culture?	Does the timing work?	What is the risk involved?
What is the level of EVR congruence?	How far does this diverge from the desired level of congruence?	What is the tolerance for variance?
What is the level of simplicity?	Can this be easily implemented?	What is the desired level of skill for the business to use it?

- Classification (Typically four categories of justification; classification is an element of prioritization, e.g., a company may rank maintenance programs ahead of transformation initiatives at a given point in time.)
    - o Compliance: Demonstrate adherence to a standard or regulation
    - o Maintenance: Maintain our operations condition
    - o Continuous improvement: Improve performance
    - o Transformation: Change the way we do business
- Strategic contribution
- Achievability assessment
- Scope
- Assumptions, dependencies, constraints
- Key deliverables and milestones
- Key risks and mitigation strategies
- Resource requirements
- Costs
- Financial benefits realization plan
- Nonfinancial benefits realization plan
- Program and project governance structure

A decision case works hand-in-hand with a program management plan—the plan to manage the program—which answers the "how" in terms of managing the processes and leading the people identified as essential to implement the desired solution(s) and realize the targeted benefits.

The program management plan is the culmination of all planning processes related to groups of projects. They are combined into a single plan in order to create a consistent and coherent set of documentation that can be used to direct both program execution and control.

The program management plan tackles the "how" of redeveloping the program governance framework and control mechanism. It determines the organization structure and required facilities, including an approach to identify, engage, and manage stakeholders; to define requirements; and, to manage cost, time, vendors, communication, quality, and risk.

Finally, the program delivery plan, which is spawned from the decision case and the program management plan, defines the explicit activities, products, milestones, and deliverables, and uses all of the governance, delivery, and management tools identified in the program management plan: for example, risk and decision logs, financial tracking tools, vendor scorecards, communication outputs, and meeting management tools.

Environment, Values, and Resources Congruence

One of the primary functions of the decision case model is to analyze the alignment between all parts of the whole business model (or system) in order to understand how the overall decision will impact the business and its environments. This analysis is done by looking for congruence (or alignment) between the environment (as key success factors), values, and resources (core competencies and capabilities).

Congruence within an organization is categorized by a particular element that is out of alignment with the remainder of the model, and according to the characteristics and impacts these misalignments will have on the outcomes of the program, thus they factor heavily in the decision-making process. These are incongruent: the consciously incompetent organization, the lost organization, the unconsciously competent organization, and strategic drift.

As illustrated in Figure 1.2, *congruence* occurs when there is an equal amount of overlap between the environment, values, and resources (EVR). The overall objective in the development of new programs and solutions is to develop new strategic initiatives, while sustaining the congruence with these three core elements.

The Consciously Incompetent Organization

In a consciously incompetent organization with misalignment, managers often appreciate the customer's need for success; however, there is either a lack of resources or lack of willingness to comprehend and internalize the changes that are required to meet those needs. In this situation, a more proactive and even entrepreneurial approach, combined with a new strategy, is required. This type of consciously incompetent organization is illustrated in Figure 1.3.

The Lost Organization

As illustrated in Figure 1.4, within the lost organization, the products, services, and markets are completely misaligned and the organizational values are inappropriate. In order to correct this misalignment, the business is required to make major large-scale changes to its strategy, structure, and leadership style, if it intends to have a future.

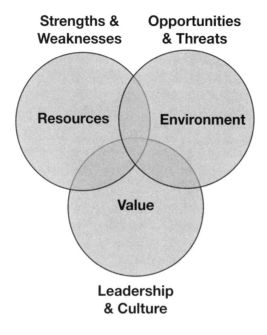

Figure 1.2   Environment, values, and resources congruence

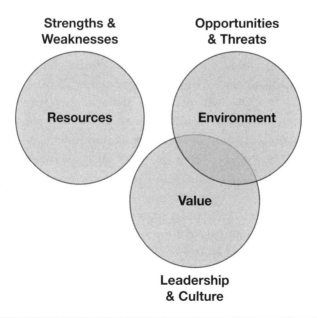

Figure 1.3   The consciously incompetent organization

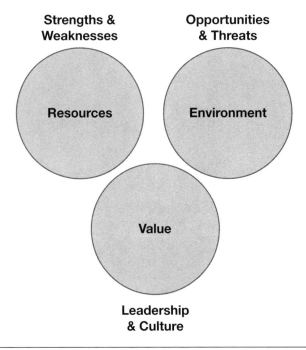

Figure 1.4   The lost organization

The Unconsciously Competent Organization

As illustrated in Figure 1.5, the unconsciously competent organization enjoys strategic positioning without any substantial or tangible commitment. This is especially true when it comes to making improvements and changes. Operations work at a tactical level with pure luck, and no real overriding strategy to achieve or maintain it. The downside, however, is that the organization's own strengths are not exploited or leveraged to its full advantage. The required change in culture possibly dictates a change of leader or leadership style.

Strategic Drift

The so-called "strategic drift" in an organization is all too common. This drift occurs when an internally cohesive organization loses touch with its environment (as shown in Figure 1.6). When drift happens, the organization requires an influx of new ideas and leadership. Ironically, there are times when the new ideas have already been captured within the company, but they are dormant in a log somewhere and have not been analyzed or activated.

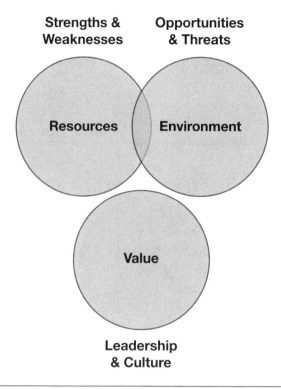

Figure 1.5   The unconsciously competent organization

Finally, this organization also requires a change in management or leadership as a means of refreshing its approaches and agendas in an attempt to realign itself with its environment.

Types of Strategic Decisions

Considering that the decision case is a model for reporting the evaluation of key strategic decisions, it is important to understand the differing types of decisions that would be evaluated and how these will impact the outcomes. There are three basic types of strategic decisions[3] that a firm has to make (shown in Figure 1.7):

1. Decisions covering alternative options/directions
2. Decisions concerning alternative methods
3. Generic strategy decisions

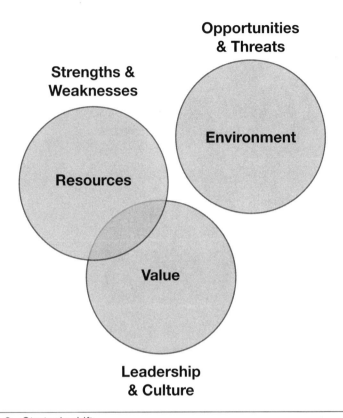

Figure 1.6   Strategic drift

These types of decisions enable the establishment of clear strategic themes and actionable plans.

Criteria for Effective Strategies and Evaluating Options

In order to compose effective strategies and perform the evaluation of the available options, it is important to consider factors for appropriateness, feasibility, and desirability.

Appropriateness

The determination of the appropriateness consists of assessing whether the proposed strategies are aligned to the overarching needs of the environment,

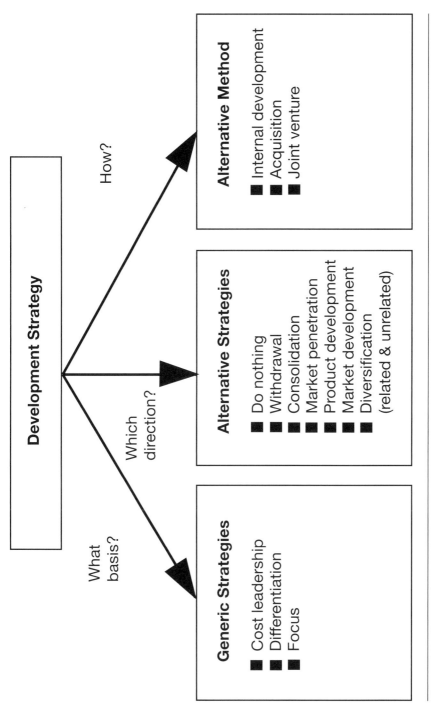

Figure 1.7   Types of strategic decisions

resources, and values of the organization. This goes back to the assessment of EVR congruency. In order to be fully congruent, the strategy must also be appropriate. This means asking some very pointed questions, such as:

- Does the proposed strategy fit with the existing mission and objectives of the organization?
- Will the business unit be able to gain or maintain a strong competitive position and make a contribution to the organization as a whole?
- Is the strategy appropriate for the current economic and competitive environment?
- Is this strategy able to take advantage of emerging trends?
- Does the strategy enhance strengths, capabilities, and competencies while downplaying or minimizing weaknesses?
- Does the strategy fit with the desired culture and values? (It is important to aim for the culture and values that are desired, especially when there is incongruence in the EVR.)
- Does EVR congruency exist with the strategy?
- Finally, is the strategy simple, understandable, and actionable, and above all, can it be communicated to mainstream employees?

Feasibility

A key criterion to consider in the development of strategy is whether or not it is actually feasible. There are times when the strategy may indeed be what is needed to bring the organization back into alignment or congruence, but is infeasible at the current time due to other factors such as business readiness or economic conditions. The following questions can provide a general guideline to determine feasibility:

- Is the strategy feasible for the available resource capabilities and capacities?
- Can the strategy be implemented effectively?
- Can the key success factors placed upon them by the industry/customers be met?
- Will the organization be able to gain and maintain competitive advantage?
- Is the strategy flexible enough to adapt in order to gain or maintain the competitive advantage?

- Is the timing appropriate? In other words, is the organization capable of adapting quickly, on demand?

Desirability

The final criterion is the level of desirability of the strategy. To meet this criterion, an assessment is performed in order to determine the ability of the strategy to meet the overall objectives of the organization and to close any identified planning gaps. In addition to this, the assessment must consider the capability of the strategy to produce specific results for either the short or long term. It is important to consider that an effective synergy leads to an enhanced concentration of specific resources in relation to the business' direct competitors. In order to understand the level of desirability of the strategy, the following questions are recommended as part of the assessment:

- What are the inherent risks to the organization posed from the strategy, and can they be mitigated?
- What are the expectations, needs, demands, and preferences of key stakeholders?

Scenarios

One of the options that many programs take advantage of, in the overall solution, is the development of scenarios. Scenarios provide an opportunity for the business team to plan appropriately for impending changes and potential risks, as well as the reality of the situation that they are going to create once the new solution is in place and operational.

In 1996, Peter Schwartz identified and recommended an 8-step approach to planning scenarios.[4] The steps in this approach are:

1. Identify the primary issues or decisions to focus on. It is important to begin scenario planning by identifying the primary, most critical decisions that will need to be made, as well as the specific mind-set of the management team who is making those decisions.
2. Identify and list the key forces that exist within the local environment. This means that it is imperative that the program manager take some time to identify the particular key factors that currently exist within the industry environment (specifically, a Five Forces Analysis): customers, suppliers, and competitors that may influence success or failure of the decisions.

3. Identify and list the driving forces or the impetus behind the need for a solution. It is equally important to identify the key driving forces (as the proverbial "burning platform") in the macro-environment, which exert crucial influence on the key factors that have been uncovered in Step 2.

4. Prioritize the factors and driving forces. This means ranking the key factors and driving forces, according to two criteria:
   a. What is the degree of importance (criticality) for the success of the decisions being made?
   b. What is the degree of uncertainty that exists about each of these factors and forces? To accomplish this, it is necessary to identify approximately two or three factors or trends that stand out as the most important and most uncertain.

5. Select the scenario logics. This means the development of a small number of select scenarios (in draft form) that outline the variations between the factors discovered in Step 4. Further, it requires the analysis of those issues until a logical pattern emerges, and a coherent story can be told by these scenarios. Specific plots for scenarios that will identify the best variations will meet the following criteria:
   a. These scenarios best capture the dynamics of the particular situation.
   b. These scenarios best communicate specific points effectively.

6. Analyze and fully define the identified scenarios. It is necessary to revisit the list of factors that were discovered in Steps 2 and 3, in order to develop the appropriate level of detail for each scenario.

7. Explore the implications of each scenario. It is absolutely critical to fully analyze the consequences of each decision, within each scenario, in order to fully understand and mitigate the risks associated with making each of those decisions. In doing so, it is important to explore these questions:
   a. What vulnerabilities have been exposed?
   b. What is the robustness of each decision under various scenarios and situations?

8. Finally, identify and select specific key performance indicators (KPIs) and milestones. In other words, identify the key indicators that will be utilized to monitor and expose the direction and trends of the change as quickly as possible throughout the process. These are the signposts

that will suggest appropriate strategic choices and mitigation tactics that will improve the position of the business "on-the-fly," so to speak.

As a final warning, Schwartz (1996) implores business teams and program managers, "Do not ignore weak signals," when it comes to scenario planning.

ESTABLISHING RETURN ON INVESTMENT

The establishment of return on investment (ROI) represents a structured approach to quantifying and delivering business value. In order for any business to take full advantage of a proposed, new, or enhanced capability or management solution, it is necessary to engage a wide cross section of the business to determine where and how business value can be best delivered, and be able to prove it. The most effective way to achieve this is through the development of a robust and realistic implementation strategy, an ROI-based decision case, and a benefits-delivery road map.

A practical step-by-step guide to building a robust, fact-based, and quantitative strategy and decision case is a useful tool in today's fast-paced climate. The decision case supports the effective decision-making process, whereas the business case is more of a foregone conclusion that supports the decision as-made, and rationalizes the purchase, instead of justifying the need for making the buying decision. It is all too common to see business cases that promise X (benefits) at a cost of Y (money and time commitment). Invariably, the end result is often at least double the cost, delivered 50% later, with at least half of the actual benefits realized.

A critical first step is developing an appropriate cost/benefit ratio. To do this, organizations first need a holistic framework of measures as applicable to their industry, vision, and goals. Further, an understanding or baseline in terms of current performance against relevant, clearly defined KPI and key risk indicator metrics is required to enable a tangible measurement of the changes effected. Finally, two key aspects of portfolio management, the ability to select—via strategically aligned and weighted scoring and prioritization criteria—and the ability to "balance" the proposed portfolio of initiatives with those key constraining factors of cost, risk, and dependencies resources, will stand the organization in good stead.

Again, a decision case is necessarily defined at a given point in time, based on available data, using reasonable assumptions based on what is understood about the environment at that point in time. Things change. Circumstances change. New opportunities or risks may arise that were not and perhaps could not realistically be foreseen at the outset of the initiation in scope. As such, despite rigor in developing the ROI case, critical reassessment should be undertaken at both predetermined points in time (frequency of review determined by the nature of the industry in terms of uncertainty, volatility, product life-cycles, etc.), and as dictated by certain unplanned events.

USING DISCOVERY PROJECTS TO IDENTIFY SCOPE

A *discovery project* is one demonstrable feature of an organization's acceptance that, while it may have clarity on where it wants to go, it does not necessarily have an understanding or road map as to how it should best get there. Running a discovery project can help with this.

Discovery projects are intended to expose a more complete picture of the current situation in order to help the organization identify the road map for the development and implementation of the solution. Typically, these projects last only a few weeks and expose many risks and issues that the business may not have even known were there. In many cases, discovery projects are also utilized to help define the overall solution.

Discovery projects yield two types of early benefits, both direct and indirect. The direct benefits of a discovery project are the ability to analyze and predict the risks and potential issues in greater detail than a simple one-hour planning session during project initiation could possibly identify. The discovery project can find out what the client's needs are, so the organization and client work closely together to create a vision and a set of shared goals for the effort. Discovery projects also yield indirect benefits in terms of enhancing the organization's ability to understand its environment and associated success factors, and its relationship between its values, core competencies, and distinctive capabilities.

Ideally, a discovery phase is undertaken before signing a contract for the subsequent phases, or at least in the full knowledge that any contract for an entire program may be subject to validation or change as part of the findings during discovery. Of course, when clients believe they clearly understand what they want, they may simple require an estimate, so that they can get started in earnest. Without understanding *why*, and some details of *what* the client wants however, any estimate would be at an order of magnitude level and, as such, of little use.

The discovery phase offers a legitimate way to ensure both the client and solution provider/team attain a shared understanding of the *why* and *what* of the initiative. Where the client is sufficiently sophisticated, they will know that this is needed. Otherwise, you have to educate your client as to the benefits of a discovery phase. In my experience, not doing this leads to significant challenges. Educating your community of contacts sufficiently before the delivery project commences will eventually bake-in this critical phase, so that it becomes known this is standard for your company/practice and is accepted by your future clients.

To reach an agreement on the need for discovery, however, the client will need to understand the benefits of doing—and paying for—this. The following five benefits should be realized as part of a discovery phase:

1. Dig deeper and find out what your client really needs vs. what they say they need.

Clients often talk about the features they want without referring to why they are needed. That is because they have already brainstormed, looked at a lot of competitors, and want to do "… something like that." Before you spend their money to "build something" per their request, you have to find out if you are building the right thing. For me, this became a moral imperative, and it will help to avoid the situation where around half of the features developed in technology solutions are rarely or never used.

2. Find out how and with whom clients are effecting changes to their businesses now.

What does the client's current change delivery landscape look like? What other partners or vendors are involved? Such background/current state questioning facilitates a look at things at least one layer under the publicly projected perception of the company—the proverbial "look under the hood" of a shiny new car, which may present a somewhat different opinion. In addition to understanding more about how to approach the solution side of change, this also enables an understanding of such management questions as: Who are the key stakeholders? What are their respective levels of commitment, support, and involvement? Do *X* and *Y* stakeholders/departments work together well?

Will you be interacting with other vendors/contractors? If such understanding is not gained early, many surprises could result in post-contract signing, which may significantly compromise your ability to be successful.

3. Work together to define the business goals and objectives for the project.

What is the business driver? What is the company trying to accomplish, and why? Once an understanding of *why* the company is embarking on this journey is gained, work together to clearly define the destination and shape the specific business objectives to be achieved. This process starts to forge a collaborative working relationship. Not working together to agree on how the organization's vision and specific objectives can be achieved, could render that one or both parties are either limited in their ability to fully realize the objectives, or that their interests/needs have not been heard. Once the journey is appropriately defined and both parties' interests and concerns catered to, a map for the journey can be created that will enable all stakeholders to fully understand where they are at any given moment. Without a destination and without a road map, your project will be wrought with wrong turns, the stress of not knowing "where we are at," and other challenges.

4. Create a road map for the project and clarify rules of engagement.

Now that the destination is known, conventional wisdom would suggest a road map be created that defines exactly how you are going to get there. Of course, this conventional view cannot work in modern times as changes, challenges, and opportunities will occur, and no one knows, exactly, where they might be when setting off on the journey. To address this current phenomenon, two attributes are essential: First, you need to assemble an intelligent group of skilled practitioners in your delivery team. Of course, this is easier said than done in an era when talent management is the proverbial "hot potato." Second, instead of plotting the journey to the smallest detail up front, take a step back and apply a set of "journey navigation rules" instead. We know the destination and why we want to get there. We have an idea as to how we're going to get there, but some conditions will change.

With rules in hand, a framework approach (such as program management) is a more realistic model. To keep the analogy going, those leading the change will check in every 15 miles or so to see how the team is proceeding along the route and invoke many mechanisms, tools, and people skills along the way when unforeseen challenges or opportunities occur to ensure all of the essential components rendezvous at the agreed destination. Of course, such a delivery model not only provides appropriate control for those accountable for delivery, but it enables that high-talent team to be creative and forge their own paths to success to some extent. I'd suggest this is an environment where smart, creative, innovative, and talented performers would like to remain, which in the long term, will form a very powerful specialist delivery capability to execute changes better over time.

5. Get to know the people.

It shouldn't surprise you that the most important factor in a project is whether you like working with the people or not. The discovery phase is an opportunity to understand their individual needs and how best you can tailor your services to the individuals in the organization. Each person and department is going to have a different need. Each of the individuals also has general career goals and needs. If you think that your client is a company or a product, you are wrong. The company is people. You are not delivering a solution for them or to them. You are effecting change with them. What is more important, the technical details of a project, or whether this is a team that you can ride with through the peaks and valleys of your journey, taking on and enduring through countless challenges together?

To illustrate the importance of discovery, Figure 1.8 depicts the key questions and activities leading up to and including discovery as a significant part of a successful delivery life cycle. That does not however, mean that these types of projects are without problems and issues of their own. These issues include disconnects between project segment staff, using a boiler-plate approach, and inappropriate identification of scope.

Very often, the discovery project is staffed by senior resources who do not ultimately work on the actual project itself. The reason for this is to have someone with experience to help uncover and identify the potential issues and the best mitigation strategies, along with defining the solution. To make matters worse, the project is usually staffed by lesser qualified and inexperienced resources that will not have the necessary experience to deliver on promises made by the senior resources.

While the logic is sound, what it means is that there is a disconnect between the senior resources and the real-world application of that planning. Without adequate documentation in place about why key decisions were made in the discovery phase, the project team is left struggling to implement a plan that they may not fully understand.

Another concern related to senior resources is that often, they will outline the ideal state and not the road map for achieving it in incremental stages,

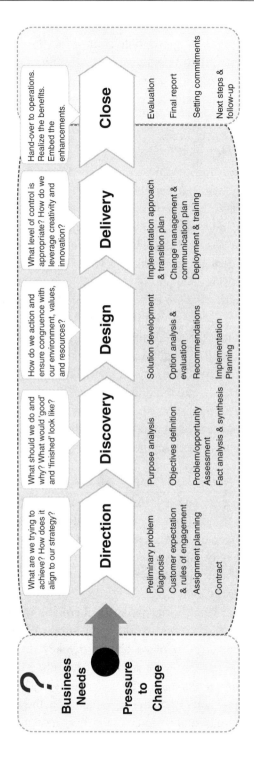

Figure 1.8   Importance of discovery within the life cycle

according to the feasibility for the particular business. This not only creates a disconnect with the project's primary resources, but also with the business itself as it struggles to reconcile the two views.

The next issue with discovery projects is that the team has likely utilized a boiler-plate approach. This means they have taken a one-size-fits-all template and filled it with generic (vanilla) information about what many companies find or don't find when it comes to the particular type of project that is being initiated through a discovery phase. Unfortunately, what this means is that many of the specific details, risks, and issues about this exact company and its unique situation are not going to be accounted for.

Finally, the risk of discovery projects is the inappropriate identification of scope. Regardless of the approach and staffing models leveraged in the discovery project, it can be difficult to get the participation required to establish a solid foundation of scope for the project. Many of the discovery resources are still developing trust and can only hope to get participation from executive sponsors, working sponsors, or technical sponsors, and usually get the bare minimum amount of participation from the bare minimum number of resources for the time that they are on site.

This does not mean that all discovery projects are bad or are doomed to failure. What it does mean is that companies who are using the discovery approach must be aware of what needs to be done and how to run a really well-planned discovery project. It also means that these companies must ensure that the discovery team clearly articulates plans which are specific to the company's own individual situation.

The reality is that discovery is a part of the planning foundation and sets the project up for success or failure. To be done thoroughly, discovery and project planning must include a needs analysis, identification of goals and objectives, analysis of the problem to be resolved, a "10,000 foot" and "5,000 foot" view of the solution, a project plan, scope, a strategic plan, and risk and impact assessments, including mitigation strategies, a communication plan, a change management plan, an overview of the architecture, resource estimates, an estimate for how much time it will take, a cost estimate, a service level agreement with the project, and kick-off meetings. It must deliver the solution definition and scope for the overall project, at a bare minimum.

VALIDATING SCOPE

A critical key to success in every project rests on the ability to verify that the project is indeed "doing the right things." This means that scope must be validated.

In order to achieve this, it is important to clearly define the problem, business needs, and desired results. Scope can be compared against these factors in order to determine alignment and the following questions can be asked to help with validation.

1. Problem resolution:
   a. How many pain points are identified as part of the problem?
   b. Does the item in scope solve a pain point for the business or customer?
   c. How many pain points are resolved by the scope?
   d. Does any item in scope limit or restrict the resolution of specific pain points?
   e. Is there another solution which would resolve more of the problem?
   f. Is there overlap in the problems that items in scope can resolve?
2. Desired business results:
   a. Does the item in scope deliver any of the required business results?
   b. How many of the results can be delivered with this scope item?
   c. What is the priority of the required business results?
   d. How many high priority results can be delivered with each item in scope?
   e. Does any item in scope prevent or impede the full delivery of the required business results?
   f. Is there overlap in the results that items in scope can deliver?
   g. Do any of these items in scope compete and override other items?
3. Taxonomy:
   a. Can the needs, problems, and required business results be categorized?
   b. How closely does scope fit into these categories?

The importance of asking these questions is in the evaluation of how well each item identified in scope either resolves a problem or delivers a desired business result. In evaluating this information, project managers, sponsors, and business analysts can be assured that they are indeed working on the right things, but they can also leverage this information in deflecting requests for scope changes that do not align to the problems and required results.

Create and leverage a weighted matrix to conduct this evaluation and ensure that the business team can see the logic behind the prioritization and weighting in order to support governance of scope as the project moves through its life span.

REFERENCES

1. Lao-Tzu (aka Laozi) *Tao Teo Ching*, circa 168 BC.
2. Relfe, Stephanie. 2014. How to Know Your Life Purpose. *Health, Wealth, and Happiness*. http://www.relfe.com/life_purpose.html.
3. Johnson, G., Scholes, K., and Whittington, R. *Exploring Corporate Strategy*, 8th ed. FT/Prentice Hall, 2008.
4. Schwartz, Peter. *The Art of the Long View: Planning for the Future in an Uncertain World*. Doubleday, 1996.

This book has free material available for download from the
Web Added Value™ resource center at *www.jrosspub.com*

THE EVOLUTION OF SCOPE ON A PROJECT

Here is the truth: Scope evolves and fluctuates. Scope is not a static and rigid target as it was once perceived. *Evolution* is the change of characteristics and traits over successive generations. *Fluctuation,* on the other hand, is the change in quantity over a series of processes. In other words, the specific items of scope can change individual characteristics, and can increase or decrease when items are added and removed from scope. This means that at any given point in the life cycle of a project, scope can fluctuate as it evolves.

The critical aspect of this reality is that the evolutionary journey should be managed within agreed thresholds and tolerances, and in-line with overall expectations of those accountable. Of course, this exposes a troubling dichotomy that continues to perplex business—the notion of controlling the corporate ship (predictable revenue and profit, hitting objectives, high-performing staff, etc.) versus enabling the "magic" to happen in terms of realizing true creativity, innovation, and genuinely enriching the lives of the employees, which, while perceived as the antithesis of command and control, I would argue requires merely a different leadership and management paradigm over the mechanistic model created at the time of the industrial revolution. This model still dominates today, despite the dawn of the information age decades ago. Perhaps a key driver behind this book is that the scope of desired or required initiatives navigates the dangerous channel between the shores of control (sustaining and preserving) and innovation (creating and disturbing), leading to a new "control" paradigm.

WHAT IS SCOPE?

Scope is the list of items that will be produced by the project. In other words, it is the sum of the targeted solution. The traditional notion of scope is that it is fixed. Scope flowed from corporate, senior leaders. After shaping scope at that macro level, its scope found itself rolled into a large dough ball, to be passed to the project manager to meticulously transform it into a culinary masterpiece.

The project manager would take this high-level mandate—to build a car, for example—and start the process of creating a fuller articulation of what was desired, from many viewpoints (chassis, engine, body, electronics, etc.), so that s/he may eventually play back a robust, SMART (specific, measurable, achievable, realistic, time-bound) contract statement (charter), and plan to achieve this objective for formal approval. Once approved, perhaps after several rounds of review and editing, the project manager has an agreed mandate to execute. Traditionally, the esteemed triple constraint rule takes over, whereby the project manager seeks to balance the constraining factors of time and cost with the approved, and now fixed, scope. Essentially, delivering to scope should, in theory, keep time and cost to deliver in line with initial expectations. Deviation from scope and the original management plan can impact one, or both, of the other constraints.

Let us expand the car analogy further. The high-level mandate from corporate may be that they require a new car. But a "car" means different things to different people. Even remaining at the high level, further elaboration would be required, perhaps by asking the purpose the vehicle was supposed to serve, how many were to be produced, what sale price was targeted, what niche of the car market was targeted (if for mass production), what geographic region, and so on. At this stage, there would likely be sufficient information to initiate a project—in that the team could take these high-level expressions against a number of criteria and formulate a plan, and cost and time estimates to produce the vehicle. When we get into project execution however, the team of specialists that comprise the project gets into a lower level of detail and requires specificity to ensure various standards: regulatory or safety requirements are adhered to and questions (invariably through articulation of risk, issue, or formal change management mechanisms established within the project) inevitably surface during this process. For example, does the car require a traditional, hybrid, or electric power train? Such questions may have profound implications on other components, and design and build facets of the car, as well as a significant impact to original time, cost, and scope constraints—more or less of any of these three constraining factors, required as a result of being specific about a particular aspect of the project's scope.

Herein lies a dilemma with scope. Corporate governance requires that enough certainty is known up front to ensure an initiative can be genuinely approved—a meeting of the minds having occurred—that the delivery of the project is desirable in terms of the corporate strategic objectives and achievable within the current governance and delivery paradigms. Traditional project management also states that the role of the project manager is to deliver what is asked for and to stipulated time and cost thresholds. One can easily see that the degree to which the desired solution can be "known," or the degree to which the targeted solution is truly a "unique, novel, transient endeavour" (the Project Management Institute's definition of a project), is a key role in how much scope may fluctuate, refine, and evolve as the project progresses.

HOW AND WHY SCOPE CHANGES

Scope is the high-level set of characteristics that defines the targeted solution. That target however, can change as the understanding of the problem or strategy (or even alternative solutions), are analyzed by the various stakeholders. The target is going to be looked at from various perspectives and vantage points, from inception of the idea to a project team's decomposing it into the requirements, design, and code through to the scripts produced to validate that the scope was achieved via a working solution. However, looking at an object (in this case, scope) from differing vantage points does not necessarily mean that the object changes. Therefore, it is important to understand how, when, and why scope changes.

In the past, nearly every change to scope was viewed as "scope creep." That is not the case. *Scope creep* occurs when the requirements, design, or development dictates or implements a feature that does not meet the objectives or the needs of the solution being produced. Scope creep is extraneous and unnecessary. If however, scope is changed as a result of the requirements, design, or development processes in order to meet the objectives and business needs, it is a valid evolution or fluctuation in scope.

Evolution

Evolution is the change in individual characteristics and traits of scope. Throughout the life of a project (as illustrated in Figure 2.1), evolution typically occurs as each item within scope is refined from a vague understanding

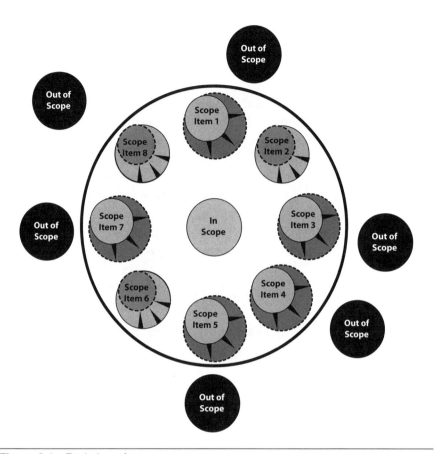

Figure 2.1 Evolution of scope

to a more defined and concrete solution. One of the key reasons for evolution is that as characteristics are solidified, the team incorporates other factors that present themselves at various points during the project.

Call Center Modernization Scope (Part A)

On a project to modernize the work scheduling module for a large call center, the scope included the following item:

"Modify and Deactivate a CSR Profile"

However, through analysis of the details and full characteristics of the item, it evolved to a more accurate descriptor:

"Manage Employee Profile"

In the Call Center Modernization (Part A) example, the scope item evolved because it was determined (through analysis of the need), that more characteristics were needed in order to better describe it within scope. In fact, where the original characteristics were merely to "modify and deactivate" profiles, the revised traits included adding, editing, duplicating, activating, and deactivating profiles. Since changing this requirement did not necessitate removing the requirement, it merely evolved, and did not fluctuate.

Fluctuation

Fluctuation in scope occurs when the amount (quantity) of items listed in the high-level scope either increases or decreases as the process of analyzing the problem and the strategy is conducted. This fluctuation is depicted in Figure 2.2. What this really means is that the actual scope items are not just changed (as they are in evolution); instead, items are either added to or removed from scope.

Call Center Modernization Scope (Part B)

On the same call center modernization project, the scope also included the following item:

"Loans to Other Departments"

However, after analysis of the project factors, coupled with the full characteristics of the item, it was removed from scope and postponed until a later product upgrade.

In the Call Center Modernization (Part B) example, the scope did fluctuate as the item was removed. This decreased the amount of items that were in scope. However, it also increased the amount of items that were considered out of scope.

Reasons for Changes to Scope

There are many factors that cause scope to fluctuate and to evolve as the project moves ahead. The most common reasons for changes to scope are:

- Changes in either corporate need or strategy, as driven by internal or external environmental considerations
- To correct misinterpretations of business needs

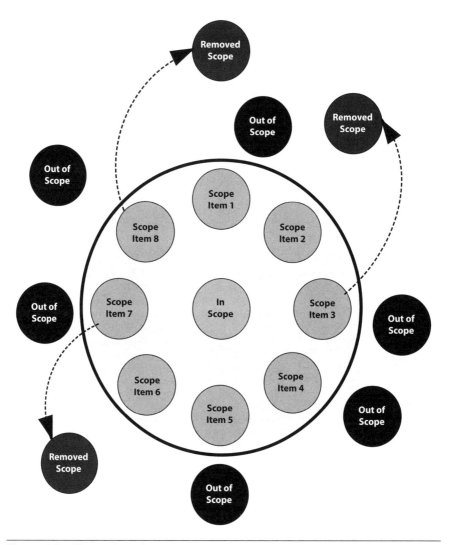

Figure 2.2   Fluctuation of scope

- To leverage new opportunities and/or technology not available at the outset
- Changes in either initiative priority or available budget
- Changes in either assumptions made or constraints identified
- Changes in company leadership
- To add feature requests made by the business stakeholders and sponsors (in and out of appropriate change controls and governance)

There are two key points that organizations must be aware of when reviewing the previous list. First, an understanding that scope may and does evolve as greater detail and specificity emerges in line with the project's progress; and second, a willingness to embrace this fact as an opportunity to put mechanisms in place for proactively managing this reality.

EMBRACING FLUCTUATIONS AND CHANGES IN SCOPE

The imperative on projects in the past was to make considerable efforts to reject changes in scope because these changes were seen as negative. However, the tasks and activities within the life span of projects actually means that the team is essentially decomposing and refining a very high-level concept into an intricately detailed solution. Ultimately, that means that at the outset of the project, there could be many aspects and attributes (traits or characteristics of scope) that are unknown. These unknown aspects and attributes can only become known as the project life cycle progresses. Figure 2.3 illustrates the progression from uncertainty to increasing certainty as a project progresses.

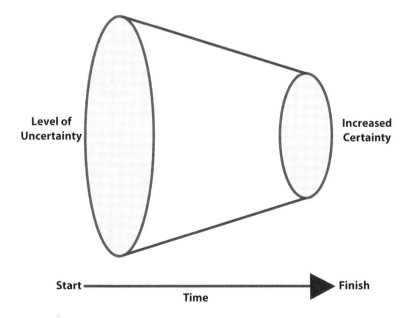

Figure 2.3   Progression of certainty across the project life cycle

What this means is that *scope* is actually a benchmark or a baseline from which to start the project. The project is a living organism. Provided that the project keeps its focus on delivering the objectives and results needed by the business, and that fluctuations are evaluated and monitored, there is absolutely no reason that scope cannot shift as the project evolves to attain those objectives and results.

Indeed, it is contended that scope will and should shift to meet the quality and overall solution expectations of those accountable. As in life, there are often many paths that lead to the same place, so to assume we can appropriately define and therefore, fix scope early is folly. But apprehension is rife among leadership about embracing uncertainty. Simply put, this is a more involved, demanding (and accountable) journey than holding a manager to account for a defined, fixed scope.

INHERENT RISKS WITH SCOPE

Scope is a critical component of the change landscape and decision-making processes. Changing scope, for positive reasons around leveraging an opportunity, or less positive reasons (such as spending cuts), impacts many other elements. For example, scope change may have significant impacts on an enterprise's architecture (current, transitional, or targeted state), which may have far-reaching effects on other desired capabilities. Similarly, scope change may directly impact the roles and skill-sets required, changing the makeup of staff accordingly. Changes to scope also require due care and attention as the very feasibility of the initiative could be impacted, where the full ramifications of a seemingly innocuous request for change are not determined early.

Unless significant research and development, feasibility assessments, discovery, prototyping, and other activities or techniques have been employed, it is unlikely that the high-level scope, targeted benefits, and estimates around time, cost, and resources required to deliver the desired scope will prove definitively accurate. There are many reasons for this uncertainty, the most common being that the true level of detail, quality requirements, or complexity of creating the targeted solution was not or could not have been known upfront. As unknowns, the time, cost, and amount of work to be done typically increase, largely because our natural tendency is to be optimistic and we simply can't flesh out all the possibilities or larger-scale initiatives at the outset; this is simply infeasible. If we dive even deeper, we don't know if the team, which has yet to be formed, will fulfill its respective accountabilities in the manner envisioned.

Performance metrics may also be unknown; less rigor could be applied, creating unforeseen issues. Such unknown factors are significant contributors to those high-level statistics which are direct measures of project success. Of course, if in the fullness of time, we all accept that a project to do A was always going to cost X and take Y length of time for a typical team to perform at Z level, but we didn't or simply couldn't have appreciated that before we dove into the initiative. So, was that initiative a failure? I'd suggest that it was more an estimation issue. Then, a really difficult question surfaces: had the true cost, effort, time, etc., been known up front, would the initiative have been approved at all? This philosophical debate points back to the discourse in Chapter 1 where a balance between doing the right things (priority, selection of initiatives) and doing things right (project management and solution delivery) is critical to success.

To minimize the prospect of huge shifts in the triple constraint factors, it is vital to understand what a project is within the company or the industry setting at hand, and to what extent the pre-project analysis and proving activities are all helping to build clarity in respect to scope. These can and do differ tremendously by sector, industry, and geography, and the objectives that the initiative is trying to attain. For example, building a new commercial aircraft has fundamentally different needs, cost structures, delivery techniques, timelines, and associated risks than a project to refurbish a family owned coffee shop.

Appropriate estimation and planning are also crucial. To that extent, the working environment should foster the creation of initiatives that are not "padded" to the point that the cost/benefit case renders it unapprovable, or similarly, that estimates are so poor that major "surprises" are experienced downstream. The ability to estimate will ideally lead to realistic estimates and something that provides an appropriate benchmark against which to assess the initiative in question. This is, however, a cultural concern. Further, a competence around estimation is something that many companies do not invest in as part of their critical value chain activities.

This book has free material available for download from the
Web Added Value™ resource center at *www.jrosspub.com*

![3]

STAKEHOLDER ENGAGEMENT AND INVOLVEMENT

One of the leading causes of project challenges and failures is the lack of involvement by stakeholders and user groups in the development process. According to Murray and Crandall (2006), a lack of user involvement occurred in 29%[1] of failing projects, while ineffective stakeholder management occurred in 51%[2] of failing projects. That means that over half of projects being executed will not be able to effectively engage and manage the stakeholders who are responsible for contributions, key decisions, and sign-off.

There are a variety of reasons for this low percentage; it is not quite as simple as they do not have time or that they lack interest in the project. First and foremost, there is often a lack of understanding about the role that stakeholders play in the project, and project teams do not engage stakeholders in meaningful ways. In addition, project teams do not collaborate with stakeholders to the degree that is necessary and there is often a lack of formal communication architecture in place to guide and facilitate communication. Finally, others may intervene between the project team members and the stakeholders.

STAKEHOLDER ENGAGEMENT

Stakeholder engagement and building relationships are really the first steps in setting and managing expectations. The truth is, while many business teams and people will come in with their own preconceived expectations, it is the job of the project team members to level-set those expectations. Ultimately, those expectations must align with what is going to be achieved by the project team, the functionality that they will see in the solution, and the results that this solution will have on the business.

In order to effectively engage stakeholders, we must understand the differences between needs, wants, and egos. Many people, including stakeholders, project managers, and team members, often confuse needs with wants. It is the result of this confusion that shows up as poor requirement definition, unused features, or excessive change requests.

Where needs are tied to specific results, the business objectives, and the desired situations, "wants" are very personal and will change dramatically, depending on the stakeholder involved. It is important to note that underlying needs do not change as frequently as wants, simply because wants are tied to the solution and needs are tied to the problem.

Operating on the assumption that needs and wants are one and the same, team members generally meet with stakeholders to ask them what they want. That is where we get stories about users wanting to name the corporate server after themselves, so that they can log into a system with their own name on it (totally true).

The first rule of stakeholder management is to establish and build a relationship with each person and to understand the power dynamics at work on the team. The second most crucial factor is to establish, adopt, and socialize a formal communication architecture for the project. Where the relationship builds trust, the communication architecture enables collaboration that not only supports but also enhances expectation management through a greater sense of transparency.

COMMUNICATION ARCHITECTURE

Communication architecture is the framework for communication and change within an organization. It is primarily a strategic framework with tactical activities for the management of both communication, and changes in steps and stages, as events occur within the life of the organization. These events include projects.

This framework is comprised of elements that are divided into four primary categories. These are: policies, tools, plans, and artifacts. Policies are rules set by the organization about things that are done within the company. Tools are those technology-based applications which enable communication to occur (e-mail, website, posters, etc.). Plans are the project-centric plans for the accomplishment of certain tasks, and artifacts are those documentation sets that will be left behind after the project to support the growth of the organization through learning. At the project level, the organization utilizes corporate tools and adapts instances of them for specific uses, and they leverage the policies to build project-specific plans and artifacts.

Policies

Policies are the rules that govern the communication of an organization among its various interest groups. These groups include shareholders, management, employees, customers, vendors, competitors, regulatory bodies, and the general public.

Many companies utilize a public relations team to manage all external communications, and designate personnel to address the media, public, regulatory bodies, shareholders, and even competitors, but they rarely utilize a policy to govern internal communications amongst their internal teams and departments. The benefit to employing a communication policy is consistent and planned messaging.

Communication Policy

At the project level, communication policies can support the team in the delivery of key messages, and in setting and managing expectations. All of this leads to a cohesive team and a more polished execution and delivery.

The Christmas Letter

The Christmas letter is a piece of project communication that will live in infamy in one organization.

Several years ago, an insurance company decided to change the way it penalized drivers for behaviors that they determined to be risky. In order to announce this new initiative and to give drivers the opportunity to change their driving behaviors, the project team sent out a letter just before Christmas.

The letter basically stated that the recipient had received the letter due to their "bad driving habits and behaviors." It went on to state that if they did not change these behaviors immediately, they would get a few extra bills the following year, and they would be required to pay them or lose their driver's license.

> This did not go over well. The call center, which had been reduced to skeleton staffing over the holidays, was inundated with calls from angry drivers demanding to know where the company got off calling them a bad driver.

The insurance company letter story illustrates the need for a communication policy. While the team members were well-meaning, there was no policy in place to vet the letter through any other group, or to have the messaging directed through a central group. This would have ensured that the letter first met certain criteria and would have (hopefully) prevented this situation from occurring.

While this example was a large-scale project that impacted approximately 140,000 angry customers, it is not unique.

Employee Attitude Forces Policy Adoption

A company once initiated a project to migrate from multiple Windows platforms, Lotus 123, and Corel WordPerfect to updated Windows and Microsoft Office versions.

During the project, a team of analysts was responsible for contacting each business unit to discuss the impending migration, and talk about the needs of that department, so that documents could be converted to the new formats, and the business unit could migrate seamlessly.

One of the analysts did not have the magic touch when it came to dealing with people, and in his attempts to schedule reviews of the documentation, several business units became incensed and angered over his "like it or lump it" attitude. Needless to say, the project team was getting several angry phone calls every time he spoke to anyone in the business units.

Eventually, the project team defined and implemented a communication policy and appointed a single point of contact (who was not this analyst) for making these calls. In the end, it was a much better scenario for all involved.

A communication policy has, at its core, a clear set of directions and expectations that must be met before the team can begin to distribute communications. In effect, it is a service level agreement for how the project will communicate with everyone outside the project team.

In order to create a communication policy, it is important to identify:

- A main contact person and an alternate contact person.
  - o Who can the employees contact if they have questions?

- o What is the person's role, title, e-mail address, and phone number?
- o Who is the alternate contact?
- o How will they get regular information from the project team?
- o Are there standard frequently asked questions (FAQs) about the project, process, or new system?
- o What is the schedule for change/implementation?
- o Is there a website that people can go to for more detailed information?
- • Response times. Projects should identify the standard response times for each of the following events:
  - o Acknowledgment of communications (receipt), such as letters or e-mails.
  - o Provision of the requested information in the initial communication.
  - o Closure of request for information once the information has been sent and accepted.
- • Response formats. Determine the response formats. Typically the format will be the same as the incoming formats with follow up via e-mail to confirm details or report requested information.
- • The specific events or triggers that constitute a crisis for the project.
  - o How will the team communicate in a crisis?
  - o To whom will the team communicate in a crisis?
  - o How will situations be escalated in the event of a crisis?
  - o Who will communicate in a crisis?

Once the communication plan has been established, it is critical that it is shared among the team and the business, and enforced. By sharing the plan and enforcing it, teams ensure that they will be successful and members of the business will feel more confident and comfortable with the changes occurring around them.

Tools

A well-designed communication architecture contains both outgoing and incoming communication channels. Those channels include combinations of informational (outgoing channels) and input activities and funnels (incoming channels). While the outgoing channels disperse information out from the project team, the incoming channels provide opportunities for the business and customers to respond, and to provide their thoughts and inputs into the new solution. In this way, the business is provided with very specific and direct methods and opportunities to contribute throughout the project.

Many projects make two common mistakes when they plan change management strategies. First, they only consider cost when it comes to communication architecture, or they only consider outgoing channels as valid, and ignore the incoming channels altogether.

This mistake is made under the assumption that requirements elicitation is when stakeholders and users will have an opportunity to provide input. Unfortunately, this is often a false assumption because many requirements are most often generated by working with subject matter experts (SMEs). All too often, those same SMEs make assumptions based on their own personal experiences or opinions.

In addition, the channels themselves tend to be one-sided because they are intended to send information out from the project. Finally, by waiting for requirements activities to begin, it is far too late in the project to begin collaboration. This makes the buy-in process that much harder and actually increases the likelihood of changes to scope.

Input Funnels

Input funnels are those tools that bring information from outside of the project, to its team members so that they may incorporate the information into the project while it is executing. These include e-mail accounts, SharePoint, and social engagement forums.

While not every project will require a unique e-mail account, there is benefit to having one. Largely, the e-mail account provides an opportunity for multiple resources to monitor the same account and segregates all project-specific e-mails into a single account. In addition, it supports the transition process between resources, so it allows new resources to get up to speed quickly without having to having to gather a mass mailing of previous e-mails.

The following questions should provide a good basis for the management of a project e-mail account if one is established:

- Will a project e-mail account be used?
- Who will have access to it?
- What is the protocol for assigning items from the e-mail?

- What are the response times and policies for managing the e-mail account?

Outgoing Channels

Outgoing channels are those tools that disperse and distribute information from the project to others outside of the effort so that they understand how the project impacts them and when. It is an effective method for providing ongoing information to the business about the project in order to prepare it for the impending changes. These tools include e-mail accounts, newsletters, SharePoint forums, and project websites.

The key purpose of the project e-mail account is to communicate with others about the project. This communication may be team member to team member, team member to business user, or business user to team member.

When automatic e-mails are planned, it is important to ask the following questions about how and by whom they will be created:

- Will automatic e-mails be used to respond to queries and inform people about how long it will take to address their inquiry?
- What other types of automatic e-mails will be used?
- What will each of these e-mails say?

The purpose of a SharePoint forum is to exchange ideas about the project and to interact with the business in a way that gives them an opportunity to provide input, share concerns, and issues. It should be noted that these forums are strictly internal only and nothing is shared externally from the company.

The purpose of a project website is to post detailed information about the project. These details are often related to scheduling, preparation, and FAQs, about what each business unit can expect as the project progresses.

The purpose of a newsletter posting is to publish important information about a specific aspect or event on the project that the business community will need to be aware (and reminded) of.

Plans

The communication architecture describes the method for planning how and when communication will occur under all circumstances on the project. This plan must incorporate and align to specific corporate and project policies about communication between the project team and the extended business community (stakeholders, users, regulators, vendors, customers, and the general public).

Communication Plan

The communication plan is used to outline the routine communications between the project team members and the business team members. This plan, in and of itself, establishes expectations for project governance activities (such as status updates, reviews, and committee meetings) and identifies who is responsible for each. As shown in Table 3.1, in the Communication Matrix, the communication plan lays out the frequency of the governance activities.

Develop your communication plan to answer these questions:

- Who needs to be informed about the project?
- How will you inform them (e-mail, website, or poster)?
- How often will they be informed or communicated with?
- What information will you be giving to them?
- What format will the information be in?
- Who needs a report about the progress of changes?
- How will you inform them (e-mail, website, or poster)?
- How often will you report to them?
- What information will you be reporting to them?
- What format will the report be in?

A plan enables the management of expectations because of the clear timeline for specific communications, and the mere fact that everyone has access to this plan and agrees to abide by it. The stakeholders hold project managers accountable for the delivery of updates and the performance of the governance activities outlined in the plan. The project managers, in turn, hold the team responsible for performing the governance activities under their purview.

Escalation Plan

The escalation plan outlines a clear plan for escalation when issues arise that must be managed and addressed by the project and/or the business teams. This plan establishes expectations for key decisions and accountability for those decisions as the need arises within project execution.

Table 3.1 Communications Matrix

Communication Type	Communication Purpose	Delivered By	Audience	Communication Format	Frequency
Identify the general descriptive title of the communication. See examples below:	Describe the purpose of the communication.	Who on the team is responsible for delivering the communication?	Who will receive the communication?	Which format type is the communication delivered in? (There may be more than one type.) Use the Project Documentation checklist to identify if a specific template should be used.	How frequently is this type of communication required? List any specific days/times, if known.
Examples:					
Status Updates	Inform of status of project activities	Project Team	Project Manager	E-mail, Use the Weekly Status Report Template	Weekly, Friday, 12:00 P.M.
Review	Discuss current progress and set weekly goals	Project Manager	Project Team	Meeting	Weekly, Monday, 9:00 A.M.
Status Reports	Inform of status of project activities	Project Manager	Client Project Manager, Project Sponsors	E-mail, Report	Weekly, Monday, 12:00 P.M.
In Process Reviews	Inform of status of project activities, provide updates to work plan, and provide performance reports	Project Manager	Steering Committee	PowerPoint Presentation, Report	Monthly, First Tuesday of the month, 10:00 A.M.
Steering Committee Meetings	Discuss issues and changes affecting project outcomes	Project Manager and selected Team Members	All	PowerPoint Presentation, Report	Semi-Monthly, Second and Fourth Tuesday, 10:00 A.M.
Quality Review(s)	Provide objective review of projects to ensure adherence to policies, processes, standards, and plans	QA Mgr	Project Manager	Report, Meeting, 1-on-1	Quarterly

The escalation plan supports the management of expectations by detailing the responsibilities and accountabilities for critical decisions that will impact the outcomes of the project. This plan crosses the lines between project team leads, project managers, stakeholders, and sponsors in that all of these individuals may be listed as part of the escalation process. The process itself outlines key decisions at various levels of authority in much the same way that bank tellers have a monetary authority level. This level indicates the size and types of decisions that persons can make.

One consideration that must be made in developing the communication and escalation plans is how to communicate in crisis situations. On a project, a "crisis" could be anything from ill-worded letters sent out to thousands of customers, breaking a seemingly disparate system during deployment, or an excessive numbers of defects.

By having a crisis communication plan in place, should a crisis occur, the business and the project team will know exactly what should be said, to whom, and how it should be phrased in order to ease the situation. In addition, there will be a plan in place to determine the need for additional resources, when they should be in place, and at what location, in order to support the effort.

Change Management Plan

Change management really begins at the outset of a project, and arguably, with the idea of doing the project. It starts with the announcement that the company is trying to achieve a particular goal, and it can be as simple as saying, "We will be looking at ways to achieve our goal of … blah, blah, blah." A further statement may look like, "We will be forming employee focus groups to help us to find ways to achieve this goal."

While there may not be a tangible project or solution to reach that goal, the company is doing two things: including the employees and informing them that change might be coming. This does not necessitate that something must be changed, but when the employees have the opportunity to get involved at this stage, they can help to identify the right solution. A further statement may look like, "We are forming employee or customer focus groups to help identify opportunities and ways to help us achieve this goal." This helps the employees to take ownership over the achievement of the goal and provides them with a degree of buy-in right away.

From a project perspective, whether this has been done or not is inconsequential. What does matter is that by the time the project is in the midst of initiation and scoping, it does leverage the directed steps (elements) of change and sets the foundation for success by ensuring that key project definition activities are completed.

The directed steps to be followed within scope do not require a change management team. However, they do have to be done by everyone in the team and be managed by the project manager and business analyst, in order to be successful. These directed steps are: inform, involve, evolve, monitor, and observe. These steps can only really be effective when time and care is taken to prepare for them by identifying the project vision, assumptions about change, constraints of change, establishing a point of contact, and development of the project communication plan.

Change Management Done Well

Several years ago, a large utility company decided to acquire another, smaller local utility company in order to extend its customer base. The company made a broad announcement to all of the employees, customers, and vendors of both companies.

They worked hard behind the scenes of the acquisition to ensure that no customer lost service as a result of the acquisition. All systems and networks could be merged and switched over on Day 1, and all employees understood the new organizational structure. Projects to blend the human resources, merge networks, transfer power from the smaller grids, and establish new processes for vendors were initiated.

Throughout the years leading up to the final merger (Day 1), communication and forums were regular, and employees were asked to help the process and begin collaborating with their counterparts from the other company. By the time Day 1 actually arrived, it was business as usual. Everything was transferred over seamlessly, and the old systems were literally shut off.

Every project done by the utility company in the example went the same way. It went smoothly because they leveraged communication and involvement through a carefully planned set of change management steps. Contrast that situation with the next story about an insurance company's change management.

Who Needs Change Management

An insurance company acquired five smaller companies in about as many years. There was no planning for the acquisitions, and communication to the employees was limited at best. Communication was so bad that one of the smaller companies was actually convinced that they had purchased the larger company!

Everyone was left feeling confused and insecure. It turned out there was good reason for that feeling of insecurity. Some of the companies were run as subsidiaries, and some were amalgamated into the larger company. For those that were amalgamated, the employees were given six months' notice before being terminated.

Unfortunately, within the six months, several projects to merge the systems took place. The employees on notice were either disappearing or completely uncooperative. It made the merging of the systems and collection of corporate tribal knowledge virtually impossible. The project team members were helpless to deliver the promised scope.

The project vision is not always defined, or at least not consistently well-defined. However, it is the one guiding statement that brings people on board, allows them to maintain a consistent focus to their activities, and ensures that the deliverables they will produce align to that vision. It is the unifier. People can be in conflict about how to achieve that vision, but as long as they can be reminded of a strong vision, they can get behind it and common ground can keep them together.

The vision answers (in short, precise, and powerful messaging) the following questions that will guide the team:

- What is this project intended to accomplish?
- What will the business achieve through the results of this project?
- How will that benefit the company?
- How will that benefit individual groups?
- How will that benefit the employees/resources of those groups?
- What DON'T they want?

Once the vision has been established, it is important to identify the assumptions about the upcoming changes. To do this, the following questions can be helpful:

- What does management assume about the flow of change?

- What does management assume about the role of employees in change?
- What does management assume about the willingness and openness of the employees to accept change?
- What does management assume about the empowerment of resources during change?
- What do the employees/resources assume about the changes?
- What do they assume about the project?

Next, it is important to identify the specific constraints that are being placed on the changes by the company, its regulators, vendors, and customers. These constraints will have a direct impact on scope and will impede the ability to deliver and will impact the rate of adoption, if they are not met. The following questions will support the identification of these constraints:

- What (if any) limitations have been placed on the changes, as far as timing?
- What (if any) limitations have been placed on the changes, as far as budget?
- What (if any) limitations have been placed on the changes, as far as how to involve employees?
- What (if any) limitations have been placed on the changes, as far as how or when to inform employees?

The purpose of both the communication plan and policies within change management is to ensure consistent messaging is distributed by the project team, and to keep the business united and working toward the common vision through the activities. Letting people know that change is coming is a critical factor in change management, as it gives them time to mentally and emotionally prepare for the new situation.

Inform Your Target Audience

Inform your target audience about upcoming changes, in addition to employees:

- Identify and invite management level resources, including program managers, project managers, and team leads who are responsible for ensuring the buy-in, adoption, and ongoing compliance of their functional and project teams.
- Set up a meeting and invite the above list of people to attend.

- Ensure that you identify location, equipment, facilities, snacks, and content, and include this in the meeting invite.
- Identify and inform the attendees in the meeting invite of the types and levels of participation expected.
- Identify and inform the attendees in the meeting invite of the goals or results that you expect to achieve in the meeting.
- Identify the format and timeline for achieving these results.

Involve the Target Audience

It is best to involve your audience in stages. Not every group or level of the business has to have complete input or control over the project in order to have buy-in. In fact, input and control at specific stages and on specific details actually increases the level of buy-in and makes change management easier because people realize their time is being valued.

After the first meeting of managers, it is appropriate to move down to the user groups and other employees (who report to the managers) to get them involved. These participants will be encouraged to contribute to the discussions, review the training materials and content, and make recommendations for improvements to the materials and content prior to the training sessions with other groups and team members.

One of the important things to keep in mind is to identify people within this group who seem obstinate or against the change, as well as those with additional questions and seek to spend time with them in small groups or as individuals. These individuals can become the best champions for change on the project, and will actually advocate for it once they have buy-in.

Artifacts

Artifacts are those documents that must be created during the project in order to better manage it and to report back to the stakeholders and sponsors. These include status reports and issues logs.

Status Reports

Status reports fall under the governance activities as outlined in the communication plan. These reports provide routine updates to the project managers, stakeholders, sponsors, and even the project and business teams. Each report contains information about the progress of the deliverables and the work against the project plan, risk factors, and issues that could stall that progress, and identifies support required from stakeholders and sponsors to mitigate those risks and issues.

Status reports enable the management of expectations in that they provide opportunities for proactive mitigation of those factors that would otherwise interfere with the development and implementation efforts. This report also provides ongoing identification of expectations for those deliverables that are off-track and those that are on-track, and how they are being addressed and when they are expected to be completed.

Issues Logs

An issues log is the central repository for all of the key issues that arise on a project. It details the issue, the source of the issue, possible options for resolution, and responsibility and accountability for that resolution. Typically, issues are logged with a time and date stamp for both entry into the log and resolution.

The issues log is a crucial element of the management of expectations in that it tracks the progress of ongoing issues that will impact the ability of the project and the project team to be successful. When these issues are not addressed, or they are not addressed in a timely manner, it not only impacts the ability to be successful, but also the team morale. Once issues are logged, it creates the expectations that they will be addressed and the team will be able to move forward.

By logging resolutions, the team can see the progress made and that every effort is being taken to ensure that they are indeed successful. This in itself promotes confidence and collaboration. However, as the next section illustrates, the lack of planning and tracking is interpreted as the expectations not being important, and the lines of communication break down and reduce the effectiveness of the project team.

EXPECTATION MANAGEMENT

As previously stated, stakeholder engagement and relationship building are the first critical steps in establishing and managing expectations. In other words, managing expectations cannot occur unless those expectations are clearly defined up front. However, measures and performance indicators must be established to track the progress against defined expectations.

Setting Expectations

The most critical ingredients to setting expectations is having open and honest discussions at the outset of the project. In doing so, you establish a clear set of outcomes, success/fail criteria for those outcomes, and how they will impact the business results. These up-front and frank discussions demonstrate that the business groups have been heard, and that the project is aligned to the needs and objectives of the project.

It is by providing this recognition that the project team begins to instill confidence of success within the impacted business groups. Having this confidence from the business is crucial to success because it is the difference between getting sign-off and getting the runaround.

Missed Expectations

Recently, a short discovery project was initiated to define a solution to replace a legacy claims system. In this case, the entire workflow had to be considered manual for the purposes of defining workflow and estimating the final solution because the majority of the existing system was defective, and it did not have the functionality or capacity to handle the workload.

After the first week, the business did not know how the work was going to progress, what the deliverables were, how they should look, or what the final results of the discovery process would be. This was a clear indicator that expectations had not been properly set.

So, just why is it that expectations are not consistently set at the start of a project? In some cases, the expectations are overlooked; in other cases, the expectations are assumed; and quite honestly, sometimes the project team is simply inexperienced or does not want to be held accountable for delivering on the expectations, just in case they mess up.

Managing Expectations

It is important to maintain the expectations that have been set by using open and consistent dialogues throughout a project. This is accomplished by having similar discussions throughout the project life cycle and through the establishment of the communication plan, escalation plan, status reports, and issues log.

When consistent messaging, plans, reports, and issues log are absent, both the business and the project team members feel as though there is a lack of transparency. The perception of the loss of transparency leads to mistrust and decreases confidence.

Mismanaged Expectations

Let's look back at the legacy modernization project (Missed Expectations). Throughout the subsequent weeks, there were many conversations between the project team members and the business about what was going to be delivered, how it was going to be created, and what it should look like.

These conversations all sounded exactly the same. The key reason was that the business did not understand the expectations and had to keep coming back for clarification. This demonstrated that not only were the initial expectations not set, but also that the team was not working to manage those expectations.

The next step in managing expectations is to keep communication lines open. As the legacy modernization project story illustrated, managing expectations did not happen the way that it should have. This was in part because they were not properly set at the start of the project, but also because there was no consistent and ongoing dialogue with the business throughout the project life cycle, and no plans, reports, or logs in place.

The key elements that enable the project team to manage expectations are the communication and escalation plans, status reports, and the issue logs. Each of these will enable and support appropriate communication with the various business groups and stakeholders in order to ensure that their needs and their expectations are being met.

In addition, they also instill confidence in the stakeholders by dictating and establishing consistency in the frequency of messages and updates. Basically, the stakeholders know what to expect and when to expect it. The reports provide a tangible progress report to showcase the ongoing status of the project.

Impacts of Mismanaged Expectations on Relationships

As the discovery project progressed, the trust and confidence that the business had for the project team broke down and it became a very contentious environment. There was an increasing amount of gossip and conflict, and the project team began to fail because there was little in the way of team communication.

It is crucial to project success that expectations be set and managed so that there are no assumptions, everyone is on the same page, and there are no hurt feelings later on.

One of the hallmarks of escalating conflict is repetition in the message. When someone expresses the same concerns over and over again, it is an indicator that the person does not feel heard. Another thing that happens when a person does not feel heard is that they begin to raise their voice. Both of these signals accompany conflict escalation because the person becomes quite vocal with anyone who will listen and this will in turn, cause others around them to choose sides; the team becomes polarized.

In the case of the business and technology collaboration and working relationship, it is critical to demonstrate how the work being done will generate the deliverables that will meet the expectations. This not only eases any potential conflict, it also shows the business how and when they will get their needs met.

In addition, it is important to use the same language as the business as a means of demonstrating understanding, but it is also important that all project team members are delivering the same message about the objectives, process, progress, and outcomes. When the team consistently delivers the same messages to the business, it not only builds confidence and trust, it helps to maintain the expectations that have been set at the start, and again when those expectations have changed.

By delivering the same message consistently, the project team demonstrates cohesiveness and buy-in to the solution. In other words, they believe in what they are doing, are all on the same page about how to do it, and agree on what the results will be. The direct result of this is that the business will be more accepting of both the project and the expected results.

Lost in Translation

One of the problems that surfaced in the legacy modernization project (Mismanaged Expectations), as the relationship imploded both inside the project team and with the business, was that the project manager, business analyst, enterprise architect, and data architect were giving different stories to the business about what was going on and what the outcomes would be.

> This did nothing to instill confidence in the business that the team was capable of delivering.
>
> Further, the differing stories created a deep divide between the project team and the business. The project manager was consistently intervening between the project team and the business in an effort to control the flow of information. Unfortunately, this made it impossible for the project team to perform and create the needed results.

Setting and managing expectations is a "two-way street." The project team, and the business stakeholders and sponsors are responsible for setting the expectations that they have with the rest of the team, and then supporting the development of the methods and framework to manage those expectations.

In the long run, the setting and management of expectations helps everyone to "just get on with it" because there is confidence, transparency, and comfort with what is going on around them.

> ### Mismanaged Expectations, Predictable Results
>
> In the legacy modernization project, one of the key issues was that there was no communication plan in place. One could argue that the plan was unnecessary because it was only a six week discovery project. However, it also meant that there was no clearly defined plan for progress reporting (status updates), or keeping the business in the loop about what was being worked on, by whom, and how much effort it was really taking in order to get the job done.
>
> For the project manager, this was not done for two reasons: if progress fell behind schedule, they could not be held accountable because they had committed very little in terms of milestones and governance, and also so that they would not overburden a short project with additional documentation that was deemed unnecessary.
>
> Instead, the project manager opted to provide "water cooler" updates to the sponsor on an ad hoc basis. Unfortunately, this led to diminished trust, confusion among the business, and some "watermelon" reports that were green on the outside but red on the inside.

The real essence of setting and managing expectations is having appropriate communication both with the business at all levels and among the project team members. Again, the key elements of communication for the purposes of expectations are having open discussions at the outset to present the mission, continually remind people about the objectives, keep the lines of communication open, and demonstrate process consistency.

GETTING SPONSORS, BUSINESS OWNERS, AND USER GROUPS INVOLVED

The key to any successful project is to ensure that the business is involved. As previously mentioned, setting and managing expectations are critical parts of setting the stage for that involvement and keeping it going throughout the project.

However, for a variety of reasons, it can be challenging to rally the business to get involved and to stay involved. The result, when this challenge becomes too much to overcome, is that there are increased numbers of change requests, schedule and budget overruns, and inappropriate software features are developed and implemented, but then never used.

RASCI Matrix

One of the ways that projects work to support the business and ensure that they are actively involved throughout the project is to define the RASCI matrix. The RASCI matrix outlines the roles and responsibilities of the project team members and the business team members.

The matrix supports expectation management in that it defines roles for who is "responsible" (R) for performing key tasks, who is "accountable" (A) for ensuring that they are completed, who has a role in "supporting" (S), who "contributes" (C) to key tasks, and who is merely "informed" (I) of the results (shown in Table 3.2).

Why Some People Contribute and Others Don't

Defining roles and expectations in the RASCI matrix is no guarantee of involvement by the business. Again, there are many challenges and factors that go far beyond the scope and control of the project team.

In fact, at any given time, there are office politics at work, family issues, personality differences, overloaded work schedules, feelings of being cheated by the company, a lack of buy-in about the need for change (no burning platform recognition), leftover grudges from past mergers, and the list of factors simply goes on and on.

However, in spite of these other issues, the project team has a responsibility to get the business involved and contributing. That means understanding

Table 3.2 RASCI matrix (roles and responsibilities table)

Describe the roles and responsibilities of specific team members and stakeholders in the development and management of these requirements.						
Name	Position	R	A	S	C	I
	Project Manager		X			
	Testing SME				X	
	Interface SME				X	
	Business Unit SME				X	
	Business Unit SME				X	
	Business Unit SME				X	
	Business Unit SME				X	
	Business Analyst	X				
	Business Unit Manager				X	
	Business Unit Manager		X			
	QA Lead				X	
	Development Lead					X
R—Responsible A—Approver S—Supports C—Consulted I—Informed						

the personal needs of the business team members and working with people (including their personal baggage) to ensure that they contribute. At the end of the day, this translates into project success and enables the development of a quality solution for the business.

In addition to working with personalities, the project team must also create opportunities for both the business as a whole and individual business team members to contribute to the project. By creating opportunities to contribute, the foundation has been laid for that contribution to occur.

Opportunity Does Not Guarantee Contribution or Increase Participation

One of the main issues that arise on projects is the lack of contribution. But just creating opportunity is not enough. There is an assumption that inviting the business to meetings is creating the opportunity, and that the business will simply show up and contribute. This assumption leads to challenges with getting "time with the business" and effective contributions throughout the rest of the project. Again, this goes back to setting expectations and to working with individual personalities.

On projects, creating opportunities to contribute is a matter of respecting people's time, meeting their personal needs, asking for clear and specific inputs or feedback, and providing adequate time to contribute. Just because people may seem content or may even seem to be involved, does not mean that they actually are. In fact, it could be that they simply do not feel really welcome. Or, it could be that they feel left out, unimportant, or even that they do not know how to contribute to the project. On the other hand, it could also be that they were contributing before a certain other person arrived, or even that something else occurred that caused them to shut down and stop contributing.

The reality is that people either will or will not participate for a variety of reasons that may be completely out of the control of the project team. However, when the project team makes the effort to identify personal needs of the individual team members, and then to work with those members on a personal level, these issues can be successfully set aside.

Without meeting some of the personal needs of individual team members, the opportunity to contribute may sometimes go over like a ton of bricks. In fact, when opportunity is presented in a meeting with heavy tension and with participants who are shut down, the person may feel confronted and could shut down even further.

Types of Participation

In order to overcome personality conflicts, tensions, and reach those who are shut down, the project team must be able to identify the types of participants who they may be dealing with. There are four primary types of participants: the Active Participant, Non-Participant, Heckler, and Hijacker.

The Active Participant

The active participant is the person that comes to the meeting prepared to contribute and to get work done. They are not usually quiet, and they play well with all others in the room. The active participant has no problem contributing ideas and is quite open to discussing the ideas of others in order to explore the value of the individual idea.

The active participant thrives in an environment where all participants are encouraged and welcome to contribute. They are all about the ideas and the merit of those ideas. Further, they don't take criticism of their ideas as personal insult; they welcome it.

However, the active participant will become frustrated when the goal of a meeting is not met, the work is not done, and others are either not contributing or pushing others around. The project team will quickly lose this person's respect if they cannot manage the other personalities on the team because they want to work on and are motivated to complete the tasks.

The Non-Participant

The non-participant is the person who sits at the back of the room and does not contribute. They are shut down and do not want to be in the meeting. They would prefer to be at back their own desk doing work, or doing anything but contributing to the project. If the non-participant is asked to give input in a round-robin meeting, they will usually not say anything and opt to pass.

The non-participant is a person whose ego has been injured in some way at work or even in the same meeting that is going at the moment. It is possible that they had contributed an idea several times and it was ignored by the group, they were passed up for a promotion, or another team member is bullying them. No matter what the scenario, the fact is that this person generally feels unimportant, disengaged, disempowered, and disenfranchised.

The active participant and the non-participant are a good pairing for breakout sessions because the active participant will acknowledge and explore the ideas of all others as well as their own, and will help the non-participant to feel included and important. The active participant would champion good ideas, regardless of the source, and ensure that the valuable contributions of the non-participant are incorporated. This validates the non-participant and renews their feelings of worth and importance.

The Heckler

The heckler openly and loudly disputes ideas and attacks credibility. They will attack and dispute the credibility of the facilitator, manager, solution, company that they work for, department that they work for, and even others in the room. When one attack is countered, they will launch another attack on some other aspect.

Hecklers deflect attention away from themselves because they do not want anyone to know that they may not be able to understand or that they do not believe in what is going on.

The heckler needs clarity, guidance, and support to help them to understand either the benefits or just what is going on. They need that clarity, guidance, and support *outside* of the meeting.

While this person is good at calling others out, they do not want to be called out in return. In fact, calling the heckler out in public may actually cause them to shut down and become a non-participant.

The heckler needs extra attention to help them either understand or buy-in, so the best way to manage this person is to give them a personal demonstration, to coach and mentor them, and to ask them for questions while they are out of the meeting setting. Once the heckler has started feeling confident in their own level of understanding and buy-in, or at least a feeling like the facilitator is a person that they can trust, they will begin to contribute effectively.

The Hijacker

The hijacker is the person that tries to take over control of the meeting. Typically, they feel as though they should be the leader, so they will make every effort to take control by redirecting conversations, steering meeting agendas off course, having side conversations, and working against the leadership behind the scenes. It is simple: the hijacker does not respect the authority of the leader because they want to be in their shoes. Typically this person is feeling a degree of supremacy, but at the same time, they are also often feeling a degree of being jilted. Perhaps in some way, they feel passed over.

What a hijacker needs is an ego boost, public recognition, and public attention. They most need to feel as though the leader is their ally. Remember that they may be feeling passed over and they want recognition, so if the leader gives it to them, they will respond positively. While this does not usually work on the first few tries, keep going and it will pay off.

The best way to manage the hijacker is to give them some time to speak during meetings, give them public praise, offer them time to discuss their burning issues after the other agenda items are covered, ask them to facilitate break-out sessions, or ask them to lead when the leader is going to be away.

Creating the Right Conditions and Environment Increases Participation

Do not be too surprised if the first few meetings are not very productive despite best planning and efforts. Until the four main participant types are identified, it is going to be difficult to manage the room and to accomplish any productive amount of work. That being said, there are ways that the project team can set up and structure meetings so that people are encouraged to both attend and to contribute.

There are a few key things that any project team member can do in order to increase the likelihood of success in getting stakeholders, business users, and technology teams involved and actively participating. These key things leverage the communication architecture and include conducting routine informational activities, creating input funnels, and running input activities.

Informational Activities

There is not a human being alive that does not need to feel important in some way, shape, or form. This need is innate. It means that a person's job, and how well they do that job, becomes a part of their personal identity.

Further, when something new comes along that challenges or threatens a person's identity, the person needs to have an opportunity to provide input into the new "situation," and to have their concerns heard and questions answered. This provides people with the feeling of being in control. It is the unknown that makes people feel as though they do not have control, and this feeling that creates the threat.

Projects that do not take these factors into consideration are doomed. They could implement a solution made of gold, and the business would still revolt against the project and the solution.

Projects must start with a high-level set of activities that provide information to the executives, and then begins to get those executives involved. Once that involvement has started, information must be dispersed to the business and customer communities in order to alert them to coming changes.

While informational activities, at this point, are not part of an intensive process, these activities do enable people to prepare themselves mentally and emotionally for impending change. These informational activities must be able to provide basic information about what the business and its customers can expect, and who will be impacted and how. In addition, this information should also provide details about the expected participation from each impacted group, where they can find more information, and how to contact the project team with any questions, comments, or feedback.

It is important to remember that "buy-in" means "believe-in." There is a lot of energy and excitement in starting a new project. The best way to obtain buy-in from people is to get them excited, get them involved, and show them how to carry it forward.

When people are informed that change is coming, it is new and exciting, yet scary all at the same time. The project team must anticipate and overcome people's fears of being replaced or phased out, or even suddenly being incompetent. These fears are overcome by collaborating with the business.

Many times the project teams can identify a single person or a group of people who are obstinate and have barricaded the way for change and the new solution because they don't believe in it. By working with this person or group, by understanding their needs and finding ways to meet their needs without changing course, you will find a new champion.

In fact, the loudest and most outspoken adversary can become the project's biggest champion. When this occurs, this person supports the initiative and it becomes a grass-roots movement.

However, knowing and understanding the types of participants is crucial to being successful in hitting this tipping point. It is equally important to understand that the role of the project team is to set up a customer-centric experience and to view each of these groups as an intrinsic part of their customer base.

This fundamental change in attitude will ensure that both teams are encouraged to collaborate in an innovative space and environment where all contributions are valued and important to the success of the project.

REFERENCES

1. Murray, M. J., and Crandall, R. E. (Winter, 2006). *IT Offshore Outsourcing Requires a Project Management Approach*. SAM Advanced Management Journal, 71(1), 4.
2. *Ibid.*

This book has free material available for download from the
Web Added Value™ resource center at *www.jrosspub.com*

IMPLICATIONS OF BUSINESS ARCHITECTURE

Business architecture has been described as a "blueprint of the enterprise that provides a common understanding of the organization and is used to align strategic objectives and tactical demands."[1] Companies establish both the framework that describes all of the internal and external entities (customers, vendors, and regulatory bodies) associated to their organization, as well as the means of governing that framework. This framework represents the flow of work and information into and out of the organization across this architecture.

OVERVIEW OF BUSINESS ARCHITECTURE ELEMENTS

Business architecture is the visual framework that illustrates the essential business elements of "who, what, which," and "where," per the National Institutes of Health model (shown in Figure 4.1) in relation to the enterprise architecture (information and technology). These elements provide a means for the business and technology teams to articulate the capabilities of the company as they relate to the current project and the greater enterprise architecture. These abilities are articulated in terms of what the business does (its products and services); for whom (its customers); where the company sells its products or provides the services; and which specific data are needed to tie all of those elements and pieces together.

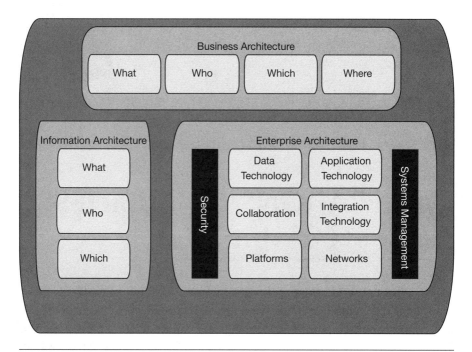

Figure 4.1   National Institutes of Health business architecture model

The Zachman Framework[2], however, articulates the business elements in terms of the project, i.e., the work performed and the data captured. By analyzing this framework, one can see the specific activities and details that would have a direct correlation and impact on scope. Table 4.1 illustrates the Zachman Framework for the purposes of this discussion. The framework represents a matrix for contextual, conceptual, logical, physical, and detailed models. Each row within the framework represents a complete model from that perspective or level of detail. If these are broken into the various types of models represented by the rows, the descriptors for each element would be contextual, conceptual, logical, psychical, and detailed representation.

Contextual Level

Across the contextual level of the Zachman Framework, the matrix illustrates the corresponding tasks and deliverables according to the elements of the business architecture being represented. These are:

Why: Goal List—This list represents the underlying high-level organization goals and objectives. On a single project, it would illustrate the project goal.

Table 4.1 The Zachman Framework

	What (Data)	How (Functions)	Where (Location)	Who (People)	When (Time)	Why (Motivation)
Contextual (Scope)	List of data needs	List of business processes	List of locations where the business operates	List of organizations/entities important within and to the business	List of events & cycles	List of goals & strategies
Conceptual (Enterprise Model)	Semantic model	Business process model	Logistics system	Workflow	Master schedule	Business plan
Logical (System Model)	Logical data model	Application architecture	Distributed architecture	User interface model	Process structure	Business rule model
Physical (Technology Model)	Physical data model	System design	Technology architecture	Presentation architecture	Control structure	Business rule design
Detailed Representation	Data definition	Program	Network architecture	Security architecture	Timing	Business rule definition
Functioning System	Data	Function	Network	Organization	Schedule	Strategy

How: Process List—This list represents all of the known processes. These processes can be formally documented or tribal knowledge. On a project, this list represents the processes that are related to the goals of the project, and identify direct and indirect impacts of the project.

What: Material List—This list represents all of the organizational assets. On a project, this list illustrates the assets that will either be impacted by or needed for the work to progress and to develop the project results.

Who: Organizational Unit and Role List—This list represents all of the organization units, sub-units, and identified roles or entities (customers, vendors, internal departments, regulatory bodies) that interact with the organization both internally and externally. On a project, this list depicts the stakeholders, sponsors, and all of the groups which will be impacted by the project and its results.

Where: Geographical Locations List—This list represents all of the locations important to the organization. On a project, this list represents only those locations that will be impacted by the project and its results.

When: Event List—This list represents all of the triggers and cycles important to the organization. Again, on a project, this list represents only those which will be impacted by the project and its results.

Conceptual Level

The conceptual level of the Zachman Framework describes the models of the business and technology systems:

Why: Goal Relationship Model—This model identifies the specific project goals that support core goals and objectives in a hierarchy format. It is intended to illustrate the alignment between the project and the strategic goals of the organization.

How: Process Model—This model depicts particular processes with their corresponding descriptions, inputs, outputs, and extension points. They illustrate how the work will flow through the new business architecture.

What: Entity Relationship Model—This model identifies and describes the organizational assets, such as data or hardware components, and their relationships to one another.

Who: Organizational Unit and Role Relationship Model—This model identifies the key enterprise roles and units, and illustrates the relationships between them. At the project level, this model identifies the key stakeholders and user groups that will be influenced and impacted by the project.

Where: Locations Model—This model identifies the organization's locations and the relationships between them. At the project level, this model identifies the locations that will be both influenced and impacted by the project.

When: Event Model—This model identifies and describes events and cycles which are related by time. At the project level, this model identifies the steps and stages of the workflow as it progresses, including the prerequisites and dependencies.

Logical Level

The logical level of the Zachman Framework describes the control and flow of information as follows:

Why: Rules Diagram—This diagram identifies and depicts the business rules that control the processes. At the project level, this diagram identifies the control gates for process governance of those processes being impacted, as well as the specific impacts to the rules themselves in order to align to and control the new processes.

How: Process Diagram—This diagram identifies and depicts the processes and the corresponding transitions and extension points. At the project level, this diagram identifies the individual workflows that are to be impacted and changed, either directly or indirectly, as a result of the project solution.

What: Data Model Diagram—This diagram identifies and depicts the data entities with their corresponding relationships to other entities. At the project level, this diagram identifies the specific data sets that will be impacted as a result of the project solution.

Who: Role Relationship Diagram—This diagram identifies and depicts the roles and their relations to other roles by types of deliverables produced across the processes and workflows. At the project level, this diagram identifies the roles which will be influenced or impacted by the project solution.

Where: Locations Diagram—This diagram identifies and depicts the locations used to access, manipulate, and transfer specific entities and processes. At the project level, this diagram identifies the geographical needs of the individual processes and solution components.

When: Event Diagram—This diagram identifies and depicts the events as they are related to each other in sequence. This includes any cycles that occur both within events and those which occur between particular events.

Physical Level

The physical level of the Zachman Framework describes the specific and granular details of the business models:

Why: Rules Specification—This specification articulates the business rules in a syntax that contains the name of the rule and precise logic in order to describe it.

How: Process Function Specification—This specification describes the process function in a technology specific language. The hierarchical process elements described in this function are correlated by specific process calls.

What: Data Entity Specification—This specification describes the data entities. It defines each entity by name, includes the description and attributes, and describes the relationships to other entities.

Who: Role Specification—This specification describes the functional roles that perform the work and the individual workflow components at the granular level.

Where: Location Specification—This specification describes the physical infrastructure components and their respective connections to the enterprise architecture around them.

When: Event Specification—This specification describes the transformation between event states that occur across the workflow, into and out of the organization and its systems.

Detailed Representation

The detailed representation level of the Zachman Framework expounds:

Why: Rules—The detailed representation articulates the intricate details of the appropriate business rules.

How: Process—The detailed representation illustrates the granular details of the identified business processes.

What: Data—The detailed representation describes and itemizes the intricate details of the necessary data fields and entities.

Who: Role—The detailed representation describes the details of the related organizational roles.

Where: Location—The detailed representation illustrates the details of the locations.

When: Event—The detailed representation articulates the details of the appropriate events and their corresponding transitions.

RELATIONSHIP BETWEEN SCOPE AND BUSINESS ARCHITECTURE

On projects, business architecture is often directly changed or impacted. In fact, many projects are initiated in order to fix or develop programs in support of one or more of the elements of business architecture. This means that architectural elements can either directly impact the scope, or they can actually be a part of it.

If projects leverage the Zachman Framework, it can be fairly straightforward to depict the relationship between the elements of business architecture and the work that is to be performed, together with its resulting deliverables. The important thing to note is that this depiction can provide a clearer visualization of the far-reaching relationship, and thus, the impacts of architecture on project scope (and vice versa), as that scope fluctuates throughout the project life cycle.

In reality, scope and business architecture have almost a yin and yang relationship. One cannot exist without the other; they can transform into one another, and can arguably be opposite ends of a cycle. Where it gets tricky is that an imbalance in one does not necessarily affect the other.

Business architecture simply could not exist without having been defined and the mechanisms having been built at some point in time. The same is true for scope on given projects. The scope cannot exist with business architecture because it defines what will be built and delivered on the project in relation to the overall architecture.

Both scope and business architecture can be said to transform into one another. Where architecture represents the mechanisms and framework for the business and can be used to define scope on a specific project, scope represents what new mechanisms are being built to support it, and in what time frame.

Both scope and business architecture can be considered opposite ends of a cycle because where the architecture begins to age and break down, or lose its effectiveness, scope is then defined to rebuild new elements to replace these elements. When the scope has been developed into a tangible product or new program for the business, it becomes a usable element of the architecture.

An imbalance in scope may affect the outcomes of the project and impact the ability for the solution being developed to be effective in supporting or redefining the business architecture. However, an imbalance in the architecture does not always translate into an item in scope for that particular project. There are many other factors such as budget, priorities, and strategies that may dictate which elements of business architecture are needed, required, or even broken. Those elements may not get corrected or fulfilled until a much later date.

Print Services Project

A number of years ago, an insurance company was in the process of transitioning from one print services vendor to another. During this project, there were a number of changes to the business architecture that had to happen before the transition could be completed.

One of the more significant changes was to the secure check process, which dictated how the paper for checks was handled, how the data for checks was managed during the printing cycle, how checks were numbered, who had access, and ultimately what should be done if a check was destroyed in the printing process. This represented a significant part of the business architecture for claims processing and payments.

The team had to determine the best new process, and how it fit with the capabilities of the new vendor, as well as fit the new enterprise architecture. They then had to create a new automated process and test run that process in sync with the old process before the new vendor could be official and the existing vendor could be removed.

In the printing services project story, the team was effectively changing the business architecture in that they changed the who, what, where, and how of the process for printing all documentation, including the checks used to make payments on approved medical claims. The architecture changed as a direct result of the project; however, that project was only initiated to change it as a means of meeting a strategic objective.

IMPACTS OF BUSINESS ARCHITECTURE ON SCOPE

Known business architecture elements that are relevant to the particular project are typically represented as items within scope, constraints, and assumptions. Basically, this means that this architecture is part of the project and places limitations on it, or the stakeholders are making assumptions about the project based on the current understanding of the architecture.

Unknown business architecture, on the other hand, cannot be adequately or appropriately represented within the scope or planning. These elements are represented by placeholders in the planning documentation through assumptions. The stakeholders will often attempt to account for unknown architecture (among other unknown elements) by making assertions about how particular situations will be handled should they arise. These assertions become part of the assumptions and constraints of the project, and can provide some guidance to the project team about how to manage the discovery of unknown business architecture as the specific details become exposed during the project life cycle.

However, this is not always the case. In fact, one of the biggest issues and challenges facing projects is that during inception, many project teams include little consideration for business architecture. It is assumed that these considerations were either already made by the business or that they will be made during the requirements or design phases. The problem with this assumption is three-fold: limited up-front information about the architecture, lack of setting and communicating related expectations to the project team, and a lack of leadership by business analysts to drive it forward.

First, when the business decides to initiate a project, the architecture itself and the full extent of the solution within the context of that architecture, is limited at best. In other words, the business may not be aware of all of the nuances of the implications and effects that the problem has on the business architecture. What they do know is where it hurts them the most and that it must be fixed. Worse, if it is not a problem that they are trying to solve, but are instead attempting to build new programs in support of a long-term strategy, they are often focused on a single business area.

In both cases, the business representatives do not necessarily perform the rigor and due diligence in making the decision to move forward with the identified solution. What it means is that there could be key areas impacted by the decision and the new program, and those will not be identified until much later. Once they are identified, those impacts will affect the scope of the project, and this usually translates directly into cost.

In addition, stakeholders and business units may look at both the problem and the solution with "tunnel vision," meaning that they may not consider factors outside of their own purview. These factors may be deemed as unnecessary and irrelevant, and critical elements of business architecture are overlooked.

Overlooking critical elements can have direct and adverse impacts on the development of requirements, as well as the overall solution (are we building the right things?). The key to resolving this issue, therefore, is to ask the right questions of the stakeholders and users about architecture. These questions should elicit exploratory conversations that enable the stakeholders and users to consider situations and elements of business architecture, as well as corporate strategy and integration points with other business units.

This is the approach that will enable the project to fill in any gaps in the information and to generate a more complete solution. In the end, this solution will fit seamlessly into the business architecture around it.

On the other hand, when the considerations for business architecture are left to the project team, this expectation is not always communicated. When the team identifies extensions and nuances of issues that will impact the business architecture and those have not been considered or accounted for, the team must work to renegotiate the scope of the project through change requests in order to ensure that these issues do not impact the quality of the product that they are working to deliver. Again, this translates directly into cost through time delays, increased resource needs, and even changes to asset requirements.

Across many projects, in general, there is a lack of business analysis leadership driving the solution forward as it relates to business architecture. The analysts are too reliant on the business to produce relevant information at needed intervals without a lot of prompting. Unfortunately, this means that key questions are not being asked, and some of the critical detail about business architecture is at risk of being missed altogether.

Computer Systems Migration

Around a decade ago, a large utilities company decided to migrate its desktop systems to a newer operating system. It was decided that they would also migrate to newer versions of MS Office at the same time in order to reduce costs.

Before sections and departments could be migrated over and have their computers reimaged, the team would conduct an assessment of the documents and the applications required for that area. The document assessment was to determine the need for conversion to the new formats, and the application assessment was to determine the compatibility of those applications for being run on the new Windows operating system.

The original scope of the project was to migrate every one of 6300 desktop systems over to the new platform. However, during the compatibility assessments, it became apparent that a specific mapping application utilized in the planning and geographical surveys section was not compatible. The team had to contact the vendor to determine the date of their next upgrade in order to make it compatible.

In the end, the desktop systems utilizing this mapping application had to be removed from scope and could not be migrated until the new product release, so that the survey teams could still perform their work.

While the computer systems migration story illustrates the impact of business architecture on scope, it still makes the point that there are times when scope will change in order to accommodate limitations of architecture that are uncovered during the project.

There are several reasons why business architecture and scope influence each other, and not all of those reasons have to do with their relationship. These are: ongoing overlapping or conflicting projects, undocumented business architecture (tribal knowledge), and unknown risks and issues of the existing architecture or systems.

At any given moment, there are projects going on in nearly every company to resolve issues or to add desired architecture. However, some of these projects may be overlapping with others in another part of the same company. These projects are intended to produce similar results, resolve similar problems within different divisions, or contain features that will perform the same tasks as other project solutions.

This overlap occurs when the stakeholders initiate a project without consulting, communicating with, or getting input from other divisions about how widespread the issues and their respective impacts are. It also occurs when single divisions define actions to address the corporate strategy that is related to their own unit without that same consultation, communication, and input.

In other words, both problems and strategy are addressed in isolation from the rest of the company. This means that business architecture as a whole entity is not viewed as a cohesive unit, and it reflects in the fluctuations in scope when projects compete or remove scope, which is redundant.

Let's face it. Redundancy costs companies by increasing the cost of software and architecture maintenance, in addition to the development costs of producing functionality that is already in scope on another project or exists within the enterprise architecture.

The real issue here is that it can be difficult to discern the stop and start points of workflow within the business architecture. Left unchecked by governance and change control, project scope can be a moving target that changes as the understanding of the architecture changes. This is exactly why the idea of scope exists at all: to set parameters that draw boundaries around those items that will be worked on and those that will not.

Another key issue that many companies face is that there is often a pervasive use of tribal knowledge throughout its daily routines at every level of the organization. Tribal knowledge can be thought of as undocumented architecture. Much of this knowledge is taken for granted by those who utilize it and do not consider writing it down or formalizing it to manage it properly.

Unlike unknown architecture, tribal knowledge is known, but is not documented in a coherent and manageable form. Where some unknown architecture can be represented in scope under assumptions and constraints with placeholders, tribal knowledge can become part of the scope itself through engaging and collaborative discussions with the stakeholders and users.

Stakeholder involvement is critical for the collection and analysis of tribal knowledge. Each will ensure the full discovery of undocumented business architecture elements, as well as their respective risks and impacts. These will lead directly to a more complete definition of scope and will lend to change control later on in the project life cycle.

Finally, unknown risks and issues of the existing architecture or systems influence scope in the same way as both tribal knowledge and unknown architecture. Again, without uncovering key elements of business architecture through collaboration with the stakeholders, the full extent of risks and issues cannot be understood or planned for. This goes directly to the rationale for utilizing placeholders in the assumptions and constraints that will support the management of these risks and issues as they become exposed during the project.

Unfortunately, not all risks and issues are exposed with the discovery of tribal knowledge and unknown architecture. It is incumbent upon the project team to perform analysis and to identify the associated risks and issues from these two elements.

USEFUL TECHNIQUES FOR EXPLORING BUSINESS ARCHITECTURE

In addition to plotting the elements of business architecture on the chart of the Zachman Framework, there are two other tasks that can be adapted and performed within a relatively short period of time. These will enable the project team to explore business architecture and expose unknown architecture, tribal knowledge, and unknown risks and issues. These are gap analysis and cause and effect tables.

Gap Analysis

Gap analysis is a method utilized for analyzing a particular object or element, and identifying the differences between multiple states (in this case, steps and stages in the workflow across business architecture). Gap analysis is defined here as a means of identifying all elements of business architecture (known, unknown, and tribal knowledge), as well as any associated risks and issues. In exploring business architecture, gap analysis is an important tool for identifying the gaps in both knowledge and documentation.

Cause and Effect Table

"A cause and effect table, also known as a decision table, maps the various scenarios against potential outcomes."[3] In this case, scenarios are architecture workflows with various combinations of preconditions, trigger events (causes), and the potential outcomes (effects) mapped out in a simple table. By using the table format shown in Table 4.2, the project team can see the architectural elements coupled with the results of each combination. This will enable them to gain an understanding of the full architecture, and what needs to be considered in planning and defining scope. However, it also enables the team to gain a better understanding of other external architectural elements (outside the project) that will be impacted by the scope of the current project.

Table 4.2   Cause and effect table

State	Filed (in doc mgmt system)	Not Filed (not in doc mgmt system)	Status	Priority
Existing	X		Active (used and edited)	Medium
Existing		X	Active	Medium
Existing	X		Active Historical (used but not edited)	Medium
Existing		X	Active Historical	Medium
Existing	X		Obsolete Historical (not used or edited)	Low
Existing		X	Obsolete Historical	Low
Non-existing		X	Active	High
Non-existing		X	Active Historical	High
Non-existing		X	Obsolete Historical	OUT OF SCOPE
Future	X		Active	OUT OF SCOPE
Future	X		Active Historical	OUT OF SCOPE
Future	X		Obsolete Historical	OUT OF SCOPE

REFERENCES

1. Object Management Group, Business Architecture Working Group.
2. Zachman International. The Zachman Framework Evolution. http://www.zachman.com/ea-articles-reference/54-the-zachman-framework-evolution. 2009.
3. Davis, Barbara. *Mastering Software Project Requirements: A Framework for Successful Planning, Development & Alignment.* Plantation, FL: J. Ross Publishing, 2013.

This book has free material available for download from the
Web Added Value™ resource center at *www.jrosspub.com*

SECTION 2:
MID-FLIGHT CHANGE
CONTROL

5

REQUIREMENTS DEVELOPMENT LIFE CYCLE

Every successful development, manufacturing, or engineering process dictates an evolution of the product through a series of stages and transition points between those stages. Requirements are no different, but so many people do not seem to have this perspective, or at least it gets forgotten in the midst of the work and the great scheme of the evolution of the project.

Requirements evolution is not synonymous with *project evolution*. This is true whether the project evolves through the stages of initiation, planning, design, development, and test (the Waterfall Model), or the stages of product vision, product road map, release plan, sprint planning, sprint review, and the sprint retrospective (the Agile Model).

Requirements evolve from high to low level in much the same way that any other literary work evolves. It is important to remember that requirements essentially go from vague ideas and feelings to highly detailed and articulated specifications.

The most appropriate stages to achieve these detailed requirements are needs analysis, elicitation, analysis, specification, and validation (shown in Figure 5.1). It is important to recognize that requirements do not start at elicitation. In fact, they begin with identifying and understanding the needs of the business and the project, and only a portion of this information will be revealed in elicitation. Therefore, the remainder of this information must be obtained through needs analysis. It cannot be ignored or omitted because this information provides context and focus to the requirements, and may actually influence them.

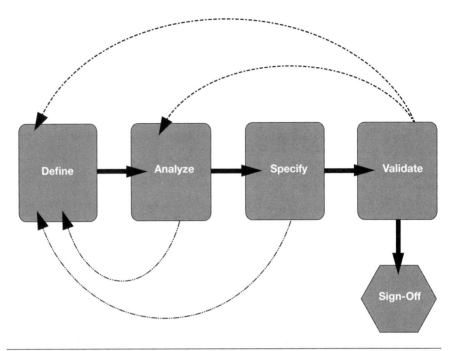

Figure 5.1   Requirements life cycle

RELATIONSHIP BETWEEN SCOPE AND REQUIREMENTS

Individual requirements are initially derived from the project scope and are subsequently articulated into increasing levels of detail and granularity through the requirements development life cycle. To say that requirements must trace back, or are even related, to scope would be an understatement. In fact, as illustrated in Figure 5.2, requirements are an extension of the scope, which lead directly to the development of the tangible solution or product.

Project scope, therefore, must be in place and communicated to the team *before* requirements activities begin. While this may sound obvious, it is not always obvious to the project manager or to the business analyst why this information is so crucial to requirements tasks. Consider two scenarios, A and B, for project scope communication. In each scenario, the criticality of the need for scope in the development of requirements was underestimated. In each situation, the cost was different, but the net result was the same: there was no context for the overall solution being built.

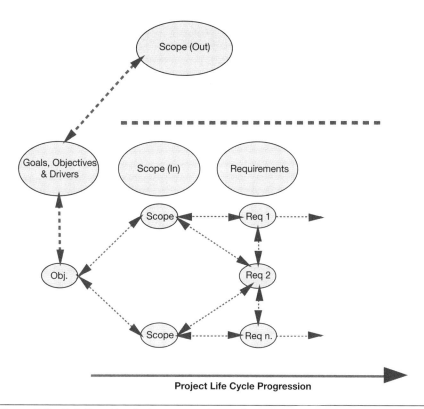

Figure 5.2   Relationships between requirements and scope

Scenario A: Project Scope Communication

The business analyst on a project was struggling to document requirements. The team had been working hard for several weeks and interviewing business stakeholders. The artifacts that they produced were not well organized and they had not yet been able to draft a single requirement, in spite of all of the meetings and the looming deadline.

A quick interview with the business analyst revealed that the team did not understand and could not identify the scope of the project or the needs of the business. In other words, they did not understand what they were doing and why. The analyst was subsequently replaced because they were unable to write requirements that aligned to scope and they didn't consider the needs of the business.

Scenario B: Project Scope Communication

The project manager was withholding the project charter, scope, and even the project plan from the project team. In regular meetings, the project manager advised the team of what needed to be done and when.

Repeated requests from the team usually went unanswered. The project manager believed that because it was their job to generate these documents, that they were private. This project manager did not realize that the team needed these documents to guide their efforts and to provide context to their deliverables.

The result was that the development team had one interpretation on what was being built, and the business analysis team had another interpretation. Unfortunately, with limited communication, no one realized this until it was too late. The product built was not only misaligned with the business need, it was built in complete isolation from the requirements.

The project was four times the estimated length and more than six times the estimated cost. In the end, the project was quietly shut down after implementation because of the lack of alignment to business need.

IMPACTS OF REQUIREMENTS ON SCOPE

When requirements change, it does not necessarily mean that scope will change. Conversely, requirements are more likely to change when the project scope changes. While requirements are derived out of scope, it is important to understand that there are several reasons for changes to requirements that may or may not result from fluctuations in scope.

That being said, changes to requirements often do lead to scope creep when the changes directly impact scope, however those changes are not always the ones that get made and others get made in their place. In understanding the difference, it is important to analyze the reasons for changes to requirements. The reasons for fluctuations in scope will only be discussed here as they relate specifically to their impacts on requirements, since these have already been discussed at length in Chapter 2.

The most common reasons for changes to requirements are:

- To impress or satisfy the business stakeholders and sponsors.
- To correct for fluctuations or misinterpretations of scope.
- To add further necessary details required by the architects, developers, or testers.

There are times when the changes to requirements may seem ad hoc or haphazard. It can be hard to differentiate between the reasons why they are changing when things are moving so quickly and the resources are in the heat of the moment. In truth, it is only when the forensic review is conducted that teams can start to analyze and understand what has really happened.

Impressing or Satisfying the Business

Impressing the stakeholders is twofold. On the one hand, the business analysts or the project team want to "wow" the stakeholders and the business so that they get the sought-after kudos. On the other hand, the stakeholders and business analysts, and even the project manager, often lose sight of the real consumer and audience of the requirements document.

When analysts and the project team want to impress the stakeholders, they often begin adding "extras." In some cases, these extras are necessary. However, for the most part, they are simply added in order to impress the business stakeholders.

These extras can be necessary when the requirements development process reveals missed yet critical functionality, which must be added in order to make the solution useful (meet the need) or usable (enable that solution to fit into the architecture or ensure that it can be used for its purpose).

In some cases, requirements are added to impress the business. In these instances, the requirements are either added discreetly (the stakeholders are unaware) or at the request of the business. The important thing to note here is that they are "extra" because they have no real traceability to the scope and business objectives, and feasibility analysis and other due diligence have not been completed. Even when the business requests these extras, the request may not follow the appropriate process of due diligence.

Periodically, business users make requests for features and functionality which are inappropriate. If these are included in the solution without due diligence and understanding feasibility, it is called scope creep.

It is important to note that people will take control where they feel that they can have it. In terms of requests for additional functionality made by the business, this means that end users may opt to request functionality that is neither feasible nor necessary simply to gain a sense of control. However, that is not the real problem with these requests.

When the business requests new functionality, these requests must be routed through the change control process without exception. Unfortunately, this is not always the case. While change control is in place in part to manage changes, it is also a process for vetting and prioritizing those changes, and ensuring that they are well defined and developed before being allowed into the solution.

The problem is that the necessary requirements are often underdeveloped, when adding new functionality begins to happen outside of the change control process, when an inappropriate prioritization takes over. In other words, the analyst begins to add unnecessary functionality before addressing the necessary (and often critical) functionality. Ultimately, they spend more time on unnecessary functions and not enough on those that are mandatory.

This can result in delays and loss of scope in the project in order to meet the project schedules and budgetary constraints. It can also result directly in unused software features. Consider that an estimated 42%[1] of implemented features are never used and only 20%[2] are used all the time.

The $64,000 Dilemma

If one were to perform some basic math, the net result is that for every $1 million spent, the result is about $64,000 in useful functionality. That is over 15 times the cost for the delivered value.

Let's break that down: industry statistics in 2012 showed that only 32%[3] of projects are successful.

32% of $1 million = $320,000 (successful project rates)
20% of $320,000 = $64,000 (implemented features used all the time)
42% of $320,000 = $134,000 (implemented features never used)

As if focus and inappropriate prioritization of these extras were enough, too many people associated to the project do not have clarity or a full understanding of the real audience of the requirements documentation. With this lack of clarity, there can be differences in perspective about whose language the documents should be written in: business jargon or geek-speak.

The answer is simple: geek-speak! Why? Simply, because of how the document is used, not who signs off on it. Ownership is not even a part of this conversation.

When writing the requirements documentation, use language that targets the right audience. It is important to remember that while the documents are prepared on behalf of the business, they are really for the developers and testers. The training materials and support manuals are for the business audience.

Consider this example: marketing materials are prepared on behalf of and owned by the business; however, they are used to communicate to customers. Therefore, they are written in the language of the customer and not the business. This means that in writing requirements, they must be written in the language of the developers and testers.

The stakeholders and sponsors must verify that the features meet the business needs and then sign off on the document. The architects, developers, and testers will then utilize the document to guide the design, build, and test activities.

When the analyst changes the verbiage and taxonomy so that the stakeholders and sponsors can understand it, they often water it down and lose the technical depth required by the other teams in order to perform their tasks and activities. The stakeholders and sponsors are business people, and that means that they usually communicate in a very different way than those in technology (hence the original impetus behind defining the business analysis role).

Accounting for Fluctuations or Misinterpretations of Scope

As discussed in Chapter 2, scope fluctuates for many reasons. Some of these reasons are directly related to or impact requirements. These include requests made by the stakeholders and sponsors; corrections to the team's misinterpretations of the business needs; and the desire to impress the stakeholders and sponsors. Scope also fluctuates as a result of business changes such as budget, priority, assumptions, constraints, need, strategy, and leadership.

When scope is increased, requirements must be reviewed to ensure that the additions are covered. Conversely, when scope is decreased, the requirements must be reviewed and scaled back.

More often than not, requirements will change as a result of these fluctuations in scope, or they may not. The review will identify the impacts of the fluctuations on requirements and determine if requirements should be added or removed. However, sometimes changes to scope are really only changes to the interpretation of the business need (or the way it has been articulated), and in this case, the requirements themselves may acquire new details.

Adding Further Necessary Details

There are times when requirements change simply as they evolve throughout the life cycle and ambiguities are exposed. These details are most commonly required by the architects, developers, or testers in order to perform their own tasks and activities.

It is important to remember that requirements will almost never be written in stone (at least they shouldn't be). Quite frankly, they will simply get to the various baselines before being managed through the change control process. They get to these baselines by evolving throughout the requirements life cycle. The baselines simply represent points in that cycle, wherein everyone agrees that the current version is a good point to move forward from, in the performance of dependent tasks.

That being said, requirements evolve in the same way that the solution itself evolves from vague idea to tangible outcome. The important factor is to understand the impacts of changes of requirements on scope and vice versa.

Due diligence in tracing and analyzing those changes are critical to success. In the end, significant changes to scope and requirements impact the cost and alignment of the solution to the business need.

Scope creep can happen at any stage of the requirements development life cycle, just as it can at any stage of the project life cycle. It is managed throughout requirements development by following a clear set of tasks and activities, and by managing the stakeholders involved in the development of those requirements.

OVERVIEW OF REQUIREMENTS STEPS AND STAGES

Requirements evolve from scope through the life cycle development stages. These development stages are elicitation, analysis, specification, and validation.

At every stage, requirements are becoming increasingly detailed and are at increased risk of not aligning to scope. It is possible that the defined requirements do not align to the project scope because they describe functions not in scope, or there are functional gaps.

Every single requirement must align and be traceable back to an element or multiple elements within scope. Likewise, every element within scope must also have corresponding requirements. They are codependent, not interdependent, in that one cannot exist without the other. In a sense, scope and requirements are like the yin and yang of the solution.

Consider the fundamental requirements behind the yin and yang concept:

- Interdependent—The elements are interdependent in that there is a symbiotic relationship; neither can exist without the other.

Requirements cannot exist without scope, and scope cannot exist without requirements in the development of a solution. Anything less spells failure.

- Opposites—Scope and requirements are opposite ends of a cycle. In this case, they are opposite ends of the solution definition cycle.
- Mutual consumption—An imbalance in either scope or requirements affects the other. In this case, missed scope means absent requirements and vice versa.
- Inter-transformation—Both scope and requirements can transform itself from its original form into the other. Requirements can become scope, and scope always becomes requirements.

ELICITATION

Elicitation is the primary stage for collecting requirements through research. This research includes reviewing various documents, as well as conducting interviews with the various stakeholders. In this stage, the analyst first identifies the functional areas and features of the proposed solution from the project deliverables developed to this point (especially the scope document) in order to begin developing the requirements.

Next, the analyst researches the architectural (business and technical) documentation in order to uncover the internal workings of the business, such as business rules, regulations, and environmental factors that may impact the specific requirements, and ultimately, the solution development.

Finally, the analyst will conduct a series of working sessions with the key stakeholders in order to capture details about the problem or objective, as well as the needs of the business. These details, coupled with the architectural information, will be translated into requirements.

Implications of Elicitation on Scope

As previously discussed, some business users will ask for new features and functionality. It stands to reason that they will ask for these during elicitation, when they have access to and the attention of the analysis team. Therefore, it is incumbent upon the analysts to be cautious about driving these sessions and keeping the business participants focused on the primary objectives, and to direct new features and functionality into the change control channels for scrutiny and evaluation by the stakeholders and sponsors.

That being said, it is also important to understand that uncontrolled sessions are not the only threat to scope during elicitation. Another threat to scope occurs when it takes too long to get work done, or when the appropriate business team members are difficult to get together.

Each of these threats can impact scope by causing a time box for the requirements and the project life cycle. This time box often forces stakeholders and sponsors to break the project into phases or to reduce scope.

The most successful analysts in the elicitation stage will be those who are assertive and demonstrate leadership, as well as solid negotiation skills. These skills will enable the analyst to work with the users and to channel their energy into building the right set of requirements for the defined solution. It is the skill of the analyst, in this stage, which will directly reduce scope creep that results in time-boxing.

ANALYSIS

Once the analyst has captured the details of the problem, objectives, and needs in elicitation, they begin to analyze those details in order to derive the specific requirements that will define the solution. These are defined in enough detail so as to enable design, build, and testing. This level of detail, however, is unachievable without first analyzing the captured information. It is in the process of analyzing that this information is functionally organized and decomposed in order to understand how the functionality can be delivered, and how that will align to the project scope.

Analysis leverages techniques such as gap analysis, scenarios, activity diagrams, use cases, and cause and effect tables in order to derive the necessary details for each functional element. Each of these techniques provides the analyst with an opportunity to view the feature sets defined in scope and the high-level requirements from an almost three-dimensional perspective (user, system, and business) in order to evaluate the completeness of the information and to generate the appropriate and applicable requirements.

Implications of Analysis on Scope

Within analysis, the analyst often uncovers details or information that may directly impact scope. Some of these details will either increase or decrease the scope, depending on the nature of the information uncovered.

The important part of these discoveries is to understand how these details impact scope, and how they will impact the overall success of the project. The analyst must also understand how to determine if there is an impact, how to articulate that impact to stakeholders and sponsors, and how to push these items into the change control process once they have been articulated. In due course of the analysis tasks, the business analyst is "primarily investigating, evaluating, and scrutinizing the information extracted from the input sources and documentation as part of the evolution process. In doing so, the analyst must model the information, conduct a gap analysis, organize, and prioritize the requirements."[4]

It is the task of modeling requirements that will reveal both new information and the potential impacts of that new information on scope. It is, however, through the gap analysis that the analyst will uncover all impacts and risks to scope. The analyst will then utilize the gap analysis to articulate those impacts to the stakeholders and sponsors.

Gap Analysis

Gap analysis is a method for analyzing two or more processes and identifying differences between multiple states (in this case, current and future states), and identifying the differences between them. Gap analysis is utilized as a means of creating the plan to move from the present situation to the ideal situation, which has been identified by the business. Within the analysis stage, gap analysis is an important tool for identifying the gaps in requirements by locating logical inconsistencies.[5]

The gap analysis document is most impactful when it contains an individual gap, as well as all of its associated risks, and details a single document. As such, each document contains the following elements:

- Project identification
- Author of the gap analysis document
- Gap type (routine, realignment, or peripheral)
- The process, system name, or reference to where the gap was located
- Gap description
- Impacts to the existing project
- In scope or out of scope
- Risks and impacts table

There are three types of gaps: routine, realignment, and peripheral. Each of these will have some influence upon scope. It is important to understand each of these types of gaps from a high level in order to understand the level of influence that each will have upon the project.

Routine Gap Analysis

Routine gap analysis is the performance of gap analysis within the daily routine and within the context of the current project. Routine gaps identify and explore the differences between the current and future states as a part of identifying additional requirements for the current project.

This type of analysis may expose gaps or overlaps in scope that will impact the project. It is necessary, when this occurs, to call attention to these gaps or overlaps by generating the gap analysis document and then escalating that information to the stakeholders for decisions about how to proceed. This escalation is best handled through the change control process, which is utilized as part of the governance structure of the project.

Missing Conditions in a Ferry Project

Several years ago, a team was building a new web-based application for making reservations on a public ferry for multiple routes. The initial documentation and requirements were scarce and not well detailed to design and build the new web application. There was a lot of tribal knowledge on the team, since many of these resources had worked together before, and some resources worked for the ferry company.

A new project manager and business analyst on the team forced everyone to start thinking about the documentation to help the new resources ramp up, and to support the new development effort. As a means of understanding the project, the new analyst conducted a gap analysis and discovered that there were whole business needs that did not trace down to elements within scope; further, that the needs did not trace down into requirements. Further gap analysis also revealed that there were requirements that could not be traced back to scope and business objectives.

In the Ferry Project case, the analyst uncovered several pieces of missing functionality, as well as additional unnecessary functionality. This type of gap analysis helped to improve the requirements and ensure alignment back up to scope and to the business needs, and ultimately eliminated the potential scope creep.

Realignment Gap Analysis

Realignment gap analysis should occur when the project or its deliverables are off track and must be reworked in order to proceed successfully to complete the project and deliver the solution. This type of gap analysis will identify areas that will enable critical decisions on the part of the stakeholders and sponsors about how best to recover from the project situation.

Realignment gap analysis impacts scope, when the project or its deliverables are so far off track that the project must be broken into phases, or scope must be reduced in order to meet the constraints. Remember that when a project is broken into phases, scope is impacted. While the overall set of phases will probably deliver the functionality in the long run, it is important to understand the priority and impacts of these functions on the business. This analysis will help to determine the scope of each phase.

A Driver Program: Broken, Phased, and Broken Some More

A number of years ago, a company was implementing a new driver penalty program. Things on the project were not going well. The initial start of the project was not delivering, and was overtime and budget. So, the sponsors agreed to break it into more manageable phases for the project team.

The first phase of the new approach implemented with nearly 400 defects. The analysis team had to support fixes, so they conducted both a root cause and a gap analysis. These analyses revealed that the development team had worked from a completely different design that had nothing to do with the requirements and had no traceability back to scope. In addition, it was discovered that the information services department had decided to segregate its code into four primary server farms instead of one.

In the Driver Program situation, the sponsors were able to understand the critical issues and the team was better able to take immediate and corrective action. The realignment gap analysis helped the team to realign the project, get Phase 2 back on track, and deliver the needed functionality with only two defects.

Peripheral Gap Analysis

Peripheral gap analysis is useful to help the analyst uncover gaps on the peripheries (extremities) of the project that they are working on. These gaps are less likely to be addressed by the project because they are usually found within another application or are part of the architecture that is out of scope.

However, by developing the gap analysis document and escalating that to the stakeholders and sponsors through the change control process, the project team is providing critical information which could be used to influence the scope or other projects in order to correct the issues. If nothing else, the business management team then has the information necessary to initiate a future project in order to address the identified gaps.

Exposed Network

Several years ago, a company was implementing a Microsoft Windows operating system patch onto all of its systems. When it came time to roll the patch out to the independent investment brokers, a discussion arose about how to set it up so that they could log into the network and update their systems for compliance.

Much to the shock of the project team, the sponsor announced it was not necessary because they did not enforce any operating system requirements, and further, these individuals did not have to log in to connect, they simply had open access. Further investigation revealed the network was not locked down and accessible through a secured portal, as is common practice.

In the Exposed Network story, the discovery of a peripheral gap presented a massive security risk to the investment firm, but was outside of the scope of the project. The gaps were connected because of the need to review the security protocol for the project in order for the team to be successful. The analyst submitted a solid gap analysis document to the sponsors, and left it for their review and future action.

SPECIFICATION

Specification is the stage where the low-level requirements are authored. These requirements are intended to be consumed by the design, development, and test stages of the product. In order to suit the needs of these subsequent stages of project life cycle, requirements must be testable.

Testable requirements are quantifiable, easy to design, and are readily consumable by other teams to develop the accurate solution and functionality.

This means that testable requirements are logically complete, consistently worded, accurate, unambiguous, concise, explicit, logically consistent, and feasible:

> Testable requirements are those which can be measured, are definitive, and have clear parameters for the functionality to be performed. Untestable requirements tend to be ambiguous in nature and leave a lot of unanswered questions for the other team members to fill in the blanks with assumptions.
>
> The problem is that the architects, developers, and testers may all be making different assumptions about how to fill in those ambiguities. It is the differences and discrepancies in these assumptions which will directly result in defects within the solution.[6]

The primary activity in this stage is to create a draft of the requirements document and to incorporate the details derived from the analysis tasks into this document. The techniques employed here are basic technical writing skills.

Many companies do not utilize a specific requirements management tool despite increasing availability. To this end, the analyst is more likely to author the requirements document within a word processing application such as Microsoft Word. Where they do have access to a tool, analysts can author the requirements directly into the tool (assuming that the feature is available).

Implications of Specification on Scope

The biggest implication of specification on scope is risk of ambiguity. Where ambiguity exists, the other teams make assumptions about the missing elements, and this in and of itself can lead to scope creep, high defect levels, and unused functionality.

High defect levels and unused functionality both cause misalignment to scope and business needs. In an effort to correct this, the team may resort to increasing functionality to attempt to realign the solution.

According to the Meta Group (2010), 60 to 80%[7] of the average project budget is spent in fixing poor requirements. Unfortunately, the majority of these poor requirements are not discovered until testing and implementation. Discovered in testing, these are considered issues; later on, after the solution has been implemented, they are considered defects.

The connection between scope, issues, defects, and cost is clear. If issues and defects are high, the company spends more, but gets less value in return.

As this situation progresses, the company is often forced to reduce scope as a means of attempting to control costs. In the end, the company loses.

VALIDATION

Validation is the most critical of the stages within the requirements process. It is the stage where requirements are both verified and validated. Where verification refers to the process of ensuring that the prescribed functionality aligns to the scope and the desired objective, *validation* refers to the process of ensuring that the individual requirements are testable (complete, consistent, accurate, etc.).

As with analysis, the primary techniques in validation are use cases, activity diagrams, cause and effect tables, and scenarios. In addition to these activities, the validation stage also leverages a peer review, and a set of ambiguity discovery activities. These discovery activities include specialized reviews, workshops, and management.

It is the validation stage that ensures requirements are ready for the subsequent design, development, and test activities. These validation activities are a critical part of rendering the requirements into the final deliverable for sign-off.

Implications of Validation on Scope

The most significant implications on scope that arise out of validation are a direct result of the ad hoc approach to these activities. In many cases, validation activities are sparse and almost nonexistent. The problem is not the desire to cut corners or not to validate, it is quite simply that far too many business analysts, and project resources in general, do not know *how* to validate.

Validation is more than going to the business and asking them if they think that the requirements are correct. Let's face it: the average business person will really only know so much about what should be in the requirements. On top of that, they will get bored trying to cram this dry and technically glorious piece of literature into their already busy schedule. It's about as much fun as watching paint dry.

While not every business person will have this much difficulty wading through it, it is important to give them the short version in the walk-through so that they can understand the gist of what is being developed, and to not be upset if they show up to the meeting without having read the entire requirements document.

So, if requirements are not properly verified with the business for alignment to the scope and objectives, there is a huge risk that there will be anomalies. There could be extra items, and there could also be large gaps.

In addition, if requirements are not properly validated, they will not align to scope and objectives, we *guarantee* it. Validation is where the technical team helps to fill in some of the missing elements and identifies ambiguities, which they will have to make assumptions about later. Remember what they say about assumptions? They make a "fool" out of "you" and "me."

REFERENCES

1. The Standish Group. 2012. Chaos Manifesto: The Year of the Executive Sponsor. Versionone.com. http://versionone.com/assets/img/files/CHAOSManifesto2012.pdf
2. *Ibid.*
3. *Ibid.*
4. Davis, Barbara. *Mastering Software Project Requirements: A Framework for Successful Planning, Development and Alignment.* Plantation, FL: J. Ross Publishing, 2013.
5. Ibid.
6. Ibid.
7. Meta Group, 2010. http://www.galorath.com/wp/software-project-failure-costs-billions-better-estimation-planning-can-help.php

This book has free material available for download from the Web Added Value™ resource center at *www.jrosspub.com*

GOVERNANCE

WHAT IS GOVERNANCE?

There are a number of layers of governance within corporations. At the highest level, corporate governance refers to the system by which corporations are directed and controlled. *Governance* provides the structure through which a corporation sets and pursues its objectives, while reflecting the context of the social, regulatory, and market environment. The governance structure within an organization stipulates the distribution of rights and responsibilities among the various participants (board of directors, executive leadership team, managers, and other stakeholders), and specifies the rules and procedures for making decisions in corporate affairs. Governance is also a mechanism for monitoring the actions, policies, and decisions of corporations.

Governance Of and Within the Organization

A board of directors is the body of elected or appointed members who jointly oversee the activities of a company or organization. Typical duties of boards of directors include:

- Governing the organization by establishing broad policies and objectives
- Selecting, appointing, supporting, and reviewing the performance of the CEO
- Ensuring the availability of adequate financial resources
- Approving annual budgets

- Adopting the strategic plan
- Accounting to the stakeholders for the organization's performance
- Setting the salaries and compensation of company management

Falling within, and subservient to, these overarching governance features that impact the direction and control *of* the organization, guidance for those accountable for affecting change *within* the organizational context is also required. Governance, then, in the context of a change program delivery environment is required to provide clarity for both the framework and delivery control mechanism for programs to deliver their objectives—in a consistent and sustainable manner—while remaining within corporate visibility and control.

Program level governance concerns those areas of corporate governance that are specifically related to program activities, such as finance and accounting, human resource management, risk and issue management, quality systems, operations and performance, information technology, member and stakeholder satisfaction, sourcing and procurement, contract management, legislative compliance, and information management. Program specific governance requirements should integrate with existing governance and control frameworks, as these should provide the necessary structure and visibility. For companies undergoing change, governance manifests itself in two ways:

- Effective governance ensures that an organization's project portfolio is aligned to the organization's objectives, delivered efficiently, and sustainable in that the project's outputs (and associated benefits) are fully integrated into the operational, *business-as-usual* environment.
- The Program Steering Group and other key stakeholders are provided with timely, relevant, and reliable information to enable informed decision making.

An effective program governance and control framework should pay its way by enabling project delivery success, specifically:

- Improved coordination of existing functions and processes
- More efficient people and resource management
- Reduced cycle time and delivery costs
- Improved quality of project deliverables
- Early identification of project issues, budget, scope, and risks
- Reuse of knowledge and the ability to leverage that knowledge on future projects

- Improved accuracy of project estimates
- Improved perceptions of the project management organization by key stakeholders/partners
- Reduced time to get up to speed on new change initiatives
- Enhanced benefits realization

While governance necessitates a controlling aspect, it is important that *control* does not become a synonym for constraint. To be successful, programs require clear and open governance. Programs require the ability to negotiate and manage required resources, and to adjust as the program and/or organizational setting requires, while working within and aligned to the overarching corporate governance attributes. The key aligning factors are the outcomes and benefits targeted by the program as endorsed by the organization. The critical aspect to enabling programs to be successful, while ensuring alignment to the broader corporate standards, policies, strategies, assets and activities, is visibility. The program approach, plans, and tools to be used should relate to the fundamental governance themes of the organization, as shown in Table 6.1.

Tactical and Strategic Governance

The different layers of governance within an organization are analogous to the disciplines of portfolio, program, and project management. Portfolio management is directly related to the higher level, corporate governance and is typically the domain of the executive leadership team and board of directors. It is linked to corporate strategy in that it concerns the management of the portfolio of "investments" targeted by the leaders of the corporation (to achieve specific objectives and the overall mission of the company) and is focused on the achievement of outcomes. At the other end of the spectrum, projects are specific, more tactical management activities that focus on delivering discreet outputs (performance), which ultimately should link to the enablement of desired capabilities that in turn enable outcomes and targeted benefits at the corporate level to be realized.

As discussed in Chapter 1, these two layers naturally reside as one safeguards that the organization is "doing the right things" while the other is charged with "doing things right." Where organizations effectively enable high performance against the correct objectives, then this can only serve to optimize the prospect of the company remaining competitive and relevant in respect to its chosen market segment.

Table 6.1   How typical governance themes are addressed by a program management capability

Governance Theme	Description	Addressed by
Stakeholder engagement	Stakeholders are engaged at a level commensurate with their importance to the organization and in a manner that fosters trust	Stakeholder management plan Communications plan
Leadership and management	The "who" in terms of the business, user, and supplier stakeholders for the three layers of the project management team; Directing (steering group), Managing (project management), and Delivering (team management)	Project organization structure Defined project roles, responsibilities and accountabilities Signing authority matrix
Project mandate	Investment appraisal, selection, and ongoing justification for the project supported by relevant and realistic information that provides a reliable basis for authorization decision making	Prioritization Scorecard & Demand Management (Gate 0) Business case Benefits realization plan Information management and reporting
Planning	A design of how identified products/outputs that are fit-for-purpose can be produced (when, where, by whom, at what cost, etc.)	Charter Project plan Planning and estimation Techniques Gate review process Tolerance (scope, progress, cost, risk, quality, benefits) Contingency (for risks) All project specific sub-plans*
Monitoring and controlling	Disciplined, pragmatic, and proven delivery methods and controls are systematically applied	Project life cycle Project management methodology Work packages Risk and issue management Project change control Health checks and quality reviews Gate review process Tolerance and contingency management
Reporting	Clearly defined reporting criteria and risk and issue escalation paths	Checkpoint reports (team) Project status report Executive/Program dashboard Risk and issue management Requests for change

Note: Includes scope, cost, benefits, communications, contracts, procurement, interface, implementation, test, quality, resource and schedule management plans, and risk response plan as may be required.

Portfolio Steering and Performance Management Groups

To clearly reflect these two layers of governance related to delivery, corporations create structures of governing bodies that oversee those "what are we doing" and "how are we doing it" elements. Various names are assigned to such bodies, such as steering groups, advisory boards, committees, etc. as may suit the industry sector, culture, and accepted naming conventions. Essentially, these bodies will need to discharge the same mandates. Two clear and pragmatic structures are offered below.

The Portfolio Steering Group

A steering group acts in a governance and stewardship capacity by providing direction and leadership on matters that impact the portfolio of initiatives in scope when it is composed of the appropriate, and accountable leadership personnel. Members of leadership will specifically:

- Organize a portfolio of activities to ensure the operational needs of the company are met;
- Endorse the delivery schedule, resources, and associated budget for the required initiatives within the portfolio;
- Provide guidance, direction, and formal decisions to enable a clear mandate for the delivery team;
- Provide direction to ensure outputs are delivered in a controlled, fit-for-purpose manner, while ensuring internal and external stakeholder communication and delivery expectations are met;
- Resolve specific issues and risks escalated by the team; and
- Approve requests for change to approved portfolio mix and delivery sequence/pace.

The Performance Management Group

Comprised of key management-level personnel, a performance management group acts in a tactical, delivery focused capacity by providing day-to-day management oversight and direction on matters relating to the successful delivery of the approved projects within the portfolio of change initiatives. Members of this group will specifically:

- Monitor that projects within the portfolio are delivering to specification by reviewing and proactively challenging the monthly project

performance information (typically summarized via an information dashboard);
- Address actual or forecast variance to specification, authorizing remedial action as required within the approved project tolerance parameters; and
- Resolve specific issues and risks escalated by the team, again within their authorized mandate in terms of those project tolerance factors of risk, budget, quality, benefit, time, and scope.

DECISION MANAGEMENT AND THE STEERING GROUP

Both performance management (tactical) and more strategic steering group structures are empowered to make decisions within an agreed mandate. While both groups have important roles to play, the scale and resultant impact of decisions made by the steering group warrant an appropriate level of rigor to be applied when defining and establishing such a body.

The steering group must ensure that any program has a clearly defined chain-of-command with a formalized decision-making process. Terms of reference for structures and accountabilities for the program roles must also be defined, as shown in Table 6.2. The process of reviewing and directing the program should be clear, pragmatic, and proactive, resulting in a program mandate that provides for execution by the delivery team within agreed thresholds, tolerance, and levels of contingency. Essentially, the team is enabled to succeed in a framework that is aligned to and reflective of all the corporate governance elements.

A critical success factor for the steering group is to ensure that this governance model is woven into the approach and specific plans of the program at hand, while enabling the program and providing its day-to-day custodians space to think and perform. There are a number of things the steering group may wish to involve to achieve this challenging aim:

- A management by exception approach should be adopted, whereby directions or formal decisions are requested of the steering group, where agreed implementation or outcome-based performance parameters are at risk.
- Similarly, where unforeseen issues arise, rapid turnaround times should be supported by the steering group, so that opportunities can be seized and problems resolved in a timely manner and ultimately, implementation does not stall.

Table 6.2   Structures and accountabilities for program roles

Role	Accountability	Responsibility
Steering group	Enable utilization of new capabilities. Achieve corporate objectives.	• Authorize vision, decision case, and benefit realization plan • Align initiatives to corporate strategy and plans • Authorize the program mandate and endorse the funding • Approve the progress of the program against strategic objectives • Advise and support the business sponsor • Engage, influence, and gain commitment from key stakeholders • Balance program priorities with ongoing operations • Approve requests for change
Business leadership team	Critical business inputs to the program. Safeguard alignment to business operations.	• Ensure correct resources are available for the program • Communicate and promote the business vision • Validate the program of projects, associated costs, and benefits • Drive identification of additional project requirements • Resolve program and project risks and issues
Program board	Outcome and benefit realization. Alignment to strategy. Decision case viability.	• Define decision case and delivery approach • Maintenance and achievement of the blueprint and road map • Define risk profiles for the program and constituent projects • Monitor and control delivery to agreed parameters • Ensure integrity of the benefits realization plan • Resolve strategic and directional issues between projects • Provide operational assurance through the program delivery life cycle
Portfolio delivery office	Benefit auditing, program assurance, delivery stewardship	• Provide specialist delivery and benefit management resources • Oversee benefit delivery life cycle (support and guidance) • Ensure compliance (finance, health) to agreed process and quality standards • Oversee alignment of project constraints and dependencies

• Concurrent delivery work streams and an understanding of other activities that can move forward or push out the delivery schedule, for example, also limit the risk of implementation delays.

Effective steering groups also recognize and accommodate a learn-by-doing philosophy, whereby lessons learned and proven approaches are "baked" into the program by virtue of predefined formal review gates. In addition to governance around deliverable focused activity, mechanisms should also exist to ensure defined delivery processes are not being circumvented.

Organization Structure and Associated Roles and Accountabilities

If performance management and steering group structures are empowered to make decisions within an agreed mandate, it stands to reason that decision management must occur within an organizational structure that promotes actionable decision making, and then has the ability to push those decisions into action at lower levels of the overall team. Figure 6.1 illustrates such an organizational structure as it relates to the associated roles that would be required to govern the model. Figure 6.2, on the other hand, illustrates the organizational structure as it relates to the specific accountabilities that are required in order to ensure coverage of all of the related action items.

Decision Management: Principles of Decision Making

Assumption: decisions are final and should last in perpetuity, or at least for a significant period of time. Effective steering groups should think more in terms of a series of decisions, each essentially building upon the last as the change journey progresses; more unknowns become known; and the team knowledge, strength, and delivery capability increases with experience.

Taking action, even when in the fullness of time and with the benefit of hindsight, the decision made was less than optimal, is invariably better than making no decision, or worse, waiting for the ingredients to be furnished to make the "perfect" decision. In the fast paced and ever evolving business environment of today, those charged with steering change initiatives need to be both comfortable and competent with making decisions where full data and information is likely not present.

Forum for Decision Making: The Steering Group Meeting

The purpose of a highly effective and focused steering group meeting is two-fold: information sharing and decision making. First, for those accountable

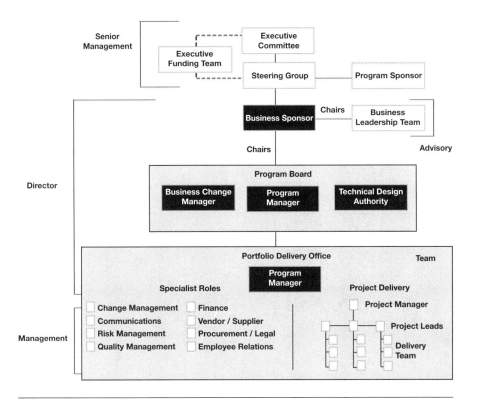

Figure 6.1   Organization structure and associated roles

for delivery to share information, this is typically in the form or combination of, a management report, scorecard with associated narrative, or management information dashboard where performance against agreed criteria with defined metrics can be reviewed. The second purpose of the meeting is to make decisions, typically as a result of the leadership being required to (perhaps by a regulator or client stakeholder), stipulate a change (perhaps as a result of a change to one or more corporate objectives), or because of some emergent factors, due to positive or negative performance or because an opportunity now exists that wasn't available when previous decisions were made and resultant plans cast.

To ensure a highly focused meeting is conducted, resulting in leaders having full awareness of critical performance criteria, and being able to provide clear direction and make decisions to enable the delivery team to be very clear of its mandate, disciplined meeting management is required.

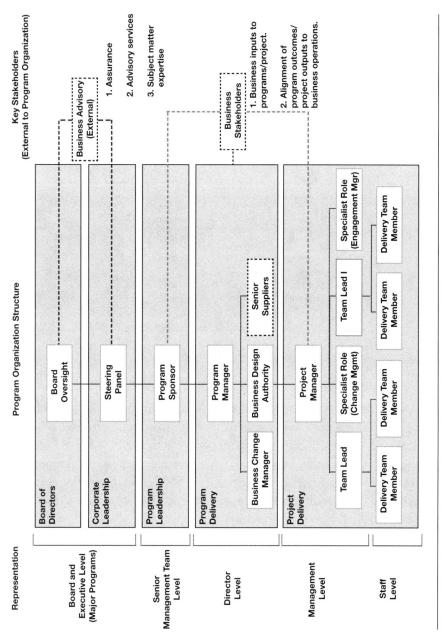

Figure 6.2 Organization structure and associated accountabilities

A meeting agenda should be issued ahead of time, along with any key supporting materials. This affords the opportunity for the steering group to be aware of the progress, issues, opportunities, and input (by way of decisions) required of them by the delivery team to ensure that they, the delivery team, remain fully enabled to deliver on the desired outcomes as set/overseen by the steering group. The agenda should clearly stipulate the purpose of the meeting convened, and articulate any specific objectives required from the meeting.

Sample Agenda for a Steering Group Meeting

1. **Purpose of Meeting:** To review the open change requests for the unemployment case management (UCM) project.
2. **Work to be accomplished (results):** We will be working to review and determine approvals for the open change requests, including the new budget amounts for each change.
3. **Expected participation:** Everyone will be actively involved in the meeting, and will be expected to contribute or lead portions of the discussion, as well as to ask or answer questions about the changes, the impacts of the changes, and the revised expectations.
4. **Things to do to prepare:** Be prepared by reviewing the open change requests and preparing some basic questions about the changes on behalf of each department.
5. **Things to bring:** Compile and bring any of the following if the departments are under your purview:
   a. How things should or must be done in the department and why.
   b. What are the results that must be achieved?

In terms of a meeting record, summary notes comprised of any key highlights or messages (salient points for the initiative), decisions made and any action items (for example, a specific person being assigned to action/implement a decision of the steering group) as a result of the meeting should be documented and issued to all participants as soon as possible post meeting. Decisions, in addition to being articulated in the post-meeting summary, should also be captured in a formal decision log as part of an effective governance control mechanism. This allows for a central place for all decisions made by date.

The decision log is an effective repository for quick access to the decision history, reviewing lessons learned or for audit requirements. Similarly, a central action register should be maintained so that those assigned with required activities are clear about what is required, by what schedule. As is the case with agreement of the original delivery activities, actions should be agreed upon by those issuing and those responsible for fulfilling the said action so that accountability is correctly vested.

The No Surprise Rule!

Projects and programs carry varying degrees of risk, uncertainty, and complexity. While enough analysis, design, and general diligence is expended up front, it is typically not possible to execute any plan perfectly—variation and small fluctuations from the "critical path" are normal.

Where significant deviations from the agreed-upon objectives (outside agreed tolerance levels around parameters such as delivery date, cost, quality, features) are expected (risk), or being experienced (problem/issue), there is an overriding duty on the management team to:

1. Make the leadership/steering group aware—typically through the formal status and information sharing (meetings) channels, including ad hoc exception reporting and issue escalation;
2. Conduct a root cause analysis of the risk/issue to determine the driving factors; and
3. Identify possible options to reduce or avoid the problem.

While unforeseeable issues can appear without warning (i.e., unexpected regulatory announcement compelling a change), "effective" monitoring and accurate reporting will often identify a growing trend prior to something becoming an issue (missed the date, features don't perform to specification, etc.). The reporting, stage authorization and gate-graduation, health assessment and quality review program governance mechanisms are solely designed to afford early and proactive management intervention by highlighting potential problems *prior* to becoming an issue that requires immediate, unplanned corrective action.

Proven Practice Components of a Dashboard

Steering group meetings are typically enabled by a summarized but structured presentation of key materials, and a dashboard for information sharing and progress monitoring purposes. The agenda structures the specific items to be discussed in the meeting and may reference any supporting documentation, for example, a report providing analysis of a specific issue. From a performance management perspective, a concise, relevant, and timely set of information is critical. To this end, a dashboard comprised of key information against defined criteria is the preferred method to invite steering group involvement.

A summary dashboard should contain all relevant information to the initiative at hand. While this can and should vary significantly between projects, companies, and industries, a typical information dashboard would comprise the core components shown in Table 6.3.

Table 6.3   Typical project dashboard components

Dashboard Component	Purpose
Executive summary	Summarize the status and forecast health of the change initiatives in scope. Typically a traffic light indicator.
Accomplishments in period	Key milestones and deliverables completed in the reporting period.
Financial summary	Inform actual financial performance and trends against plan. Variance explanation and corrective actions planned.
Resource (team) summary	Resources used and forecast compared to plan. Highlights and challenges experienced. Variance explanation and corrective actions planned.
Health assessment	Results of specific health, quality, or product review activities. Highlight assessments planned for next period.
Risk (including opportunity risks)	Illustrate key or critical risks (likelihood and impact), trend forecast of those key risks, scale (in terms of cost if risk materializes) and progress made in terms of implementing agreed risk strategies and mitigation plans.
Issues	Articulate key issues requiring immediate attention. Illustrate option analysis and recommended response.
Decisions	Illustrate key decisions required in period.
Key deliverables/ milestones	Typically focused on the next 90 days. Status of key milestones and deliverables by project. Variance explanation and corrective actions planned.
Overall trend	Overall status of projects in the portfolio by period. Forecast overall status.

Note: for each element of the dashboard, any variance to planned or agreed metrics/expectations, either positive or negative, should be captured in the relevant section with proposed management response articulated accordingly.

REASONS FOR SCOPE CHANGE

There are two fundamental, all-encompassing questions for organizations that are defining or refining strategy, or that are specifically planning change initiatives to ultimately achieve the corporate goals: What do we need to do? And, how do we do it?

Most organizations can typically define the "what" quite well, with strategic planning, executive away days, and a plethora of established and accepted methods, tools, and techniques for articulating an appropriate, feasible, and desirable strategy or change activity. Like all great innovators, however, while defining what to do is relatively achievable, not many organizations upon formulation of an idea, know precisely *how* to achieve the goals and objectives targeted. The "how" becomes more elusive to stipulate with certainty, the more unique, novel, groundbreaking, or paradigm stretching the aspiration.

In an environment where a detailed road map of "how" is not a realistic pursuit, one can easily understand why the scope initially outlined may need to change. Indeed, the need to change from the original scope should not be seen as a negative, but actually a necessary, positive, and enabling reality. Specific examples are as follows:

1. Tactical/Management level: Other "tolerance factors" of time, money, quality, risk, and benefits for specific initiatives.
2. Strategic Level: Changes to business objectives and direction, mergers, or acquisitions.

Fundamentally, the organizational context may itself change due to pressures, strategic-driven (planned), or emergent opportunities to change. Quite likely in this modern, fast-changing corporate landscape, a change could be a merger/acquisition, a major strategic review and overhaul, or new innovations or opportunities that emerge in the business context that were not present at the outset of the change initiative when the original strategy was defined (opportunity risk). Three drivers of strategic level change are:

1. External pressures to change
2. Vision-led (planned) change
3. Emergent (opportunity/risk) change

Whereas traditional management and leadership paradigms resist change (try and stamp out turbulence in the environment), the organization best prepared for today's reality will proactively accept that change will (and should) happen, and accept that dealing with opportunities to change is not a weakness. Indeed, acceptance of change is a significant strength that will enable the organization to better navigate, via the ability to adapt and evolve to the real world around them.

MANAGING SCOPE CHANGES

Effective governance considers and plans for how to manage changes to scope across the life of the project, as well as the overall program. In order to accomplish this, this planning must define the baseline, a management plan, and priority order.

In order to define the baseline, the charter, benefits mapping, and decision case (both high-level business and initiative scope with target benefits) are analyzed to identify the current state and a quantifiable position to assess future progress against.

The management plan is really a mechanism for monitoring and managing scope. In order to define this plan, it is important to understand the potential risks and issues, as well as the needs of the business and objectives of the project. It is these components that will enable the identification of potential changes to scope as the project progresses, and also provide anticipated means and limits for future changes. In other words, as the project progresses, this plan will provide a framework for making key decisions about requested changes to scope.

Finally, managing changes to scope requires a predetermined framework for prioritizing requested changes. One such recommended framework is the MoSCoW approach for categorizing requested changes, as they are assessed, in order to determine if they are really necessary. The MoSCoW approach is utilized as part of a gating process approach to governance in line with risk (opportunity) assessment and environmental scanning practices.

The tactical elements of managing change, utilizing the governance framework, include managing and directing the meetings. Carefully planned and executed meetings include identifying and inviting the appropriate stakeholders, creating a detailed agenda, careful crafting of key messages, up-front identification of decisions to be made (as objectives of the meetings), and clearly stated action items.

The presentation materials will be structured under categories of either: a) information sharing, or b) decisions required. This will ensure that consistent information for the same activity types (i.e., consideration of a change request) is presented to allow informed and relevant decision making in the context of the entire portfolio. This model should also align directly with a company board's reporting requirements, and therefore facilitates enablement of the board's mandate and/or simple and consistent escalation, as required.

The presentation material represents the primary document of record for the meeting. Additional outputs of the meeting will comprise key messages, action items (assigned), and a record of decisions. A decision log and action register will be used by the group to ensure activities and decisions are appropriately tracked and recorded. This should be published in a secure location.

Table 6.4 provides a strategic level example of how scope of the portfolio of investments is selected, and ultimately decomposed down to requirements, as granularity increases (initiative—scope—requirement).

Governance and Change Management

Program governance ensures decision-making and capability management activities are focused on achieving program goals in a consistent manner, addressing appropriate risks, and fulfilling stakeholder requirements. Planning and management of the changes is necessary to constantly ensure the program is on target to achieve the stated value proposition. Unlike projects, where change is first seen as something to be avoided, programs see change first as an opportunity to build value. Table 6.5 outlines the activities of each area for governance and change management.

THE MOSCOW RULES

Prioritization can be applied to requirements, tasks, products, use cases, user stories, acceptance criteria, and tests. *MoSCoW* is a technique for helping to understand priorities. The letters stand for:

- Must have
- Should have
- Could have
- Won't have this time

Requirements classified as High, Medium, or Low importance lack definition. Using MoSCoW prioritization means that priorities are specific (as

Table 6.4 Prioritization/weighted scoring model example

Element	Weight (%)	Description	Criteria
Strategic alignment	20%	The degree to which the approach directly supports the attainment of the corporate 3-year plan	Directly supports corporate strategy = 50 Some strategic imperatives = 20 Not strategic in nature = 0
Delivery risk	15%	The level of uncertainty or risk and the probability/impact of that uncertainty/risk	High certainty/low risk = 25 Typical = 10 High uncertainty/risk = 0
Achievability	12%	The degree of complexity to implement	Standard or low complexity = 25 Typical = 10 Highly complex/likely rework = 0
Resource	10%	Internal and external capacity and skill considerations	High availability of staff/partner people and skill = 25 High availability/low skill or low availability/high skill = 10 Insufficient resource/skill = 0
Timing	8%	Appropriate, feasible, and desirable timeline	Highly optimal timeline = 25 Alternate timeline that can be accommodated with minimum disruption = 10 Unsuitable = 0
Cost	12%	Investment required. Financial cost of the proposed approach	<$1m = 25 $1.1-2m = 20 $2.1-5m = 15 $5.1-10m = 10 $10.1-30m = 5 >$31m = 0
Operational benefit	5%	Level of operational need met by this initiative	Important/fully meets = 25 Important/contributes = 15-20 Moderate/fully meets = 10-15 Low/contributes = 5-10 None = 0
Customer benefit	10%	Level of customer need met by this initiative	Important/fully meets = 25 Important/contributes = 15-20 Moderate/fully meets = 10-15 Low/contributes = 5-10 None = 0
Benefit realization	8%	Lead time to operational/member benefit and return on investment (ROI)	Dis-benefit/Mandatory = 0 0-10% ROI and/or >24 months = 10 11-20% and/or 18-24 months = 20 21-30% and/or 12-18 months = 30 31-40% and/or 6-12 months = 40 41%+ and or <6 months = 60

Table 6.5   Governance and change management

Area	Task/Activity	Definition
Governance	Document management	Defines the document to be created, reviewed, or updated
	Program decision case	"Business case" for programs
	Governance structure	The program organization structure for effective delivery
	Program roles	Specific roles to manage the program & deliver its components
	Accountability matrix	Describes responsibility and accountability by product and/or outcome
	Monitoring & control approach	Specific activities and actions to manage and control the work
	Stage-gate graduation	Formal review of actual vs. plan, and/or approval of plan for subsequent stage
	Decision log and action register	Governance tools to capture key decisions made and key decision outstanding
Change management	Change management plan	Approach to manage the delivery and adoption of change
	Change control board	Formal process to manage changes to the agreed plan
	Change request	Structured document to enable the consistent presentation of requests for change

illustrated in Figure 6.3). The specific use of Must, Should, Could, or Won't Have implies the result of failing to deliver that requirement.

A Tip for Defining Project Terms

It is important to agree on the project's term definitions with the users. Preferably, this is agreed upon before the requirements are captured, i.e., before the discussion becomes emotive.

Must Have priorities provide the Minimum Usable Subset (MUS) of requirements that the project guarantees to deliver. These may be defined, using some of the following rules:

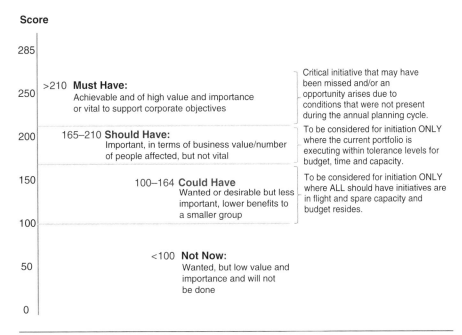

Score

285	
250	>210 **Must Have:** Achievable and of high value and importance or vital to support corporate objectives
200	165–210 **Should Have:** Important, in terms of business value/number of people affected, but not vital
150	100–164 **Could Have** Wanted or desirable but less important, lower benefits to a smaller group
100	
50	<100 **Not Now:** Wanted, but low value and importance and will not be done
0	

Critical initiative that may have been missed and/or an opportunity arises due to conditions that were not present during the annual planning cycle.

To be considered for initiation ONLY where the current portfolio is executing within tolerance levels for budget, time and capacity.

To be considered for initiation ONLY where ALL should have initiatives are in flight and spare capacity and budget resides.

Figure 6.3   MoSCoW prioritization

- Cannot deliver on target date without this.
- No point in delivering on target date without this; if it were not delivered, there would be no point deploying the solution on the intended date.
- Not legal without it.
- Unsafe without it.
- Cannot deliver the decision case without it.

Ask the question, "What happens if this requirement is not met?" If the answer is "Cancel the project—there is no point in implementing a solution that does not meet this requirement," then it is a Must Have requirement. If there is some way around it, even if it is a manual workaround, then it will be a Should Have or a Could Have requirement. Downgrading a requirement to a Should Have or Could Have does not mean that it won't be delivered; it simply means that delivery is not guaranteed.

The Business Sponsor's Perspective

The MoSCoW rules have been cast in a way that allows the delivery of the MUS of requirements to be guaranteed. Both the team and those they are delivering to can share a confidence in this because of the high degree of contingency allowed in the delivery of the Must Haves. A rule of thumb often used is that Must Have requirements do not exceed 60% of the effort. If this rule is followed, then that ensures contingency represents at least 40% of the total effort.

So is this all that the business sponsor can expect to be delivered? The answer is an emphatic "No"! While understanding that there is a real difference between a guarantee and an expectation, the business sponsor can reasonably expect more than this to be delivered, except under the most challenging of circumstances. This is where the split between Should Haves and Could Haves comes into play.

If the Should Haves and Could Haves are split evenly, with 20% of the total effort associated with each, then the Must Haves and Should Haves, in combination, will represent no more than 80% of the total effort. The remaining 20% of effort associated with the Could Haves is now the contingency available to protect the more important requirements. By most standards, this is still a very reasonable level of contingency and rightly implies that the business sponsor can reasonably expect the Should Have requirements to be met. It is just that, quite understandably, the team does not have the confidence to make this a guarantee.

A Tip for Prioritizing

Sensible prioritization, combined with time-boxing, leads to predictability of delivery and therefore greater confidence. Keeping project metrics to show the percentage of Should Haves and Could Haves delivered on each increment or time-box will either reinforce this confidence, if things are going well, or provide an early warning that some important (but not critical) requirements may not be met if problems arise.

MoSCoW is primarily used to prioritize requirements, although the technique is also useful in many other areas. It is recommended that no more than 60% effort apply to Must Haves for a project, with 40% Should Haves and Could Haves, combined. Anything higher than a 60% Must Have poses a risk to the success and predictability of the project unless the environment is well understood, the team is established, and external risks are minimal.

The hierarchy of requirements recommended by the MoSCoW approach means that requirements are identified at various levels of detail, from a high-level strategic viewpoint (during program setup or project feasibility) to a more detailed, implementable level (during design and development). High-level requirements can usually be decomposed, and it is this decomposition that can help resolve one of the problems that confront teams: all requirements appear to be Must Haves.

What to Prioritize

Every item of work has a priority. Priorities are set before work commences, and kept under continual review as the work is done. As new work arises either through introduction of a new requirement, or through the exposure of unexpected work associated with existing requirements, the decision must be made as to how critical they are to the success of the current work using the MoSCoW rules. All priorities should be reviewed throughout the project to ensure that they are still valid.

How Many of Each Priority?

When deciding how much effort should be Must Have requirements, bear in mind that anything other than a Must Have is, to some degree, contingency. The aim is to get the percentage effort for Must Haves (in terms of effort to deliver) as low as possible and to be wary of anything above 60%, i.e., 60% Musts Haves, 40% Should Haves and Could Haves. Won't Haves are excluded from the calculation, as they will not be part of this project/increment/time box. Levels of effort above 60% for Must Haves introduce a risk of failure. Unless the team is working on a project where estimates are known to be accurate, the approach is very well understood and the environment is understood and risk-free in terms of the potential for external factors to introduce delays.

Importance of the Decision Case

The best way to address prioritization initially is with a quantified decision case. This should support feasibility and be revisited during program setup.

The decision case should comprise all Must Have and Should Have requirements. The Could Have requirements should be seen as contingency, as illustrated in Figure 6.4. It is likely that contractual relationships (whether

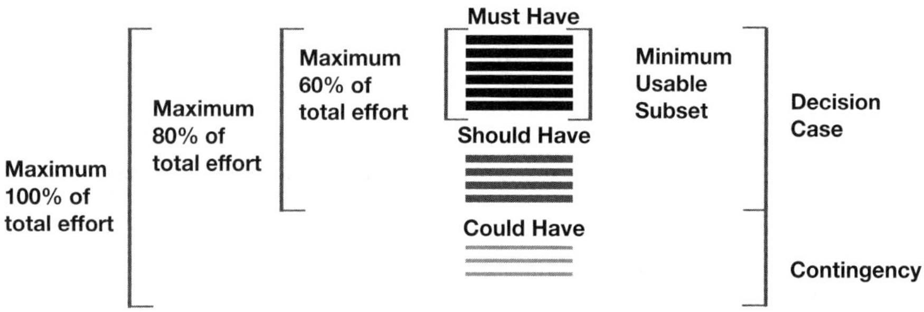

Figure 6.4   MoSCoW and the decision case

formally between organizations or informally within an organization) will influence the decision on this issue one way or the other.

This book has free material available for download from the
Web Added Value™ resource center at *www.jrosspub.com*

SECTION 3: APPLYING PROJECT AND ARCHITECTURE METHODOLOGIES

IMPLICATIONS OF AGILE ON SCOPE

There is increasing pressure on organizations to deliver working solutions to business in ever-shorter timescales without compromising quality. The processes by which solutions are developed must be agile and deliver what the business needs, when it needs it.

WHAT IS AGILE?

In this context, Agile development is a group of methods that provides a flexible yet controlled process that can be used to deliver solutions. Historically, the development methods have been applied to software development, but agile methods can be used for initiatives that have no technology element at all.

In the project context, *Agile* is a delivery method based on iterative, incremental, and evolutionary development and delivery principles, as originally defined by Watts Humphries (IBM) and Hadar Ziv (University of California). It was designed as a means to deliver blocks of usable functionality in increments through short development and delivery cycles, typically called "sprints." This "speed of delivery" represents one key differentiator between the traditional, sequential methodology known as "Waterfall." Agile principles consider requirements as uncertain and even indefinable until the end user has had the chance to work with the solution, with both requirements and the solution evolving through collaboration as the project progresses.

"Uncertainty is inherent and inevitable in software development processes and products."[1] By delivering blocks of functionality in each sprint, the end users then have the opportunity to work with and comment on the product as it is being developed and refined.

Each sprint is directed by a person called a "scrum master," and can be anywhere from two to four weeks in duration. Figure 7.1 illustrates the Agile process. In order to better understand how Agile might impact the scope of a project, it is important to understand the full life cycle process from a high level.

The product vision is defined within the initial planning. It is defined in collaboration between the team and the product owner(s). Not only does this vision clearly define the product, it also illustrates how that product will be used to support the business and its strategy, as well as who will use it and how it will be used.

During planning, the product road map is defined in collaboration with the scrum master and the product owner. This road map provides a high-level view of the requirements, with a rough time frame for developing and

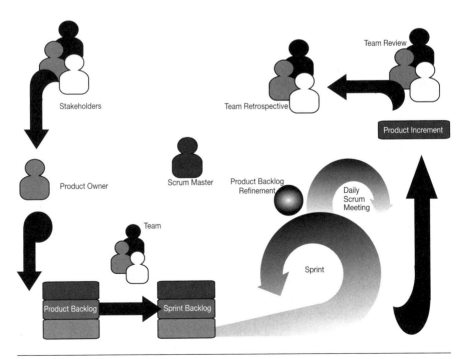

Figure 7.1   Agile life cycle

delivering those requirements. The Agile process really starts with the road map to value, which provides a high-level overview of the project and its intended objectives. Further, it identifies several key stages that will enable the project to evolve from concept to product along a clearly defined plan. These progressive stages are product vision, product road map, release planning, sprint planning, sprint review, and finally, the sprint retrospective. Figure 7.2 illustrates the Agile road map to value.

An effective *road map* contains details about the product and the effort required to develop and implement it. In this case, these details include requirements, prioritization of those requirements, and an estimation of the effort to develop and implement those specific requirements.

Next (as an extension of planning), the scrum master and the product owner collaborate to create the release plan. This plan determines the overall schedule for the release of functioning products, such as software.

To be clear, while an Agile project contains multiple releases and sprints, the release plan does not replace a more formal scheduling and release plan at the program level, as it is limited to the life cycle of the project. It plans for the release of specific features in a particular, prioritized order. To this end,

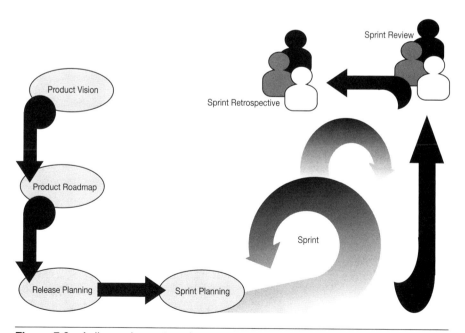

Figure 7.2   Agile road map to value

the plan dictates that the highest-priority features are released first, and less crucial features are released in subsequent sprints. A typical release plan will cross approximately three to five sprints. New release plans are created at the beginning of each release.

In the next stage, the scrum master and the development team collaborate with the product owner to plan the sprints. Again, sprint planning sessions also take place at the start of each sprint. However, in these planning sessions, the team determines the specific requirements for the features that will be in the subsequent iteration. Once the sprints have been planned, the team runs each sprint in sequence and creates the product features that have been planned for each of those sprints.

Sprints are managed through the daily *stand-up meeting*. As a general rule, the daily stand-up meeting should not be more than 15 minutes. In these stand-up meetings, participants have the opportunity to discuss the work that was completed on the previous day, tasks for the current day, and any issues they foresee that will prevent them from getting the work done.

The basic tasks for each sprint include requirements definition and analysis, as well as design, implementation, deployment, and solution testing. Unlike a traditional project model that creates as many of the identified features as possible (as identified by the needs analysis), the Agile project model focuses specific blocks of features and only those tasks which would build the particular functionality to create those features.

Within Agile, managing scope starts with identifying the road map to value and extends across planning. Filling the requirements backlog is absolutely critical to managing scope on an Agile project. This is essentially the list of features that need to be defined in order to address the product backlog. If this is not well-defined or managed, scope will still change unnecessarily.

The techniques outlined in this book should be applied throughout all projects, including an Agile project, in order to realize great results. The need for due diligence is not affected by the project methodology; it is simply scaled back to accommodate the shorter life cycle.

Next, the team conducts a *sprint review*, where the team demonstrates the working product that was built during the sprint to the business stakeholders. This review is held at the end of every sprint, and the results are used to help the team to determine the requirements for the subsequent sprint where the product does not match the business needs. In essence, this review enables the team to assess the overall alignment of the product to the scope and the identified needs in order to ensure that scope creep does not occur.

Finally, the team conducts the *sprint retrospective*. This meeting is when the team identifies and discusses the lessons learned and then plans for improvements to the subsequent sprints. As with the sprint review, the retrospective is conducted at the end of every sprint and supports quicker integration of the lessons learned into the development process.

MISCONCEPTIONS ABOUT AGILE

Some of the most common misconceptions about Agile are:

- Requirements are unnecessary;
- Agile teams deliver more functionality faster than other project models;
- Agile teams are self-organizing and do not need to be managed; and
- Agile can be applied to every project.

Over the last decade, Forrester Research indicated that Agile has shifted from an approach practiced by Agile evangelists (so-called "Agilists") to one applied by teams and companies with more diverse approaches to projects. Agile methods are still gaining popularity, a Q3 2010 survey conducted by Forrester Research revealed that approximately 39% of the 1,023 respondents cited following an Agile method.[2]

In spite of this finding, the reality is that the approach being claimed by many companies is merely inspired by the Agile Manifesto. In practice, however, its application "is constrained by both organizational culture and intuitive governance. The result is Agile adoption that is both challenging for the Agile team and that fails to realize Agile's business benefits, such as faster time-to-market, increased business value, and improved flexibility and responsiveness."[3] What this really means is that Agile is not and cannot deliver on its promise without some level-setting of expectations and some education of the teams involved. One of those challenges arises out of the misconception that requirements are unnecessary. Unfortunately, with the codependent relationship between scope and requirements, this is not possible to achieve without also impacting scope in some way. In effect, this perception puts scope, in general, at risk of not being met.

While the Agile Manifesto values "Working software over comprehensive documentation,"[4] this does not remove the need to have documented requirements before development begins. In an example of a retailer without adequate requirements documentation to support the project, the cost to support the end-product rendered the company unprofitable and put partnerships with other software companies at risk.

To Document or Not to Document at a Retailer

At one time, an online retailer had an e-commerce website that was so riddled with defects, it produced upwards of 600 error messages per day. The retailer decided to re-architect the site in order to comply with the demands of a new partnership. Unfortunately, before this could be done, they needed to understand how the existing processes worked and identify the business rules that governed those processes.

In this instance, the requirements had never been documented, so the re-architecture of the website took additional efforts to define the existing processes and business rules, which would become the foundation for the new website requirements.

One of the problems was that the team was trying to apply the principles of Agile in the development of the original website. They developed features in iterations as they were needed. To compound this approach, there was a consistently high employee attrition rate.

After two short years, there were no remaining staff who understood the functionality, while new iterations developed by new team members created overlapping functionality, and above all, the system functionality was actually delivered as separate mini-applications. This resulted in literally thousands of errors every day, which swamped the support team.

Another common misconception is that using the Agile life cycle means that teams deliver more functionality, more often than other project methodologies. This idea comes from the delivery of parsed functionality in limited iterations. This means that after the first iteration, the business could have working software, even though the functionality is limited.

One of the keys to Agile success is the concept of *continuous integration*. However, resources are required to support continuous integration, test automation, peer reviews, and end of sprint reviews. Many perceived gains in cost, scope, and time, are actually spent in these activities and really are not gains at all, during the initial projects that apply the Agile methodology.

Continuous integration is not to be mistaken for, nor does it replace, scheduling and release management of active products. A project is still the development process with a defined start and end.

The concept that self-organizing teams do not need to be managed is a misconception based on the principle identified in the Agile Manifesto, which states, "Build projects around motivated individuals. Give them the environment and support they need, and trust them to get the job done."[5] However, trust, support, and management are three entirely different things.

While management provides guidance and direction, it also frees up the team members to focus on the tasks without having to also focus on reporting back to the business and ensuring that the project is on track. Management also enables the business to identify and prioritize the features to be developed in each sprint through collaborative planning.

Trust means that team members will not be micromanaged to complete the tasks and to utilize their own judgment, skills, and experience in the completion of those tasks. Support requires that obstacles to the completion of the tasks be managed and minimized. This ensures that the tasks are completed in a timely manner.

Another misconception may be confusion over iteration/implementation of priority features versus quality. A core principle of Agile is that quality is never compromised. Reduced, key working feature sets should be divorced from the "system" being of inferior quality, as this transcends into negative perceptions of Agile being "cheap and cheerful." Quality is nonnegotiable—period!

The last major misconception is the idea that Agile can be applied to every project. Consider this: methodologies are techniques to be applied to achieve a specific outcome in the development process. This is similar to the use of specific techniques in any other construction process, such as the way to install flooring in a home varies with the attributes of both the home and flooring type to be installed. In other words, the subfloor, the load-bearing structures, and the type of flooring materials will determine the application and approach used to install the flooring.

According to Mike Cohn (2011), "the most appropriate projects for Agile are ones with aggressive deadlines, a high degree of complexity, and a high degree of novelty (uniqueness) to them."[6] This means that projects are appropriate where there is a high degree of urgency, and/or intricacy and complexity, as well as some elements of newness or uniqueness to the development team.

What Cohn is basically saying is that a project with one or more of these attributes is a great candidate for applying the Agile methodology because of the way in which the sprint delivers functionality. He does suggest however, that complexity alone is not a determining factor in the application of Agile, but this complexity is the one attribute that must be in combination with any of the other attributes in order to be successful in applying Agile.

According to Mark W. Timmis (2011), project size, requirements stage, and ability to increment are also factors in the selection and application of the Agile methodology. As to project size, he suggests, "Medium to small system projects that are relatively independent of other systems are easier to leverage with an Agile approach."[7] While he does not state why project size factors in, one can assume it relates back to the complexity of the project as suggested by Cohn.

As far as the requirements stage is concerned, Timmis suggests that Agile is better suited to more high-level requirements than those that are more granular and well-defined. The concern with this is that it leaves room for invalidated requirements and features. This does not actually alleviate the problems of unused software features, and it does little to curb the costs associated with scrap and rework. Finally, Timmis also suggests, "If it can roll out incrementally, and continuous improvement is feasible, then it is absolutely a good candidate. If not, but all of the other elements meet the Agile criteria, then this can be worked out."[8] In other words, while the ability to increment is a good factor, it is not actually a make or break factor in the application of Agile to the project.

IMPACTS OF AGILE ON SCOPE

When you consider that the scope of an Agile project is closely tied to (if not defined by) the product backlog, the question is what rigor is being applied to ensure that this backlog maintains alignment to evolving business needs. As that backlog ages, the organization must determine the life span and stale-dating for items within the backlog. This will prevent projects from going ahead with features and functionality that are no longer required, feasible, or appropriate because the needs have changed. This is a key benefit of an Agile approach to delivering business value.

The concept of a backlog is that elements are scheduled in priority within a confined time frame, so not all required elements can be addressed at any given single point in time. Backlog suggests capacity to develop is limited, and thus features are staggered over time, and a "log jam" of required features and functionality are awaiting development and implementation. Ironically, in any other sense of the word, having a "backlog" is not considered to be a good thing. Traditionally, a *backlog* refers to the accumulation of work that is waiting to be completed or orders waiting to be fulfilled, over a period of time.

It is really important for a backlog life cycle to be defined as part of the Agile governance model, in order to define the stale-dating process for features whose timeliness, usefulness, feasibility, or overall appropriateness have expired. The alternative is to continue along with planned development and implementation of features simply because they were identified as necessary at one point in time. This does nothing to alleviate overspending or to enable Agile to address product scope in the way it was intended. Therefore, all it does is prolong the development effort indefinitely, which has both direct and opportunity cost implications, among other things.

On the flip side, however, Agile can limit or prevent the ability to adequately identify an appropriate scope for a given project, and could put the entire solution at risk of becoming a hodgepodge of functionality that is hobbled together and serves no real benefit to the business. In this case, the solution will end up costing more and requiring higher maintenance than if it were developed and implemented utilizing a more traditional, linear delivery method.

This goes right back to the statement made by Dave West et al. (2011) about how solutions are limited by "organizational culture and intuitive governance,"[9] and directly results in the inability to achieve the benefits that a business may have gotten from utilizing the Agile approach (i.e., improvements to flexibility and responsiveness, as well as shorter time-to-market and increased value).

IMPACTS OF AGILE ON REQUIREMENTS

If requirements are an extension of scope (as the decomposition into its granular details or representative components), then it stands to reason that wherever and whenever Agile impacts scope, it will also impact requirements, and vice versa. While one of the primary drivers behind the development of Agile, and certainly in its rise to popularity, is the idea that erroneous requirements can be addressed in subsequent iterations, it does not necessarily mean that there is less risk associated with Agile, or that requirements are suddenly complete, consistent, or even accurate, let alone having any of the other attributes that quality requirements must have.

Where Agile is based on the premise that users do not know what they want or need until they have been presented with options, it is more likely that it is not the inability of the user, but the inability of the software team in facilitating the articulation of those business needs into a descriptive format which can be analyzed, verified, validated, designed, developed, and tested. At the outset, this means that uncertainty in software really comes from our own inability to define, predict, and communicate the user actions that complement the needs.

It can be difficult to interpret and to predict the thought processes of others when each person is a unique individual and may perform one specific task in any number of differing ways. The truth is that the onus is not on technology professionals to predict what the user will do. In fact, it is more important to identify the needed results and then to produce the mechanisms that will deliver the events, which will create those results.

As Timmis pointed out, one of the factors that has the potential to make an Agile project more successful is that the requirements are high level and not well-defined. However, that does little to alleviate the risks of misinterpretation. Essentially, what Timmis is saying is that by defining requirements only a step or two below scope means that they can't be wrong, and the development team has more opportunity to work with the business team to interpret them into more specific details, which immediately get designed and coded.

Unfortunately, this leaves too much room for interpretation and omission of critical requirements. This means that requirements are not going to be validated and will leave a lot of assumptions to the architects and developers. In Chapter 5, the discussion pointed out the need for both verification and validation to occur as necessary steps in the development and definition of requirements through the decomposition of scope. When requirements are defined at an inappropriate level (too high), verification is subjective and validation is impossible.

The real issue is that other teams downstream from requirements activities must then attempt to interpret what the business actually needs. This leads directly to inadequate testing of the features, as well as an inability to trace from testing back up to requirements. All in all, this places restrictions and limitations on the test coverage and the overall change control as the project moves throughout successive sprints.

While Timmis suggests that Agile projects are more successful, Planit Software Testing (2013) reported Agile project success rates at 52%,[10] while the volume of projects that report significant changes is 22% (as illustrated in

Figure 7.3). These rates would support the position that change is the greater challenge of Agile projects, and that requirements need to be detailed enough to support all of the activities in the later stages of the project, not only the development stage.

USING AGILE TO MANAGE SCOPE CHANGE

Before an adequate discussion on changes to scope within Agile projects, the differences between reasons for these changes must be clearly understood and defined. Technically, with requirements less defined than more traditional models, one would expect that changes to actual scope should be limited or dramatically reduced.

However, what this expectation really illustrates is that Agile, while quicker, shorter, and more engaging throughout the project life cycle than a

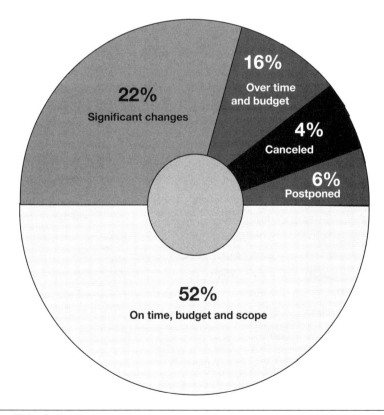

Figure 7.3 Agile success rates

waterfall approach, it is not the best means of managing significant changes to scope. Of course, this conclusion is obviously impacted by the following discussions about how Agile projects are being governed, and if teams are doing enough on Agile projects to ensure that due diligence is being done up front to define scope at the outset. It begs the questions: "Are we doing the right things, and are we doing these things right (or are we leaving it to the subsequent sprints and iterations to answer this question)?"

GOVERNANCE OF AGILE PROJECTS

As project teams adopt Agile software development methods, issues arise with traditional approaches to governance. Such approaches, which include Control Objectives for Information and Related Technology (COBIT) and the Project Management Institute's Organizational Project Management Maturity Model (OPM3)®, are often too heavy in practice for development shops striving to be Agile. An all too common fear in respect to adopting Agile— linked to a common misconception—is that control will be lost where the proverbial "reins of the horse" are loosened. Any conversation and resultant governance model of Agile initiatives will perhaps be fruitful where it provides comfort, and ideally, address satisfactorily the question, "Is it possible to loosen the reins on development teams without a loss of control and audit trails, and without a degradation of quality and service?"

From a project governance perspective, while Agile initiatives are often perceived (misconceived?) as being difficult or even impossible to govern, the corollary is actually the case. Indeed, all of the key principles underlying Agile lend themselves directly to governance. Prior to understanding how governance can flow from those principles, it is vital to understand who owns, drives, and is accountable for governance of an Agile development initiative.

A key aspect of any governance model is the organizational structure or the body or group that runs the governance program. For Agile, a critical success factor is that the governance group should seek to enable the stakeholders and team first, and control and manage second. To achieve this, the governance group must create an environment, provide clarity of mission, and elucidate pragmatic rules of engagement. To put it another way, start to create the conditions required for success.

Governance here ensures that goals, quality expectations, thresholds, and tolerance levels are appropriately defined and communicated, while enabling the team to "think" and "do" in a project specific manner, as opposed to the application of standard, boiler plate, or prescribed reaction to situations, as though they are all the same.

Therefore, a key aspect of this environment is access to resources, including access to business stakeholders, management information, knowledge, guidance, support, and mentoring, as well as a pragmatic delivery tool kit that the team can apply and adapt as required. This of course, is the antithesis of a command-and-control governance model such as COBIT, OPM3, or ITIL frameworks.

As it is vital to select the right team mix—in terms of roles, experience, skill sets, and knowledge—it is essential to establish the correct governance group. A proven tactic here is to establish a group comprised of accountable key stakeholders, typically from the business, IT, or design authority, or any vendor/partner/supplier critical to the initiative, and senior stakeholders from the user community. By bringing this group of stakeholders into the solution "tent," an "us vs. them" mentality is avoided from the outset.

Key Principles of Agile and Their Relationship with Governance

A few core principles underpin all Agile methods. The first principle is to foster individuals and interactions over process and tools.[13] This directly touches on two sub-principles: collaboration, and clear, continuous communication. These principles are, in turn, embodied fully in the concept of the self-organizing team.

The dynamic systems development method (DSDM) is a software development method that is utilized on agile projects. Much like agile, it leverages a continuous improvement approach through iterative cycles that includes heavy user involvement.

Other key Agile principles that directly encourage and warrant effective governance are central to the DSDM Atern philosophy, as developed in partnership with the Association of Project Management Group,[14] and include:

- On-time delivery;
- No compromise to quality;
- Build incrementally from firm foundations; and
- Demonstrate control.

To show how these integrate and interrelate, in the same way that staged program delivery enables an optimized, enterprise centric approach to value delivery by applying formal health and quality checks at key stages of the delivery and/or development life cycle as part of a gating process, Agile principles mandate regular and frequent "inspection" opportunity through its incremental, sprint construct. This allows rapid review and calibration through effective use of "time-boxing" as a delivery technique, for example.

As an outcome, time-boxing and the inspection that occurs during the sprint, demonstrate control, support on-time delivery, and ensure that quality is both built-in and fit-for-purpose, as determined against defined quality and acceptance criteria. In other words, demonstrable results feedback is provided to enable broader direction and situation-specific decision making. Such activities and outcomes build a reputation for timely and predictable deliveries, while affording high levels of control and opportunities to manage.

From another perspective, there are always insufficient resources to deliver all of the needs and wants (in terms of changes and new capabilities) at the corporate level. A business-driven project pipeline may, therefore, reside. At the project level, the product backlog offers a control mechanism in line with the corporate level model to manage demand, scope, and feature sets in a prioritized manner. Management of the product backlog affords regular opportunities to interact with key stakeholders (relevance, updated priority, etc.) and collaborate on the ongoing validity of aspects of scope for the project at hand.

A final thought in terms of Agile and its governance revolves around concepts such as: Enough Design Up Front, compared to Big Design Up Front promoted by a traditional approach, where design and documentation are appropriate and lead to techniques and practices such as testing early and continuously, prototyping, and proof of concept. Coupled with the other fundamental Agile principles, it is possible to see how appropriate, feasible, and desirable solutions aligned to corporate goals can be achieved alongside a natural management of the change from a people perspective, a key to Agile being to "bring the people with you" on the journey—through close collaboration and direct engagement—so that genuine involvement will nurture adoption and ownership by the ultimate recipients of the change.

STRENGTHS OF AGILE

The truth is that Agile does have an "up" side, in spite of the perceived risks of ambiguity in requirements and heavy changes to scope. In reality, 29% of failed projects cite a lack of stakeholder involvement in the project.[15] Agile dramatically changes this percent, in that 34% of projects are far more successful at engaging stakeholders and team collaboration,[16] and 40% are generally more successful at team collaboration.[17] This means that Agile projects are actually about 74% more successful than traditional models when it comes to engagement, involvement, and team collaboration (when the two highest success rates in this category are combined).

Another big strength is that Agile projects are adept at getting products to market faster. About 51% faster according to Planit Software Testing (2012), as shown in Table 7.1, reporting that Agile projects were 18%[18] far more successful, and 33%[19] generally more successful at reducing the time to market for products. For those aggressive schedules, projects which cover new technological ground, and even for projects where budgets come in influxes of cash instead of one large up-front investment, Agile can create and deliver much-needed functionality to the business as time, money, and resources permit.

Having shorter delivery time frames mean that the business is also able to be more agile in its competition against others, because it has the capability to develop on-demand functionality. That is, if the business can master the delivery of Agile projects, and it leverages these projects to their advantage under the right circumstances, and for the right types of products.

That same Planit Software Testing survey also reported that among the waterfall, V model, and Agile methodologies, the most significant changes to requirements were reported by Agile projects. This is directly attributed to an increased involvement of the business stakeholders in the overall development process. Without the means and the mechanisms to validate inputs before they can be incorporated into new products, this is simply not going to change, due to the many reasons noted in the discussion on stakeholder management in Chapter 3.

Table 7.1 Agile success statistics, 2012

Success	Team Collaboration	Time to Market	Addressing Requirements	Overall Success (ROI)
High	34%	18%	15%	14%
	40%	33%	40%	34%
	19%	30%	27%	28%
	7%	11%	13%	18%
Low		8%	5%	5%

> **An Agile Success Story[20]**
>
> Several years ago, a project was initiated at a large company to replace the existing underwriter risk assessment tool and to change how the underwriters kept track of notes on client accounts. Agile was chosen as an alternative to using traditional waterfall because the business felt it would take too long, consume excessive resources, and would not deliver exactly what the business wanted.
>
> The team was small. There was one project manager, one architect, one solution lead, one development lead with five developers, and a single test lead with three testers. The team was supported by one business sponsor and one business lead.
>
> The majority of the leads on the team were generally co-located in one central location (at least the majority of the time). The team also maintained a disciplined calendar that everyone adhered to. The calendar included a daily stand-up meeting with the entire team. In addition, this team also established a team document that contained the solution, the development, and the test components.
>
> In this case, the team was able to successfully decommission a legacy application in roughly six months. This solution already had user buy-in and a low defect rate. On top of this, the solution was built so that after any given iteration, the resulting application could have been moved into production as a fully operational product.
>
> One of the main strengths of this project was that the team had also created a solid foundation of requirements and associated test cases that could be used for any future changes or modifications.

There were several factors to the success of the Agile success story example. The entire scope of the solution was predetermined and the timing of the iterations was based on the input of the entire team. Further, a single reference document was used in combination with individual prototypes for each iteration. The project team was also co-located, had great dynamics and finally, they leveraged both engagement and feedback mechanisms.

RISKS OF THE AGILE APPROACH

In spite of Agile's strengths, a true discussion of the approach is not complete without further discussion of the associated risks. This discussion is meant to provide information to proponents in selecting the methodology for a given project so that an educated decision can be made and they are more likely to be successful.

That being said, the biggest risks in the application of the Agile approach directly result from the interpretation, misconceptions, and incomplete utilization by the resources themselves. Remember that it is the people who will interpret, understand, and then later apply the techniques. This application is going to be based solely on their biases, experiences, education, beliefs, and core competencies. What this means is that when project resources come together in any given project, and they set out to apply specific techniques according to an approach or methodology, they are all really working at the project from differing angles and levels of expertise.

An unwritten concept of Agile is a "learn-by-doing" approach. This notion applies not only to the solution (as scope evolves and incremental delivery progresses), but also to the "solutioners." It is imperative that a true team, one of differing but complementary skills, and an enabling environment (where failure is deemed an opportunity to learn, improve, and develop) reside. A high level of self awareness and self actualization exist in the most successful Agile structures, which infers a certain level of maturity. As can be said of many things, the caliber of the people can significantly impact the success or even achievability of any specific initiative. The biggest risk to successfully applying Agile is ultimately a people risk. Those leading the cause should see the hiring and selection of specialists and practitioners as something to aspire to and not fear for concerns of a loss of power, be it real or perceived. Perhaps the following tenet, which ultimately alludes to confidence and accountability, is a good one to stand by: First-class people hire first-class people; second-class people hire third-class people.

REFERENCES

1. Ziv, Hadar and Richardson, Debra J., "The Uncertainty Principle in Software Engineering." 1996.
2. Forrester Research. 2010. "Dr. Dobb's Global Developer Technographics® Survey." Dr. Dobb's Journal.
3. West, Dave, with Mike Gilpin, Tom Grant, Ph.D., and Alissa Anderson). 2011, July 26. "Water-Scrum-Fall Is the Reality of Agile for Most Organizations Today." Forrester Research, Inc. http://www.forrester.com/WaterScrumFall+Is+The+Reality+Of+Agile+For+Most+Organizations+Today/fulltext/-/E-RES60109?docid=60109
4. Agile Manifesto. 2001. http://agilemanifesto.org

5. *Ibid.*
6. Cohn, Mike. 2011, January 15. "Deciding What Kind of Projects Are Most Suited for Agile." Mountain Goat Software. http://www.moun taingoatsoftware.com/blog/deciding-what-kind-of-projects-are-most -suited-for-agile
7. Timmis, Mark W. 2011, July 22. "Is Agile Right for Your Project?" PMforward/BCforward. http://www.pmforward.com/is-agile-right-for -your-project/
8. *Ibid.*
9. West, Dave, with Mike Gilpin, Tom Grant, Ph.D., and Alissa Anderson. "Water-Scrum-Fall Is the Reality of Agile for Most Organizations Today." Forrester Research, 2011.
10. Planit Software Testing. 2013. "Planit Testing Index 2013: Project Outcomes." http://www.planit.net.au/resource/industry-stats-project -outcomes-2013/
11. *Ibid.*
12. *Ibid.*
13. Agile Alliance. 2001. The Agile Manifesto. http://www.agilemani festo.org
14. Association of Project Management Group.
15. Murray, Michael J. and Crandall, Richard E. 2006. IT Offshore Outsourcing Requires a Project Management Approach. SAM Advanced Management Journal (07497075); Winter 2006, Vol. 71 Issue 1.
16. Planit Software Testing. 2012. "Industry Stats: Project Outcomes Based on Primary Methodologies." http://www.planit.net.au/resource/ industry-stats-project-outcomes-based-on-primary-methodologies/
17. *Ibid.*
18. *Ibid.*
19. *Ibid.*
20. White, Tony. 2013. Agile Interview with Barbara Davis. Olenik Consulting.

This book has free material available for download from the
Web Added Value™ resource center at *www.jrosspub.com*

8

WATERFALL

WHAT IS WATERFALL?

Waterfall is a model to deliver change, which is essentially the antithesis of the Agile iterative development processes. In the iterative life cycle model, artifacts are defined, grown, and evolved as the initiative progresses and more certainty is established. As discussed in Chapter 7, this incremental approach is based on a premise that everything can't be known up front, and that learning and refining by doing is a key success factor. Concepts such as Enough Design Up Front are key to Agile in a concerted attempt to deliver working, relevant functionality to the organization in a timely manner.

Waterfall is predicated on a sequential approach to change whereby development is linear, with outputs of each phase of an analysis (requirements), the design, build, and test and deploy development process cascading like a waterfall into the next phase upon completion. The concept of Big Design Up Front is a foundational aspect whereby the amount of time spent in the first phase (analysis) ensures thorough inputs to the design phase, and so on. The intention is to safeguard the correctness of the required artifacts at each stage (requirements catalog, design document, etc.), thus providing 100% certainty with confidence and a clear road map to producing the overall desired solution.

Waterfall as a concept has taken hold primarily because it is simple. It is easy to understand and follow, and therefore adopts a logical sequenced approach. The sequential model theory, as illustrated in Figure 8.1, is ultimately premised on the promise of reduced time, effort, and cost, where proceeding phases of the

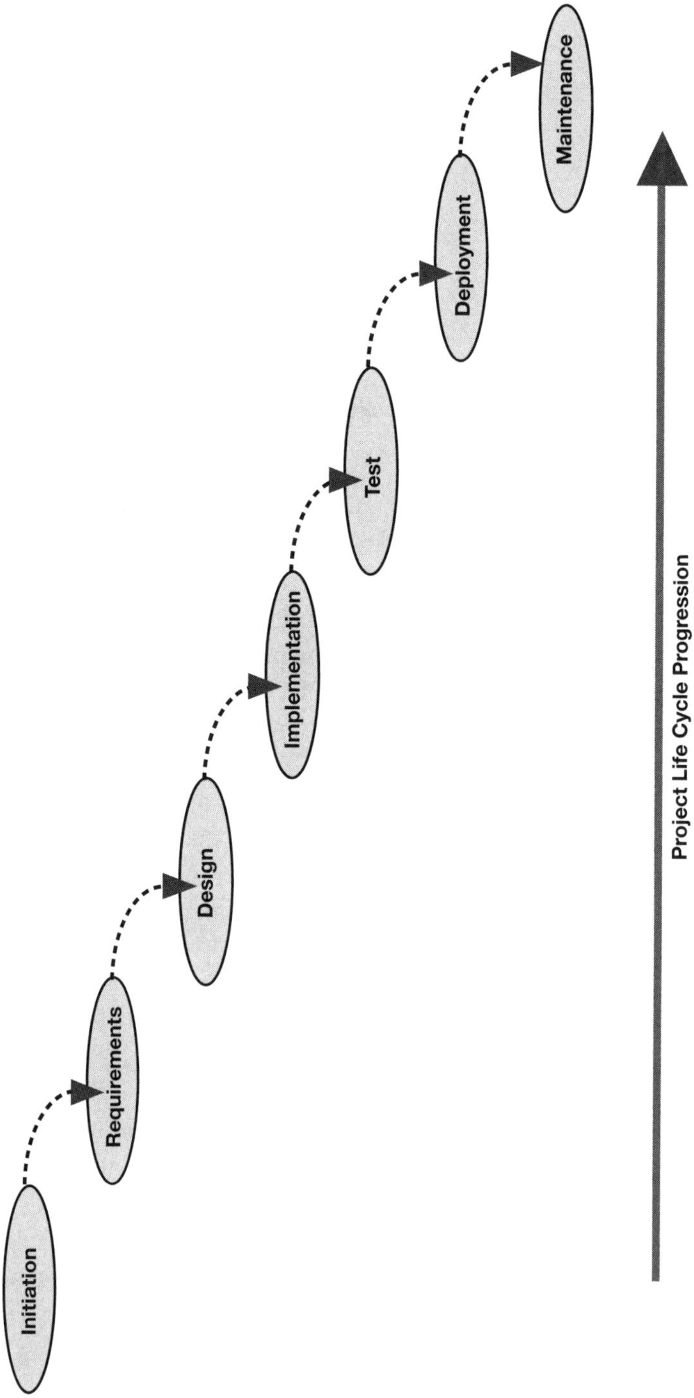

Figure 8.1   General waterfall model

life cycle are complete and correct as those downstream have a clear mandate/ foundation against which activity can be performed and deliverables produced with high certainty. For example, with a completed design document, a full set of test scripts can be developed to ensure all aspects of the design are tested and that it conforms to the stipulated technical and functional specifications.

Like Agile development methods, the Waterfall model is typically associated with the development of software. It can however, apply to projects that do not have a technology/software component. Of note is that its origins stem from the hardware domains of manufacturing and construction (as does software engineering itself), where any desired change after things have been built (for example, a multistory office tower) are either impossible or would be prohibitively expensive to affect. A key to Waterfall, then, is the freezing and formal approval of things such as scope, requirements, and specifications prior to development.

Another classic model that is worthy of note, due to its complimentary nature to the Waterfall approach, is the V Development Model, as illustrated in Figure 8.2. The *V* stands for Verification and Validation. Perhaps best viewed

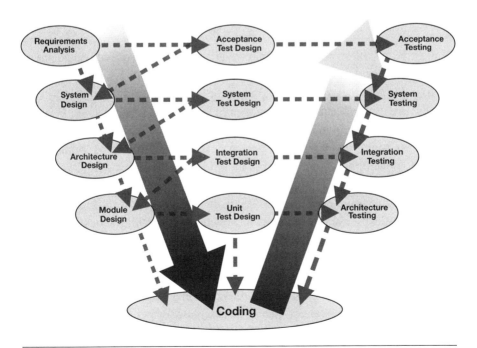

Figure 8.2   The V development model

as a helpful elaboration on the Waterfall model, the V-shaped life cycle is a sequential path of execution of processes. As in the Waterfall model, each phase must be completed before the next phase begins, but the difference in the V Model is that testing of the products planned to be created in each phase is designed in parallel with the corresponding phase of development, and provides an input into the next development phase. This balance, or healthy tension, between the verify and validate aspects of development are designed to really flesh out that the products to be produced are correct, and that the quality, functionality, and other requirements are defined, understood, and feasible as agreed by a number of project stakeholders, mostly those charged with development and testing, respectively.

We suggest that the V Model is viewed as an elaboration of the Waterfall model for two primary reasons:

1. The various test planning and designing activities occur prior to the code being written. This provides more confidence earlier in the development life cycle than afforded by a pure Waterfall model, so that the desired solution can be achieved; and

2. As some defects can be identified at each of the development phases, fewer defects will be carried forward into the subsequent phases, as may occur with a Waterfall approach.

While a Waterfall project has certain advantages around ease of use due to its sequential nature—rendering these types of development initiatives very neat to compartmentalize, manage, and monitor each stage of the process—there are some restrictions and disadvantages of such a simple model.

First, neither the world nor change within businesses is linear, simple in nature, nor stable for prolonged periods. Adopting a linear and simple approach to development in a Waterfall model may, therefore, be fundamentally flawed, as the premise is not vested in reality.

Second, the foundational premise of the sequential, Waterfall approach calls for the desired solution to be determined up front without the opportunity to model or prototype solutions, and obtain relevant and real-time feedback from stakeholders—a key feature of Agile development approaches. Often, the customer does not know to the specific level of detail, what s/he wants up front—Agile proponents stating that this can only come about through a series of iterations. This state of uncertainty may be further compounded, given the uncertain nature of estimating time and costs with any degree of accuracy.

Software Unveiling: But What About ...?

Every time I see a new software unveiled, immediately following the initial wows and gasps, it invariably leads to statements like "... and wouldn't it be good if it could also do X, Y, and Z?" Essentially, having seen the product, a window into the art of the possible is opened and new ideas flow from the audience. With this in mind, wouldn't it be powerful to do this as early as possible and capture all that energy, enthusiasm, and possible rich feature mix to actually utilize in the solution? How helpful would that be in managing the change, for those receiving it to have been a genuine part of the solution?

Expanding upon the concept of capturing potential prior to a software unveiling, the project stakeholders (non-IT personnel) may not be fully aware of the capabilities of the target technology being implemented. This can lead to what they think is possible—as constrained by their own skills, experience, and knowledge—defining expectations and requirements. In turn, this may lead to a design that does not use the full potential of what the new technology can deliver, or simply replicates the existing application or process with the new technology. This can cause substantial changes to the implementation requirements once the stakeholders become more aware of the functionality available from the new technology.

A third criticism of the Waterfall model strikes at the assumption that a design can be converted into a working solution. This may simply not be feasible and may become apparent should unforeseen roadblocks arise during the process.

Following from this criticism, and perhaps the most significant criticism of Waterfall, is that a less than optimal performance and associated outputs from the proceeding phases of development will be compounded and baked-in to the downstream activities and ultimately, the final solution. These problems may only be exposed when code is actually written and the developed solution subsequently tested—and seen for the first time by users. But going back would require significant time, effort, and cost (rework) to correct the "defects" that will only come to light late in the development life cycle. Even where defects come to light before coding, substantial rework may be required prior to continuing down the Waterfall process. Essentially, the need to rework is built into the model, not because it assumes the translation of design into a tangible, working, user-friendly product is an easy journey, or even achievable at all. Unless at completion, where a less than perfect solution is delivered, the organization simply tolerates any missing or less than optimal features, a Waterfall approach presents a real issue on all but the most simple projects.

MISCONCEPTIONS ABOUT WATERFALL

There are a number of misconceptions about Waterfall. For ease, these have been consolidated and are summarized as:

1. There is such a thing as a 100% Waterfall project;
2. Waterfall is a fit-for-purpose model on all projects; and
3. Waterfall reduces the risk and delivery uncertainties associated with all development work.

In practice, most Waterfall projects have some limited form of iterations for several different reasons, and often rely on some sort of feasibility study or prototyping by way of significant input. Further, Waterfall type approaches in the real world must incorporate feedback loops at each stage, and it is unlikely that the development/project team will get all the users' intentions documented, developed, and integrated correctly the first time—"to err is human," after all. So, one or two iterations through all the stages is a more realistic expectation.

The very advantages of Waterfall—its logical, sequenced, formal, and rigid approach to development—also hinder it in terms of its applicability to all projects. Sometimes, while an organization may know what it wants and even why, it may not know how to go about developing the desired solution and ultimately realizing the associated targeted benefits. Projects that are large (typically defined as taking longer than 12 months), poorly defined, or born of an unstable, unpredictable, or fast-changing environment, whereby the solution may not be well understood, may not be the best projects to apply a Waterfall development approach.

Another significant misunderstanding of a Waterfall model is that its very nature of driving 100% complete sequential phases of a development life cycle means that it necessarily reduces risk and/or uncertainties around delivery. While a sequential model seems a perfectly logical way to approach things, and the Waterfall model would appear to offer easy and full management control and thus generate confidence that all is well, this assumed logic and delivery confidence may be misplaced. Further, the level of risk may actually be increased as errors or omissions can be compounded through the sequential model, and uncertainty may increase as the final product is not seen until the end of the process.

When defects are unearthed, key stakeholders are often left scratching their heads, asking the rhetorical questions: "How could we have missed that?" or "How could this happen?" The perceived control offered by a sequential approach may often be nothing more than a veneer of control primarily focused on driving the right process and outputs at the expense of tracking those higher level outcomes initially targeted by the initiative. Management control in this sense, is more about restricting and resisting changes to the initiative and tracking that all features are delivered to plan and within cost estimates, rather than welcoming the opportunity to change (scope, time, cost, feature mix, etc.) where this is in the best interest of the organization as a whole. Essentially, management control here is focused on the specific project thresholds and tolerance levels and deliberately blinds itself to broader, enterprise level concerns. Where a project is really good at executing a process, but ultimately that process is delivering the wrong things, I'd suggest this not only destroys the value targeted for the particular initiative, but that there is likely an equal opportunity cost to pay as valuable resources could have been utilized on other initiatives that would benefit the organization.

IMPACTS OF WATERFALL ON SCOPE

This first step in the Waterfall life cycle is to gather information about what the customer needs and explicitly define the problem that the product is expected to solve or the opportunity to be leveraged. Analysis includes understanding the customer's business context and constraints, the functions the product must perform, the operational performance levels it must adhere to, and the other systems (business and technical) it must be compatible with. Techniques used to obtain this understanding include interviews, use cases, stories, and requirements catalogs, which capture the feature shopping list. The results of the analysis are typically captured in a formal requirements specification (for example, functional and technical requirements), which serve as the key inputs to the next phase.

With time spent up front defining and ultimately fixing the scope, a key principle of Waterfall is that once fixed, the development machine will progress and take that agreed scope and make it real.

The Waterfall approach has one critical impact to scope. First, the scope is defined at a point in time based on information available at that time. For example, if new information, new technology, a diversification into a slightly different line of business or industry arises, it is very expensive to accommodate changes after scoping, the more granular requirements have been completed, and design or development work started. The business then, would have three choices:

- Incorporate the new idea/scope via a variance or change request process, resulting in a decision to vary the scope and associated timeliness, resources, cost, etc., up or down as specific to the nature of the request for change;
- Persist with the original plan (the assumption is that the business case still stands or the project should or must still be completed—a regulatory compliance initiative, for example) in the full knowledge that the scope request for change will not be incorporated; or
- Commission another project or drive some operational changes that can accommodate all or some of the scope changes raised.

One answer to mitigating this dilemma is to ensure that Waterfall projects are not too large in scale, complex, or long in terms of the timeline. This consideration, combined with a relatively stable environment, should mitigate the risk of change being raised prior to implementation. Another solution is to restrict the use of Waterfall to those more straightforward projects, well understood change initiatives, and business domains where "bleeding edge" solutions are not typically proposed.

Similarly, scope has one critical impact to a Waterfall approach. If scope cannot be defined up front with any degree of confidence, it is difficult to see how a Waterfall approach may be an optimal development model. Waterfall is reliant upon scope being clear, known, and fixed up front. It may simply be infeasible for all projects to be able to achieve, particularly where the project is truly unique or novel, as defined by the Project Management Institute. Both the Waterfall model and the scope of a Waterfall based project would render the concepts of trial-and-error, sandboxing, prototyping, and piloting as not applicable.

Potential solutions here may revolve around a senior developer working with a mature enterprise architecture discipline to ensure appropriate rationalization, consolidation, and harmonization; and, a streamlined solution is captured in the scope. The concept of a more modular approach to development, in general, which would necessarily filter into the scope of specific development initiatives, is another potential solution and complimentary to an architectural approach to development and managing change.

IMPACTS OF WATERFALL ON REQUIREMENTS

In respect to requirements, we can again observe that Waterfall is a double-edged sword, with its celebrated strengths potentially having a negative implication.

Waterfall promotes thorough documentation of requirements. On the face of it, this should drive through requirements gathering activities from a robust and broad group of key stakeholders. Thorough and well-documented requirements gathering can provide a compelling, persuasive, and confidence boosting set of requirements that look good, and perhaps even feel right, from the perspective of key stakeholders. But there are some fundamental constrains and assumptions that can significantly impact the appropriateness and the ability of the requirements to result in fully used and enduring features.

First, in what context are requirements gathered in respect to business or enterprise wide architectural design: current, transition, or future state? Next, is the operating model within which the development will fit appropriate, feasible, and desirable for the organization? When is it expected to be reviewed, or are there any significant plans to overhaul or reengineer it afoot? How successful is the analysis approach, practice, and techniques and how skilled are the practitioners? Do we need specialist analysis resources to assist with the planned initiative? How resistant is the organization or department to change in general, or the type of change proposed, and how forthcoming will they be in enabling the delivery team?

While requirement gathering is a fundamental component of Waterfall, it is a skilled, subjective, and specific aspect that touches on, works with, or needs to integrate with other business capabilities in the organization. If the planned Waterfall initiative does not take account of or receive good inputs from a wider environmental context, then it may perpetuate the Pareto principle.

The Pareto principle has stood the test of time, and I can't tell you how many times and in how many different sectors I've observed this as more of a truth than merely a frequently occurring phenomenon. To illustrate the Pareto principle: 20% of the features get used 80% of the time. In an IPMA Forum in 2009, citing the Standish Group's Chaos study, Skip Angel illustrated that 45% of features developed for software projects aren't used at all: 19% of features are rarely used; 16% of features are sometimes used; and only 7% are always used, with 13% used often.[1]

Features are derived from requirements, which in turn are the detailed decomposition of scope. If Waterfall promotes fixing the scope, requirements, and resultant feature sets, then the risk of crystallizing the design and later development components of requirements that will be developed into product features that are never or rarely used, is also set, promoting the Pareto scale of overengineering, and ultimately, the "waste" indicated in report after report from the Standish Group.

However, this is merely the start of the issue. Imagine the true cost. "Costs" include the time, cost, and resources to develop 50 to 80% of features that potentially, the business could do without, plus the resultant complexities of integration with other developments, testing, and training people, and the cost of sustaining, maintaining, and upgrading features that if missing, would not be showstoppers. The actual and opportunity costs in this regard are significant, and should be a major consideration for any organization introducing change.

This risk of this phenomenon occurring is only exacerbated by the fact that the individuals who produce the analysis have a personal stake in their work being good. To justify their contribution, the analyst who is asked to sign off on the requirements will generally strive to ensure that they can be traced, are comprehensive as per the target operating model or concept of operations pursued, and will be expected to vehemently defend these business requirements when translating and enabling the technical development team to develop the required solution features. The very model and governance features that support formal approval of the Waterfall phases, mean it is more likely than not that "waste" may result where a solid understanding of the business context, other change, strategic intent, etc., are not adequately conveyed to the project team.

USING WATERFALL TO MANAGE SCOPE CHANGE

A common measurement of the continuum often used to define the management of software is "predictive" vs. "adaptive." Another measure is "plan driven" vs. "value driven." Waterfall is a predictive, plan driven delivery paradigm with Agile representing the corollary. This is a significant factor in determining how scope is managed.

In a Waterfall type initiative, a vision and objectives are defined, analysis undertaken, and a breakdown of the work or products required is documented; time and resource estimates are undertaken, risks accounted for, and the final estimate is the budget for the project. Such work activity is focused on answering the question, "How much is this going to cost?" Agile slightly rephrases this question, asking, "How much can be built for a certain cost?" For Waterfall, starting off with a predictable total cost paradigm, the scope can be managed as follows:

- Scope is managed to a development schedule as derived from the work and/or product breakdown of deliverables to be produced.
- Where the need for additional scope is identified—perhaps missed as part of up-front analysis and design work, and could only reasonably have been detected during development—it is defined, analyzed, and endorsed or rejected, based on importance and impact to the delivery schedule.
- Must-have scope that cannot be accommodated into the delivery schedule will cause a schedule extension, require the need for additional resources, or both.
- The resultant cost of the initiative may be impacted in a negative manner, which may cause a review of the cost/benefit assessment that forms a critical part of the business case, the business case being the rationale for undertaking the project, or not. Therefore, the focus of Waterfall is the avoidance of cost increases.
- Formal acceptance testing by the end customer is undertaken at the end of a traditional development life cycle. For gaps in relation to scope at this stage, a plan to address is formulated or the gap accepted/tolerated by the customer. This is unlikely to involve significant review and rework, however; more likely, some small change initiatives will be spawned post project and added to the major deliverable(s) at an agreed future date.
- The project successfully completes when the schedule is complete. (For Agile, the project can be successfully terminated at the end of any iteration, providing significantly more scope flexibility than the Waterfall all or nothing commitment.)

The focus of Waterfall is to safeguard the predicted schedule from cost increases due to additional work. In other words, opportunities to change are seen as negative and should be resisted. In contrast, Agile approaches strive to ensure the highest value/priority work is conducted during the estimated time. Waterfall protects the schedule through formal, heavily documented change control (governance) and scope management plans that analyze schedule and scope impacts prior to acceptance. Maintaining the original scope is the focus, with cost and time considered variables. In other words, the paradigm is to deliver everything with management to focus on the time and cost to achieve all. With Agile projects, this model is inverted, with time and cost (and quality) considered fixed, and scope being the main variable.

RISKS OF THE WATERFALL DEVELOPMENT LIFE CYCLE

One of the core premises of Waterfall, and the rationale for why it should be used, also presents one of its greatest risks—certainty. Waterfall is premised on the certainty of the preceding step, prior to spending time, effort, and money on the subsequent stage. All stakeholders will be aligned and have a clear sense of where the project is, and what exactly, they will get. However, imagine that something quite important was missed on a larger-scale software initiative in analysis, and this went undetected among the thousands of explicit requirements, remained elusive in the final design, and only became apparent during testing of the proposed completed system. At this point in the development life cycle, it may be very difficult to go back and incorporate the missing component.

Similarly, Waterfall drives a big-bang approach to delivery where, in the case of software development, for example, no working software is produced until late in the project life cycle.

It can be concluded, therefore, that the Waterfall approach may not be the optimum approach where the initiative in question is large, long (time), complex, inherently higher risk, unstable (dynamic environment where requirements may change), or truly innovative in nature, i.e., the risk of not defining all the key features the first time around on a truly pioneering endeavor.

Some criticisms also center on the fact that the Waterfall model implies a clear division of labor between, say, designers, programmers, and testers; in reality, such a division of labor in most software firms is neither realistic nor efficient.

THE HYBRID—AGILE AND WATERFALL—TAKE THE BEST OF BOTH WORLDS

Waterfall projects are never really true, pure Waterfall. Given that we humans are flawed and that we do not get things right the first time, all the time. Accepting that the scope and requirements of initiatives can and do change (often for good, positive reasons), an approach that does not accommodate such inconvenient aspects must be limited in application and/or success. Practitioners of change accept that the world is not perfectly linear and that a sequential paint-by-numbers approach is not always possible (or realistic), so while the pervading delivery methodology of an organization may be described as Waterfall, within it, practitioners execute a number of iterations (beta programs, Phase 2, prototyping, for example)—sometimes explicitly calling them Iteration 1, Iteration 2, and so on. The Waterfall life cycle, therefore, is never truly "Waterfall," especially on those more complicated projects where there are risks and unknowns to address.

So, what is Agile? Well, a very simple articulation may be that it is simply the Waterfall process that is put on a "wash and repeat" cycle. A strong Waterfall approach will invariably require two iterations because, after testing, it is realistic to assume that some defects to specification will be found that may require amendments to design documentation and certainly development rework to correct, and an activity to retest and ensure the product is now fit for purpose. While two development methods are accepted, it can be argued that these are not stand-alone, mutually exclusive methods. Why not take the best of both methods to suit the specific project initiative at hand?

WATER-SCRUM-FALL

The culture and governance rules of most organizations require the definition, planning, and cost of a proposed change before work can be sanctioned. Similarly, the notion of a fixed-price contract, either with an external client or internal teams intuitively suggests that a high degree of certainty is desired prior to signing. These constraints suggest that a good degree of up-front assessment and design are required to reduce both solution and economic risk factors. This element can be seen as the '"Water" aspect of a traditional project method. It is also precisely for these reasons that Agile adoption is challenging for the team and that Agile often fails to realize the target

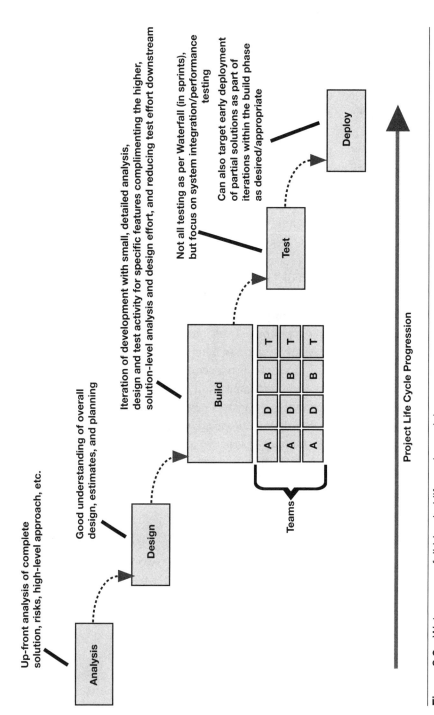

Figure 8.3   Water-scrum-fall blended life cycle model

benefits, such as increased speed to market, higher value, and improved responsiveness. The default organization structure and operating model conspires against Agile reaching its full potential. However, Agile principles can play a part here, as it is suggested that "too many early requirements are too many wrong requirements."[2] So, a compromise between big design and good enough design up-front is targeted.

The "Scrum" aspect of Agile can follow the traditional "Water" up-front analysis and planning stage, in that iterative elaboration and construction activity can be undertaken. This caters for the fact that truly novel initiatives cannot always be defined up front; learning through doing is of value; testing can be undertaken early in the life cycle; and, engaging with the business can be fostered in such a mechanism, which helps with ownership and accountability aspects of successful delivery.

The "Fall" aspect of a traditional approach tempers the Agile desire of frequent releases of working solutions to the live environment. While the intent behind the frequent release paradigm is both delivery and client focused, the reality is that many organizations do not have the infrastructure or architecture to support regular, dynamic, and flexible releases. Typically, releases are infrequent—perhaps only three per year—and are supported by heavy process, governance, data migration, testing, etc. Again, a hybrid approach will push the predominant release paradigm, yet deliberately tailor a full Agile release schedule (which is not realistic).

In the same way that the life cycle aspects of traditional Waterfall and iterative Agile methods can be tempered, the blended, hybrid approach of Water-Scrum-Fall, illustrated in Figure 8.3, also encourages the use of the right mix of practice and techniques to the situation at hand. The hybrid approach fosters those desirable factors of collaboration, discipline, and "good enough." Essentially, this simply opens a broader toolbox to select from, depending upon the specific activity in scope or problem identified. In turn, this broader toolbox provides a more robust, adaptive, and flexible approach to manage, rather than a linear, heavily process orientated and documented approach, or perceived uncontrolled and uncontrollable Agile process. In today's information age, this hybrid approach seems more feasible that the polar opposites of Waterfall or Agile, which in their purest forms, often invoke as much or greater risk than they purport to mitigate.

REFERENCES

1. The Standish Group. 2009. Chaos Report.
2. West, Dave. 2011, July 26. "Water-Scrum-Fall Is the Reality of Agile for Most Organizations Today." Forrester Research. http://www .forrester.com/WaterScrumFall+Is+The+Reality+Of+Agile+For +Most+Organizations+Today/fulltext/-/E-RES60109

Web
Added
Value™

This book has free material available for download from the
Web Added Value™ resource center at *www.jrosspub.com*

9

ENTERPRISE ARCHITECTURE

WHAT IS ENTERPRISE ARCHITECTURE?

Enterprise architecture (EA) is conceptually brilliant, but its challenge seems to revolve around the ability of individuals and organizations to grasp the rigorous and voluminous framework, methods, and accepted best practice tools to both apply it and keep it current.

EA is a detailed and complex discipline that, perhaps not helpfully—for both the organization trying to apply it or the credibility of the concept of EA itself—is defined, adopted, and used in different ways. In the simplest terms, EA is the design of the business. Much like buildings or bridges have designs prior to construction beginning, EA advocates that an organization as a structure should also be by design. Jay Forrester, author of *Industrial Dynamics*, in a speech at the Universidad de Seville in 1998, clearly stated the imperative of architecture for companies. Any organization that has been built by groups or mere gut feelings could be expected to perform about as well as a plane designed and built using the same approach: "As in a bad airplane design, which no pilot can fly successfully, such badly designed corporations lie beyond the capability of real-life managers."[1]

In an attempt to concisely answer the question of what EA is, an understanding of three aspects is helpful: enterprise, architecture, and system. It is also important to dispel some myths and misnomers about what EA is not.

Enterprise

So what is an "enterprise"? To enable a common understanding, an *enterprise* is defined as a collection of departments, business units, or services (capabilities), such as marketing, which are bound by a common purpose, set of goals, and ownership. "Enterprise" is synonymous with the terms "organization," "company," "firm," or "corporation." An enterprise can be any organization in the private, nonprofit, or government sectors.

Perhaps unhelpfully, an enterprise can be articulated at a macro-level, depicted as a list of fundamental capabilities, such as sales, operations, distribution, etc. It can also be depicted at the micro-level as specific processes or roles of people within a business service or specific process. It is suggested that better descriptions of the enterprise should distinctly classify lower, more detailed layers to avoid confusion and enable a common vernacular within the organization. For example, where, as offered here, the term "enterprise" refers to the entire company, while its marketing or distribution functions may also be labeled as discrete enterprises of their own, it may be helpful to simply refer to them as departments for the purposes of EA.

Architecture

Architecture is typically referred to in the context of engineering, planning and design of buildings, automobiles, and other physical structures. While an enterprise, in the corporate sense, typically has some physical manifestation, e.g., a head office or manufacturing plant, the planning and design of a head office is not the primary purpose of the business enterprise. Instead, it is merely a foundational asset that enables it to carry out its purpose. The planning and design of the company, what it will do, how, what people and skills it requires, how information will flow through it, and what processes, governance, tools, and practice techniques will be used, etc., all fall within the domain of the enterprise's "architecture."

As a building is the end result of architecture in the construction domain, the company itself would be the result of EA, where any EA has been done, of course. Everything we have built since the dawn of the Industrial Age has been architected in some way, shape, or form. Very few "Enterprises" have been Architected. Up until now, "Enterprises have simply happened ... somehow."[2]

Architecture is about creating things and should be applied to complex things for which it is simply impossible to remember all the details of the thing in question at once. Architecture then, is simply a set of descriptive documents required to create something. Architecture becomes imperative when you later want to change the thing previously created by providing a baseline and illustrating the design principles, environmental conditions, assumptions, and constraints at play, and the time the original object was created.

Without architecture, it is difficult to understand how complex things can be created, maintained, and sustained, especially where change is required as change. If not architected, change could fundamentally disable an aspect of an organization's capability, destroying value and possibly impeding the organization's ability to remain competitive and ultimately viable.

With several hundred years of empirical experience in learning how to create and change complex industrial products under our belts, a universally proven practice for describing industrial products is derived from the classic six primitive interrogatives. Answers to the who, what, when, where, why, and how provide a complete description of anything. Applying this approach to the construction and manufacturing of enterprises is the prerogative of the EA discipline.

System

The term "system" has a long history, dating back to the days of the early Greek philosophers. It referred to the uniting of a number of elements to form a whole. As with the term "enterprise," somewhat unhelpfully, the concept of a system has many applications, from social and cultural meanings to engineering, information, and computer sciences. For our purposes, we focus on a system from the business or "enterprise" perspective. A *system* can be said to be a representation of entities, elements, or components under concern and how their interaction, interdependencies, and interconnectedness form an integrated whole.

From the mid-twentieth century, the concept of the "system" was being applied in the business context with "systems theory," espousing principles and rules that apply to systems in general. This business view of systems defined them as a transformational process whereby component inputs (e.g., raw materials, data) were "worked" to ultimately transform into an output (e.g., steel, knowledge). Within the past 30 years, the term "system" is perhaps synonymous, and generally thought of, in terms of information systems and technology systems.

This recent, almost automatic association of "system" to information or technology "systems," is understandable due to the rise and proliferation of the level of reliance on the promises that information technology has borne over the corresponding period. Further, the concept of EA dates back to the early 1980s and is the birth-child of John A. Zachman. As an IBM employee in the Information Systems (IS) domain, not surprisingly, its original application was in terms of information "system" design and had a technology solution bent. Indeed, in 2011, Forrester's own contributor Gene Leganza stated, "Enterprise architecture consists of the vision, principles, and standards that guide the purchase and deployment of technology within an enterprise."[3]

This seemingly natural association of systems with IS, alongside the birth of the EA concept, has however, posed problems. With the integration and focus of systems predominantly being the purveyors of information technology, an articulation of the business system—independent of any technology solution—has been lacking. From an EA perspective, the importance of the business layer, business model, or business system cannot be understated, but sadly, has been lacking and generally absent.

In spite of the multitude of systems under one roof within a company, or whirring within the confines of its walls, as Zachman himself stated, "There is no Architecture. There are no 'Primitive' Models. There is no baseline for managing change. No Enterprise engineering has been done. Enterprise parts have been manufactured ..."[4] but those parts are hobbled together. They are awkward and ill-fitted.

The practice of EA, then, has largely been in the domain of enterprise technology architecture (ETA) and not a true, enterprise-wide and enterprise-layered representation. Perhaps a better understanding of a true EA, that can be fully applied to both business and purely technology domains alike, is jointly defined by the American National Standards Institute (ANSI) and the Institute of Electrical and Electronics Engineers (IEEE): "The fundamental organization of a system, embodied in its components, their relationships to each other and the environment, and the principles governing its design and evolution."[5] In its simplest form, "Enterprise Architecture is about understanding all of the different elements that go into making up the organization and how those elements interrelate."[6]

In fact, EA can be likened to the blueprint of the enterprise. This blueprint is made up of a number of diagrams, which represent the differing layers as viewed by various stakeholders within the organization. These diagrams are designed to break down silos and drive synergy across the organization. EA is the mechanism that binds the various elements of the organization together in order to optimize the often disparate people, processes, and technology components. In combination, these elements enable the business strategy to be enacted and delivered.

The Gartner Group defines "enterprise architecture" as "the process of translating business vision and strategy into effective enterprise change by creating, communicating, and improving the key principles and models that describe the enterprise's future state and enable its evolution."[7] While the term "boundaryless information flow" is a proprietary trademark of the Open Group, its definition also supports EA as being truly enterprise, and not an ETA, although it should be noted that the early architecture framework from The Open Group Architecture Framework (TOGAF) was based firmly in the IT architecture. By including other management frameworks, EA enables the enterprise to define, develop, and exploit the flow of information as a means of achieving the enterprise's actionable strategic plan. It is the role of the enterprise architect, therefore, to orchestrate planning for an organization's future and guide implementation.

A well-architected organization is also an enabler of agility and flexibility, both within and for the enterprise, balancing technology concerns with the evolving needs of the business and the desire for a coherent whole (at the macro level), while enabling individual departments to enhance and innovate (at a more tactical/operational level) within the bounds of higher-level architectural parameters. As with other disciplines, such as project management, planning, and estimation, for example, the trick is how to properly apply the conceptually sound principles and years of industrial application to the corporate enterprise. As with many other theoretically sound concepts, where application is lacking, negative, value-destroying consequences can be observed.

Rather than leveraging the promise of EA, many companies have experienced increased complexity in terms of change, with the stewards of EA often pushing a platinum, textbook standard from their generally IT housed ivory towers that is neither appropriate, desirable, nor realistic for the enterprise under concern. The association of EA within IT and the historic phenomenon of IT folks being unable to effectively talk "business" also fuels an early and instant resistance in those business people and domains who may not understand and therefore, may be threatened by their IT compatriots.

Finally, further confusion by association arises where EA has typically been the accountability of the CIO, with the traditional role of the CIO being more Chief Technology Officer or focused more around application design and technology implementation activities. We propose that the correct perception of the CIO today—the CIO 2.0—is a business savvy leader who, while business centric, has an understanding of the information technology domain (and is on point to keep up to date with developments, trends, and changes in that environment as part of the enterprise's overall environmental scanning capability), and has the ability to orientate and lead those more technically focused managers and practitioners to enable a supporting information and technology landscape aligned to the corporate strategy and business model.

According to National Grid, we must shift the concept of EA from information technology services into the business. This changes the perception "away from being the 'traffic warden' governing against technical standards"[8] to that of the guide for helping to set the direction and ensuring that the journey aligns to the business strategy.

Enterprise Architecture Methodology

There are many different methods for EA. Some of the most influential ones are described below: the US Federal Enterprise Architecture Framework (FEAF), TOGAF, the Zachman Framework, and Forrester.

United States Federal Enterprise Architecture Framework

In September 1999, the United States Federal CIO Council published the Federal Enterprise Architecture Framework, Version 1.1, for developing an EA within any Federal agency for a system that transcends multiple interagency boundaries. The US FEAF is the most recognized Federal EA. It represents a management best practice for aligning business and technology resources to achieve strategic outcomes, improve organizational performance, and guide federal agencies to better execute their core missions. It provides an enduring standard for developing and documenting architecture descriptions of high-priority areas. It provides guidance in describing architectures for multi-organizational functional segments of the Federal government. Like other frameworks, the FEAF is built using an assortment of reference models that develop a common taxonomy and ontology. It layers architecture into three distinct striations: enterprise (common or shared assets), segment (a business service), and solution (application and technology solution concerns).

The Open Group Architecture Framework

The Open Group Architecture Framework provides the methods and tools for assisting in the acceptance, production, use, and maintenance of EA. It is based on an iterative process model supported by best practices and a reusable set of existing architecture assets.

The Zachman Framework

John A. Zachman, a renowned pioneer in EA and a former IBM consultant, describes framework as a *schema*, in the sense of a system for organizing and/ or perceiving information, and an ontology (or structure) of the enterprise. Zachman is clear that his framework is not a methodology or process for creating a specific object, and that structure provides definition, whereas a process provides transformation. Equally as clear as this distinction is his assertion that processes based on an ontological structure will be predictable and produce repeatable results (for example, chemistry, based on the Periodic Table). Conversely, processes without ontological structures are ad hoc, fixed, and dependent on practitioner skills (for example, alchemy, based on trial and error).

Forrester

The Forrester EA solution provides a process framework that links EA activities to business change efforts, ensuring alignment and enhancing organizational agility. It also helps enterprise architects clarify the processes that EA organizations own and those that they influence as part of a broader practice of architecting the enterprise. As part of a strategic approach to the discipline of EA, Forrester developed its EA method *Playbook*, housing a set of high-value practices that enterprise architects should use to help their organizations plan, architect, and implement sustainable business agility.

Enterprise Architecture—from Challenge to Opportunity

Put simply, EA—when done properly—is a critical instrument for enterprise efficiency. EA impacts the effect of the business operational processes, their cost and associated risks—the key factors for company efficiency.

Forrester CEO George Colony sums it up by saying that an enterprise architect is an "internal, trusted advisor who marries the best interests of the business with long-term technology strategy."[9] While agreement with this summation comes easily, the contention here is that EA is not, or at least has not, "performed well" and has struggled to sell its wares and become accepted. In other words, the desired state of the EA role and practice remains elusive and aspirational at present.

So, why do companies need EA? Why should they provide senior management support and fund such initiatives?

Companies paved with technology need to build and control it. Technology supports the business, period—but technological innovations can be a significant enabler or even drive a business goal or key element of strategy. There is a need for the ability to design, in an aligned manner to the business functions, technology solutions that deliver value over the medium term.

EAs bring agility. You know this cliché: "Markets change fast, so your business has to keep up." If a company's technology isn't representative of what the business model requires, the organization may struggle to keep pace with its customers and competitors alike. Good EA will design the business and the technology solutions for quick adaptation. EA enables the project team and the stakeholders to know when and when not to use new technology.

Mobility and Enterprise Architecture in Banking

Depositing checks can be done via a mobile application, typically on a smart phone. There are a number of banks that now offer this capability, the driver behind it being ease, speed, and cost of use for the customers when compared to the process around depositing traditional checks that involved paper, stamps, forms, etc. Then came the smart phone. Because the early adopter bank enterprise architects had designed adaptable systems, they could offer the ability for their customers to take a picture of a check with a smart phone, and then it was deposited.

USAA, a financial service company, was the first to offer this service. When it launched in 2011, it was expecting 22 million uses of the app, however the actual number ended up being 120 million uses. Much like the way in which iTunes revolutionized the music industry, this is an example of how technological innovations could revolutionize a long-established industry such as banking.

The corollary of the mobile bank application example could be introducing an enterprise resource planning system to "fix" some organizational challenges when the business and operating models are not well defined, and doing those first may: a) ensure the right problem is tackled (root cause versus symptom); and/or, b) actually solve problems by enhancing working practices so that a large scale, complex, and costly technology solution may not be warranted.

As we often talk about business and IT, those more technical people are not typically business savvy. Likewise, those business savvy people are not typically of an engineering or technical persuasion. The enterprise architect acts as the bridge to span these two distinct but necessarily interrelated components of organizations.

RELATIONSHIP BETWEEN BUSINESS AND ENTERPRISE ARCHITECTURE

Much like the dichotomy between business and IT, so we have a dichotomy between the business view and technical perspective of an enterprise.

Often, business planning, process management, and associated disciplines such as business architecture are seen or managed in isolation of the overarching EA construct. However, the business architecture and EA complement each other well to get the best value from each other. Business architecture is one of the key enablers of the EA, making it real and when done well, business architecture profoundly improves corporate investment decision making and operating performance. Complementary to this, the EA offers much needed context for the business architecture.

The Business Architecture Special Interest Group of Object Management Group (OMG) defines business architecture as: "A blueprint of the enterprise that provides a common understanding of the organization and is used to align strategic objectives and tactical demands."[10] Similarly, TOGAF states that "Business Architecture describes the product and/or service strategy, and the organizational, functional, process, information and geographic aspects of the business environment."[11]

While the practice of EA has matured over the past few years, it is widely accepted that both the business and information architecture layers of most organizations are either:

1. not done at all;
2. are done, but in isolation of the organization's technical architecture;
3. are done, but are disconnected or ill-aligned with the business context; or

4. are done, but in the context of a technology driven governance and decision-making framework.

Where not done at all, or where done but in isolation of the enterprise technical architecture, an incongruent organization results, not only from the overarching business and technical perspectives, but from an environment (opportunities and threats), values (leadership and culture), and resource (strengths and weaknesses) view. Depending on the nature and extent of the business, and IT investment and decision-making gaps, this will lead to a "lost" organization. In a lost organization, the products/services/markets are out of alignment and the values are inappropriate. Similarly, the "consciously incompetent" organization is also congruent, where managers appreciate the needs for success (customer needs), but there may be a lack of resources or unwillingness to grasp the changes required. Or, the "unconsciously competent" organization results, which enjoys strategic positioning without any real commitment, especially to improvement and change. Finally, where business and a true EA are not in sync, strategic drift is commonplace, and an internally cohesive organization simply loses touch with the environment.

This is one of the biggest mistakes of business architecture: "Simply positioning business architecture as a layer on top of existing EA domains is a mistake. Business architecture is business-centered. Simply layering it on top of an enterprise technical architecture will result in tech-centerd silo implementation."[12] As the OMG's Business Architecture Special Interest Group states, "The business architecture defines the structure of the enterprise in terms of its governance structure, business processes, and business information."[13] In defining the structure of the enterprise, business architecture considers customers, finances, and the market to align strategic goals and objectives with decisions regarding products and services, partners and suppliers, organization, capabilities, and key initiatives. Business architecture primarily should focus on the business motivations, business operations, business analysis frameworks, and related networks that link these aspects of the enterprise together, and it should be seamlessly integrated with EA efforts within the organization.

Therefore, to meet the main challenges in establishing a true EA—that covers both planning and implementation aspects—the business architecture should be harmonized with the business context, it should be truly integrated within an holistic EA framework, and further, it should be the driver of the other enterprise level architectural domains (the information, application, and technical layers). Finally, the governance frameworks, models, drivers, and implementation facets that relate to technology decisions should be integrated into a business-aligned, business-driven enterprise governance model.

It is important to note that technology can be a driver of business strategy, a model, an enabler of architecture, and so on. With mobile, social, and other technologies changing how your employees work and how a company does business, building adaptive technology solutions has never been more challenging for IT leaders.

Using Enterprise Architecture to Manage Changes to the Enterprise

EA can be applied from a number of different perspectives to many different organizational functions. TOGAF Foundation Architecture, for example, is an architecture of generic services and functions that provides a foundation on which more specific architectures and their associated components can be built—industry reference architecture. EA can also be leveraged as the mechanism for business and technology governance, as well as technology performance monitoring. Further, as EA is about transformation, it represents a unified change framework, and therefore may form part of an enterprise "management of change" capability, an example of which is illustrated in Figure 9.1.

---

*Note:

The concept of an "enterprise management of change capability"—that is, the ability of the enterprise to change in response to both vision-led strategy and/ or the need to change due to pressures from the environment—is an overarching capability that is essential for any enterprise to remain relevant and competitive in the information age.

In a complex organization, determining the degree to which information and services is to be shared is a key benefit of architecture. This concept of "interoperability" is designed into the operating model of the enterprise in a similar way that IT seeks to integrate applications via a common look and feel, single source of data, etc. In addition to EA as a strategy to define the organizational operation, EA also provides various models to manage operations. "Enterprise architecture is the organizing logic for key business

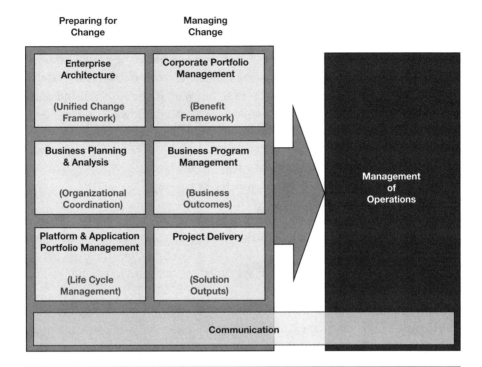

Figure 9.1   Enterprise management of change capability business services

processes and IT capabilities reflecting the integration and standardization requirements of the firm's operating model."[14]

The definition of an organization's operating model may vary based on the organizational and operational context, so a specific Business Blueprint of the organization is required. A *Business Blueprint* is a communication tool that defines a vision (typically 3, 5, or 10 years) to define or improve one or more business capabilities (practices or ways of working). Synonyms of the Business Blueprint are Concept of Operations or Target Operating Model, as first defined by IBM. It proposes the optimal design and deployment of resources to achieve an organization's business goals. As such, a Business Blueprint is a working document that brings discreet focus to one or more business capabilities existing within the wider context of the organizational operating model.

The blueprint answers the "what" and "why" aspects of transformation. The full Business Solution document, which represents the current response to the business blueprint and program and project delivery methods, addresses "how" the transformation will be achieved, and is produced later in the architecture life cycle as the business must drive any resultant and specific solution.

Key deliverables of a Business Blueprint include business review, current operating model assessment, desired future state, benefits and impacts to the organization, and change management plan road map.

Because the Business Blueprint holds together various organizational concerns, such as capabilities, processes, governance, and stakeholder views in a single cohesive fashion, and is the mechanism to link the business goals and strategy of the organization with a road map for change to achieve those goals, it stands to reason that the discipline of EA can be leveraged as a tool for managing the organization's operating model.

As alluded to above, various EA frameworks exist and no one specific framework is recommended here since factors such as organizational context, culture, timing, industry setting, and desired outcomes may lead to the use of different frameworks to suit the need or opportunity present. Arguably, the Zachman and TOGAF frameworks are the most recognized and used. We touched on the Zachman framework in Chapter 4, so for illustration purposes, we demonstrate below how TOGAF 9.2 can effectively direct the management of the operating model. (TOGAF 9.1 and 9.2 is the Architectural Framework of The Open Group, and can be referenced at www.opengroup .org.)

Let us consider the Architecture Development Method (ADM), which is the TOGAF process for Enterprise Architecture Management, as depicted in Figure 9.2. The ADM process links the vision and strategy of the organization and its business/functions with a portfolio of change programs designed to produce outcomes that together will realize the strategy. TOGAF uses various architecture disciplines such as business architecture, information architecture (data and application), and technology architecture as mechanisms for linking the strategy with implementation, and governance of change programs to deliver on the strategy.

As discussed previously, EA is not and should not be limited to IT systems. As a true enterprise framework, it can be juxtaposed against the concept of the Business Blueprint, whereby the approach, process, and specific tools used from each of the ADM phases both guide and support the development of the blueprint. A simple table that shows the relationship between EA, Business Blueprints, and effecting change is provided in Table 9.1 for ease of reference.

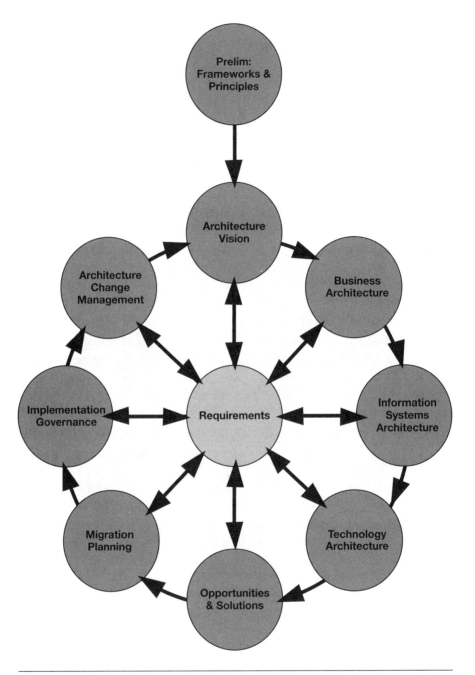

Figure 9.2   Architecture Development Method (ADM)

Enterprise Architecture and Scope

The same factors that drove the formalization of architecture for industrial products in the Industrial Age will drive the formalization of architecture for enterprises in the information age: complexity and change. There are two key viewpoints in relation to EA and scope: 1) the impact of EA on the scope of specific change initiatives, and 2) the scope—perceived or real—of affecting the discipline of EA within an enterprise.

Impact of Enterprise Architecture on Scope of Specific Change Initiatives

In Chapter 4, the relationship between and impacts of business architecture and scope are discussed. The salient points and principles articulated are applicable at the EA level as it applies to the other viewpoints of information, application, and technology architecture. Supplementary to this is the concept of ensuring change initiatives, which invariably touch on all the EA

Table 9.1 Relationship between EA blueprints and changes

TOGAF Phase	Blueprint Phase	Management of Change Response
A. Architecture Vision	Discover: what business challenges need addressing now to move forward?	Business vision, goals, objectives, strategy and road map. Business decision case.
B. Business Architecture	Value: What value is achieved by securing the right business solution?	Gap analysis, impacts, benefits and measures, capabilities and skills, business process, rules, governance, new ways of working.
C, D. Information and Technology Architecture	Viable: What is the best business solution at this time to achieve the objectives?	Full solution document, technology solution and performance metrics, validated milestone delivery plan.
E. Opportunities and Solutions	Deliver: What are the quickest ways to realize the most benefits?	Solution evaluation, vendor/partner/supplier, solution and other resource sourcing.
F. Migration Planning	Deliver: What is appropriate, feasible, and desirable, given real-world constraints?	Delivery road map, sequence and pacing, implementation, communication and change management plan, operational specifications.
G, H. Implementation Governance and Architecture Change Management	Assess: How much actual business value is being achieved?	Delivery life cycle management, delivery and operational performance, training and benefits realization, lessons to be applied.

layers, that are selected based on return on investment, value, or whatever demonstrable success criteria is relevant to and furthers the success of the enterprise.

EA both fosters and supports an integrated, harmonized approach to the selection of change initiatives. To put it another way, it can guide and ensure that appropriate principles, standards, and criteria are used to select the scope of what change, why, and when to the enterprise.

Two components of the TOGAF EA framework that impact or are impacted by the specific scope of change initiatives include building blocks—components of business, IT or architectural capability that can be combined to define architectures or deliver solutions—and the Architecture Repository, where different classes of architectural output at different levels of abstraction are housed from foundation to organization-specific solution architectures. This view of artifacts across the enterprise provides a valuable context for understanding architectural models: it shows building blocks and their relationships to each other, and the constraints and requirements on a cycle of architecture development. This is critical when understanding the scope and impact of a specific change initiative in terms of common scoring and prioritization criteria to select a change (such as strategic alignment, complexity and risk, and achievability). This also assists with planning a proposed change (dependencies, constraints, sequence, and pacing) and aspects around managing a change (estimation of time to deliver, as well as resource and cost factors).

The Scope of Enterprise Architecture

There is a significant, voluminous body of research that concludes all businesses are digital businesses. There is no such thing as a noninformation-centric business anymore—or at least there won't be for very long, because they are going out of business. Forrester has been using the term "business technology" to indicate that there is no room for having separate business and IT: it simply won't work much longer. Similarly, many companies go out of their way to articulate "business programs of change," even if heavily enabled by technology solutions. The next decade of digital business will see continued pressure for organizations to react quickly to changing conditions in the economy, market, and competition. Organizations that can change rapidly will have the best chance of thriving in these turbulent, dynamic, and often ambiguous conditions. While many organizations have established effective capabilities in respect to the more traditional value chain components such as sales, marketing, and operations, for example, a dedicated and distinct capability focused on change, flexibility, and adaptation as a key strategic enabler is not prevalent in the majority of today's companies.

By definition, EA is all encompassing—business, information, application, and technology—with factors such as people and communication transcending all these layers. It is also associated with being a lengthy initiative with unclear results. This is due in part to the relative infancy of EA and because the practice of what is a complicated discipline is far from standardized itself. Like a set of references architectures, which in practice are often significantly different from architectures of actually deployed solutions or a set of principles for building a new finance system, which are too high-level and theoretical, any solution built can be said to be compliant. Of course, the corollary of this is that when executed well, EA is perhaps the single most critical component for enterprise effectiveness. The challenge is that EA has yet to receive the reputation of being done well, with the father of EA himself, John Zachman, declaring, "It is chaos."[15] This is the very reason that corporate enterprises are in the state that they are. Far too many exist without coherent and mature processes.

The application of the Pareto principle seems highly relevant to the scope of introducing an EA discipline to the organizational capability landscape, in that a significant benefit (80%) can be derived from a relatively small (20%) effort in terms of the total required to design, implement, and establish an EA practice. Documenting the enterprise—its business, information, application, and technology pieces—as a first step will necessarily elucidate how the organization works, what processes, practices, roles, skills, what information is used, what gaps or potential deficiencies reside, the distribution of cost and risk across the enterprise helps to start gaining a considered, objective grasp on how the organization is structured and performs its primary activities as a helpful input to questions around why, and what to add, move, or change.

Without this context, it would be too difficult to understand how organizations could systematically determine how the operational performance metrics (cost, speed, dependability, flexibility, and quality) would be impacted by any proposed changes. For example, the pursuit of a cost reduction strategy of a part of the operations model, could introduce new risks where an understanding of the impact on availability and/or performance of any technology solutions is not clear. Similarly, developing a new capability, sourcing a solution without knowing the extent and nature of where it fits in the end-to-end process life cycle, or any duplication of features and impacts on its integration with other information systems does not seem an appropriate, feasible, or desirable approach to running and changing a company. Solutions and business change, if done in this manner, would be tactical in nature and siloed in application, typically leading to redundancy of features and a significantly increased cost and effort to sustain and improve both business and IT systems subsequently.

Documenting the current operating model, in conjunction with an understanding of what the company is trying to achieve (business vision, mission, goals, objectives, and strategy), strengths and weaknesses, and opportunities and threats impacting the organization, will provide a firm foundation to state the current strategic position of the enterprise. This, in turn, will enable the company leadership to resolve key strategic questions such as: Is strategy consistent with company objectives? Is strategy consistent with the environment, and how it is developing? Is strategy internally consistent? Is strategy supported by key players? Is risk/benefit favorable?

If a business is contemplating increasing its operating hours or opening new locations in different countries, for example, an understanding of the impact to security protocols and systems, business processes and structures to take account of country specific regulations, impacted IT systems, and agreed service level agreements will need to be understood to reduce the company's exposure to risk as well as negative time and cost considerations. While all of the implications across the EA domains may not be known up front, at least an assessment against a documented current state is prudent and would illuminate some guiding principles, perhaps by way of assumptions and constraints—even if at a high level. This will serve to assist the organization's decision-making process and potentially avoid some major pitfalls that are foreseeable.

Quite often, we see that as technology has led the EA space since inception, so too do technology solutions lead the way as a means of optimizing cost within IT. According to the Gartner Group, the average IT spend is fewer than 6% of the company's total spend. That means cost optimization only within IT does not bring much. As with EA, only joint efforts of business and IT can lead to noticeable results without negative impacts on company operational efficiency and sustainability.

REFERENCES

1. Forrester, Jay. 1998. Speech given at Universidad de Seville. http:// www.zachmaninternational.com/index.php/ea-articles/117-yes -enterprise-architecture-is-relative-but-it-is-not-arbitrary
2. Zachman, John. 2007. "Architecture Is Architecture Is Architecture." John A. Zachman and Zachman International, Inc. http://www .zachman.com/ea-articles-reference/52-architecture-is-architecture-is -architecture-by-john-a-zachman
3. Leganza, Gene. 2014. *"The EA Practice Playbook"*. Forrester Research, Inc.
4. Zachman, John. 2007. "Architecture Is Architecture Is Architecture." John A. Zachman and Zachman International, Inc. http://www .zachman.com/ea-articles-reference/52-architecture-is-architecture-is -architecture-by-john-a-zachman
5. ANSI/IEEE; "ANSI/IEEE Std 1471-2000"; 2000. https://standards .ieee.org/findstds/standard/1471-2000.html
6. Institute for Enterprise Architecture Development. 2001. http://www .enterprise-architecture.info
7. The Gartner Group. 2013. http://www.gartner.com/it-glossary.
8. National Grid. 2012. http://blogs.forrester.com/node/8320
9. Colony, George. 2012. "Enterprise Architects for Dummies (CEOs)." Forrester Research. http://blogs.forrester.com/george_colony/ 12-08-27-enterprise_architects_for_dummies_ceos
10. Business Architecture Special Interest Group of Object Management Group (OMG). 2012. http://bawg.omg.org/
11. TOGAF. 2001. http://pubs.opengroup.org/architecture/togaf9-doc/ arch/chap08.html
12. Heffner, Randy. 2012. http://blogs.forrester.com/randy_heffner/ 12-03-21-the_big_mistake_with_business_architecture
13. Business Architecture Special Interest Group of Object Management Group (OMG). 2012. http://bawg.omg.org/business_architecture _overview.htm
14. MIT Center for Information Systems Research, presented at the Sixth e-Business Conference, Barcelona, Spain, 2007.
15. Zachman, John. 2011. Yes, "Enterprise Architecture Is Relative" BUT It Is Not Arbitrary. John A. Zachman and Zachman International, Inc. http://www.zachman.com/ea-articles-reference/ 57-eanotarbitrary

SECTION 4:
IMPLEMENTATION
AND BEYOND

10

ROLL-OUT: MARKETING AND SOCIALIZING THE SOLUTION

Implementation is more than just "plugging in" or installing a new application or system, and then walking away. People need to adopt and use it. This only happens when people buy in to the new solution and have the chance to be a part of the process. People help support what they help build.

The most important thing that any team can do is to facilitate the process of the business achieving its goals by utilizing the new solution that they are working on. It is important to include the business throughout the project, so that by the time you get to roll out and implementation, there is not a big push-back from the business or an outright refusal to adopt the solution.

Above all else, this means two things must be done on a project: change management and documentation of the lessons learned.

CHANGE MANAGEMENT

First and foremost, change management is intended to successfully support and assist employees and other impacted individuals through the process of change. For that to happen, it is important to understand why people have a difficult time accepting change, even when the new "thing" is going to make their life a lot easier and a lot better.

Make no mistake. Change management is one part of the trifecta required for successful project execution and delivery. The other two parts are stakeholder engagement and governance, as shown in Figure 10.1. Without these

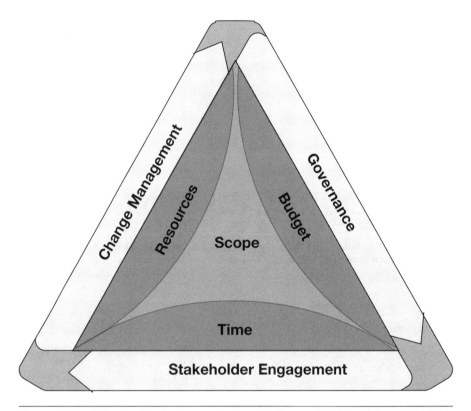

Figure 10.1   Trifecta of project execution and delivery related to triple constraints

three core elements, the project will fail because it will fail to deliver what is needed and when.

Consider this: without stakeholder engagement the project scope and requirements could be (and most likely are) inaccurate and bombarded by scope creep, and it will take longer to define them. Without change management, user groups will revolt and could sabotage the implementation, or they simply will not adopt the solution. Finally, without governance, there could be no change control to manage scope creep, control compliance, or ensure adoption after implementation.

Why Is Change So Hard?

"Change is both scary and exciting. Scary when you don't have any feeling of control over what is happening, and exciting because of the prospects of what could be."[1] Change is hard because of:

- Fear
- Uncertainty
- People adopt their job as part of their identity
- Easier to keep doing the same things
- People do not always know how to change
- People do not know how the changes will impact them

Change management is all about incorporating two major elements into your project scope through a series of directed steps. These two elements are communication and involvement. The right combination of these elements leads to a sense of control and importance for those who will be impacted and brings them on board more quickly.

By the time you reach implementation, change management should be a non-issue because the communication architecture and stakeholder engagement techniques will have been applied throughout the project. However, that does not mean there are no longer some key activities to perform, and it does not mean that the project team should not consider supplementing these techniques with either the ADKAR model or Kotter's 8 Step Change Model.

The ADKAR Model

The ADKAR model,[2] published by Prosci in 1998, outlines an approach to managing change based on the personal motivations of the individuals involved. It provides a process for ensuring that the recipients of change are guided through a carefully planned set of activities aimed at providing the Awareness, Desire, Knowledge, and Ability, and then capping the changes off with activities for Reinforcement.

The ADKAR model asserts that individuals do not change unless they are able to first develop a personal awareness that change is necessary. In many other arenas, this would be known as the impetus for change or the burning platform. It is by knowing that something is wrong, that the individual is made aware of the need for change.

The ADKAR model also asserts that people also need to acquire the desire for change. This desire can come from external sources that highlight how much easier or better the situation could be within a different reality or by utilizing a new product. It is this "grass is always greener" stimuli that creates the desire to change, and then prompts the person to take action and make efforts to change.

Next, the model asserts that what is needed is the knowledge of how to change based on the person's current reality or situation. In projects, teams spend a considerable amount of time creating the future state and planning for how to achieve the desired changes. In many cases, the business has already defined that a change must occur, and it has the desire to change. The project is initiated to determine how to change and then to further create the ability required to change.

This brings up the next point of the ADKAR model, which is having the ability to change. In part, this step can be likened to the business readiness planning that occurs later on in the life of the project. From this step, there will be an impact on scope in terms of enabling the company to create the other parts of the puzzle that are required to realize the change.

Finally, the ADKAR model asserts that individuals require reinforcement as a means of supporting the changes once they have taken place. This reinforcement can take the form of training and governance, but it can also take the form of rewards and penalties.

Kotter's 8 Step Change Model

The Kotter change model describes eight steps that will guide change initiatives to a successful conclusion. These steps are:

1. **Create or increase a sense of urgency**. This would be the same as the burning platform idea, creating the awareness that change is needed. But it also adds the idea that urgency will cause people to want to act as soon as they discover that change is needed; it will only be a matter of how to proceed.

2. **Build guiding or coaching teams**. This is where a team of leaders is brought together and those leaders work with the mainstream employee base to sell them on the changes and then works to guide those people through them. This is my champion. I find the most outspoken person against what I am doing and then work with them to get them believing in what is happening, because they make the best leaders, coaches, and guides.

3. **Create a unified vision**. Earlier project vision was singled out as a cause of major issues in stakeholder management—well, the lack of a project vision was actually to blame. However, Kotter points to the need for a strong and even powerful vision for the project team, sponsors, stakeholders, and user groups to rally around. The vision

provides focus, informs and reminds people of what is being built (why they are doing this project in the first place).

4. **Communicate the vision and achieve buy-in.** Once a clear and powerful vision has been defined, it is important—no, absolutely critical—that it be shared with everyone consistently and persistently. This is the only way to keep people on task and to acquire not only buy-in, but also to gain incremental achievements.

5. **Enable action.** A leader is any person who sets expectations for themselves and others, and then creates the environment for meeting those expectations. Charles Kettering, renowned American engineer, inventor, and businessman, said, "High achievement always takes place in an environment of great expectation."[3] What this all means is that the project team must now empower people to act, remove barriers to their contributions and success, and cheer them on.

6. **Create quick wins (short term).** "Quick wins" are small tasks that can showcase pieces of the changes to be performed in short successful bursts. These can be leveraged to help people feel comfortable and more prepared to adopt the changes once they have been implemented. Quick wins can also help to refine the idea as a proof of concept, and it gives people an opportunity to help shape the way things will be done, based on their actual working habits.

7. **Be persistent; do not give up.** Persistence is the key to ensuring that all of the hard work in making changes is not lost. It can be easy to scrap something and quit altogether, but unfortunately all that does is ensure that the business and every other project team in the future has a much harder time making any kind of changes.

8. **Make it stick.** This step is often referred to as "institutionalizing," but it is more commonly known as "socializing the solution." However, making it last is really a combination of the two. Where institutionalizing is creating the infrastructure to support the changed workflows and environment, socializing is about getting people to be willing to hang onto the changes and utilize the solution in their everyday work life.

Both of these approaches can be utilized together and combined into a single approach because they have differing levels of detail in various areas. There are some subtle differences between the ADKAR and Kotter models, but in reality they complement each other quite well, and can be leveraged in a combined approach to ensure that the change efforts are truly successful throughout the project life span.

That being said, change management within the implementation phase is all about evolving the business through training, as well as maintaining and sustaining the changes.

In order to evolve the business through training, it is important to establish the immediate and ongoing training plan and schedule the initial training sessions. This plan should include:

- Training goal: A typical goal might be to involve mainstream business users to support the transition of the project.
- Who is going to be trained? It is important to identify the target audience so that training can be customized with the right messages. This will make it easier for participants to learn, and in the long run will make it easier for them to use the new product.
- What are they going to be trained on? Knowing what specific topics will be discussed and delivered during the training is just as important as knowing who is going to be trained. This will make it easier to determine how they will be trained on the topics and what materials will be used to support the training.
- What is the material for the training? Training materials must support both the content being taught and the medium for teaching. It is crucial that the material support an extension of learning after the course because participants will take this material with them and review it as they begin to apply what they learned.
- What is the medium for training? Identify whether this training will be delivered in a classroom, across virtual settings, or online. It is important to ensure the medium will support learning of the material and effective delivery.
- What is the format for training? The training format determines how the material and content will be delivered through the medium and over what period of time. This must be considered for implementation to ensure that a minimum of two to three rounds of training can be offered prior to full hand over and implementation, as this will better support employees in the thick of the changes.
- What is the feedback mechanism for post-training comments and input? Every training session should collect and analyze feedback from the participants. This is especially important on an implementation so

that it can be used as a gauge of their comfort level and confidence in the new solution.

- Where is the training going to occur? This provides the specific location of the training. This could be a physical address and conference room number, or it can be a web meeting link.
- What are the alternate training dates available? Setting one or two dates for training is not enough. In order to be effective, training must become a part of the overall landscape with the product. It must be able to account for employee learning capabilities, styles of learning, and long-term attrition. This means a training program must be implemented with the product, and must include periodic refreshers and on-board training for new resources.
- What is the schedule for training? With the need for ongoing training in mind, it is important to establish an immediate schedule for training of all impacted resources and their managers to ensure everyone knows how to utilize the new product.
- What are the physical and personal requirements for the training sessions? Are there any special needs for participants or based on the material being presented that determines a specific location or other requirements for the location? If it is outdoors, what happens if it rains?
- What equipment is needed for the training? It is essential to itemize the equipment that will be used during the training and to test it the day before. No exceptions. There is nothing more embarrassing, painful, and frustrating than watching an instructor struggle to get the PowerPoint up and running for 20 minutes of a two-hour training session. It is an inexcusable waste of a participant's time.
- What will be included in the training package given to participants? Many training sessions utilize elements and delivery mechanisms that appeal to multiple learning styles including tactile, auditory, and visual. As a continuation of this, the sessions will provide packages for each participant that includes PowerPoint presentations, round-table discussions, hands-on exercises, handouts, and job aids.
- Who will take over responsibility for training after the project has been completed? At some point, implementation is completed and training must continue. It is important to determine who will take ownership of the training and will ensure that everyone has access to it, both as needed and for regular refresher courses.

Another key step in change management is to monitor and observe the results and impacts of both the change and the implementation progress. This means that implementation is not as simple as installing the product, turning it on, and standing back to see what happens. Implementation and change are carefully measured to ensure success and that any issues can be traced and isolated quickly so that they don't impede that success.

In order to carefully measure changes and implementation, it is necessary to identify and log key metrics and milestones for success and progress during the development and implementation of a new system. These metrics and milestones will be carefully tracked and analyzed throughout the process of implementation in order to ensure it runs smoothly and delivers as expected.

While measuring the success of an implementation is primarily carried out by testing and is certainly easier to measure and monitor with adequate rigor and due diligence in the quality assurance processes, change and people can be more difficult to assess. It means reaching out to those impacted, asking them about each stage of the process, and finding out they what liked and did not like. Still, there are other ways to tell if you are on board and the changes went well. This can be achieved by establishing and measuring the following:

- How did people respond during meetings?
- What was the overall participation rate?
- Was there anything that caused this rate to change dramatically?
- How did the response rates change? Did they rise or fall?
- What caused the change?
- What was the general feedback from the training sessions?
- What metrics and benchmarks will be used to measure adoption?
- Are there system-based statistics that can be used to highlight areas of usage or improvement?
- How and when will measurements take place?

LESSONS LEARNED

One of the best things a company can do is learn from its past successes and failures. On projects, this means documenting the lessons learned throughout the life cycle and then closing implementation with a final review. The review ensures that all of the lessons have been adequately documented in appropriate levels of detail.

The details include a standardized categorization of the lesson, as well as its detailed description. In addition to this basic information, a good log should also require descriptions of all of the risks and impacts associated with the changes. Finally, each entry should be accompanied by recommendations for the business to consider on future projects.

Lessons Learned Knowledge Base

One of the key areas where companies tend to drop the ball is in incorporating past lessons from other projects. By employing a searchable lessons learned knowledge base, mistakes should be less likely to occur, but applying the lessons learned is actually rarely the case.

The knowledge base typically contains the lessons learned from previous projects, and is an essential component of the corporate inheritance. These past project assets provide valuable insight and sources of information for future projects. Where the knowledge base is maintained separately from the project artifacts, all lessons learned must be transferred over, in order to provide a single repository for faster reference.

Lessons Learned Review

Before implementation is completed and finalized, it is important to take a forensic look at the project in order to finalize the lessons learned and to finish the log for escalation to the business. This review will give the project team the opportunity to share what worked and didn't work as they developed the product, and what they recommend for future project considerations.

IMPLICATIONS FOR DELIVERING SCOPE

Above all, the implications for delivering on the promised scope, arise out of the ability of the project team to have the new product socialized and adopted by the business. Change management across the entire life cycle is the critical success factor. Any project can deliver a product made of pure gold, and if change management has not been done well, it will not matter; the business will be slow to adopt it.

To be clear, adoption and socialization are two different things. Adoption is when the business users begin to utilize the new product in their everyday routines. Socialization is when they all believe the product is beneficial to them and makes that daily routine easier as a result of using it.

That is precisely why every project needs a business champion: the person on the business side who will rave about how great it is and why everyone should try it. The champion will turn the implementation into a grassroots movement and will have everyone believing it was all his or her idea. That's completely fine, because then, change comes from within.

One important note here, is that the champion is not the sponsor or anyone from management. The champion is someone who is at the same level as everyone else and has some influence over what they think and how they feel about doing their jobs. There is an element of trust there, but no one really wants this person to be unhappy, because then everyone will know just how unhappy he or she is. Worst of all, their work life will be unhappy until the champion is happy.

REFERENCES

1. Davis, Freyda. Interview with Barbara Davis.
2. Prosci. 1998 "The ADKAR Model." Prosci.
3. Kettering, Charles F. (1876-1958). 1934. *Scientific American*.

Web Added Value™

This book has free material available for download from the
Web Added Value™ resource center at *www.jrosspub.com*

HANDING OVER TO OPERATIONS (BAU)

Ultimately, at the end of every project, the solution must become the responsibility of the business and its operations team. This is more than simply implementing the code or dumping the final solution into the laps of the business and expecting them to pick it up and run with it.

Business as usual (BAU), or *operations*, is the day-to-day management of the organization's regular activities. These activities must be consistent in order to ensure that the organization has the capability and capacity to meet its objectives and to achieve its goals. Table 11.1 illustrates the relationships between operational BAU and program management. By defining and understanding the roles more precisely, the entire transition from a tactical project to BAU operations is made efficient and more thorough.

Hand over is where the project team lets go of ownership and responsibility of the solution that it has delivered, and releases it into the organization; operations then takes responsibility for it. Successful transition and hand over looks both backward and forward. In effect, hand over is bidirectional.

In looking backward, the team focuses on delivery and readiness for that delivery to occur. Completion of the business readiness review and relevant preparatory items is the trigger for the hand over. When the business readiness criteria have been met, it means that the following statements are true:

- ALL deliverables and outcomes have been formally accepted by the business stakeholders and sponsors.

Table 11.1   Relationship between operational and program management

Program role	Business-as-usual role	Relationship
Program board and responsible owner	Main board	• Overall development and transition progress • Major exceptions to project and guidance • Maintaining leadership
Responsible owner and program manager	Finance	• Funding control and release • Budget management • Change control (major changes) • Gateway reviews • Benefits management
Responsible owner and program manager	Program office or enterprise portfolio management office	• Progress tracking • Change control (major changes) • Benefits management • Guidance on resource management • Internal standards • Gateway reviews
Program manager	Resource owners	• Sign-off on release of resources • Program management
Organizational change manager	Impacted business as usual (users)	• Change leadership • Sign-off on future state • Change communication • Benefits ownership and realization
Tactical delivery team	Project team (including PM, BA, architects, developers, and QA)	• Project management • Transition planning • Business readiness • Transition management • Handover
Tactical operations teams	Such as human resources or customer service	• Contribution to deliverables • Review of deliverables • Advice on specific policies/standards

- ALL third-party agreements and working arrangements have been negotiated and authorized. This includes contracts, master services agreements, service level agreements (SLAs) and inter-working agreements that define the client–supplier relationship, and multi-supplier interworking when relevant.
- The solution is ready for live operation.

Looking forward, on the other hand, focuses on the operations of the business and relevant teams, and ensures that they are ready, willing, and able to accept responsibility for running the new solution. However, this can only occur when certain conditions are met. These criteria for hand over most commonly include the following:

- ALL support and maintenance protocol are in place and prepared, such as a help desk.
- ALL preparations for the business operation to run the new solution have been successfully completed, such as initial training.
- Appropriate cultural and behavioral changes have been socialized and normalized.
- Business readiness criteria have been achieved.

TRANSITION AND OPERATIONAL ACCEPTANCE

During the transition from project delivery to operational control, the focus shifts to managing suppliers that are part of project delivery and preparing to manage other operational suppliers (standard vendors). Suppliers that are involved in the delivery of the project can be managed as with any other part of the project delivery. Business change managers, on the other hand, will be heavily involved in working with (managing) suppliers, according to the new protocols of changed operations, by:

- Managing and coordinating the departure of existing suppliers whose services will no longer be utilized or required. One of the considerations here is that an established working relationship may extend back years.
- Ensuring that all appropriate SLAs have been secured as part of business readiness.
- Ensuring that the mechanisms for managing the administration and execution of new or revised contracts have been established.

All of the business readiness considerations must now either be in place or have actionable plans with time frames for delivery. The business must know how to support the new solution and who will do it. Above all else, they must know how to use the new solution. In addition, the business must have new SLAs in place, and they must also have the ability to learn from the project that they have just completed. This means that the sponsor must sign off on the new solution, but that they must also ensure that people will use it, it delivers on its promised benefits, and it can be supported and maintained.

Activities that take place during transition typically include:

- Executing the transition plan
- Executing the leadership strategy
- Executing the stakeholder leadership plans and testing their effectiveness
- Updating the benefits realization plan (if necessary)
- Preparing operational support and maintenance infrastructures such as the help desk
- Establishing the benefits management mechanism
- Preparing to manage operational supplier contracts
- Negotiating and authorizing the operational supplier contracts
- Initiating and executing the transitional governance framework for transition and hand over to manage changes, which occur during the transition process.
- Completing the sign-off of deliverables and outcomes for the new solution
- Confirming business readiness
- Handing over sign-off by the appropriate operational management group(s).

Transition Factors

The truth is that the transition process and its elements will vary, depending on the type of solution being implemented. While this book has largely assumed that the audience is more interested in the implementation of new technology, it may not actually be the case. In fact, the solution may be new organizational structures, new business processes, or new technology. While fitting the new solution into place, one could assume a level of transferability of the checks and balances. It is especially important to call them out and discuss them below.

New Organizational Structure

The implementation of a new organizational structure occurs when the solution changes how the company is organized and creates a new reporting model. An example of this would be the addition of a new department to manage mobile business programs. Changes to organizational structure are the only time that ownership is not going to be a factor in implementation because the new organization is ultimately owned by the business group it reports to, and there will be managers and supervisors assigned to manage the group in the same way that a business owner is responsible for making key decisions about processes and technologies.

These changes are significant, however, because they alter a larger part of the company than new business process or technology. In fact, it will bring with it new processes and even new technology in order to support the new organizational structure and to help the business achieve its strategic goals. Consequently, this type of implementation requires a lot more change management and more extensive training. The change management planning and guidelines, outlined in Chapter 3, can be leveraged to ensure that everyone knows what to do and when and how it all impacts them for the better.

New Business Processes

New business processes are always attached to organizational change, but they also often accompany new technology. This is because some of what the business does in terms of processing (in other words, how it performs certain parts of business) are dictated by the tools they currently utilize, but also because new technology is often intended to update and change how work is being performed.

As a necessary part of the changes to workflow, business rules will often change as well. While it may seem that this discussion was primarily and best covered within the Chapter 4 discussion of business architecture, this discussion is intended to serve as reminder here that ultimately, changes to workflow are inescapable as the business evolves.

The implementation of new business processes (i.e., workflow) requires both change management and extensive training so that the new processes are effectively implemented. By ensuring that people are comfortable with the new processes, know exactly how to leverage them to their advantage, and know how to increase their personal productivity and effectiveness, they will not only readily adopt the new processes, they will own them.

New Technology

The implementation of new technology occurs when new software or hardware is introduced into the business as a means of supporting the completion of specific work functions (elements of work or entire workflows) in more effective and efficient ways. Implementing new technology brings a host of complexity in terms of systems integration, as well as new processes and potentially new administrative roles. It is important to understand how the new technology will not only benefit the company, but how it will evolve over time as it is utilized throughout the product life cycle.

In projects which implement new technologies, change management which is performed throughout the project by leveraging the techniques outlined in Chapter 3, will enable a lighter load during implementation. This means that by the time implementation is in full swing, the business stakeholders and users should be eagerly awaiting the new technology. This leaves the need for a short- and long-term training plan in order to enable the business users to continue being successful despite changes in resources or management (or even organizational structure, for that matter).

The Impacts of Implementing COTS, Cloud Solutions, and SaaS Products on Sarbanes-Oxley Compliance

Compliance activities can go more smoothly by asking some key questions during a transition in business organizations, processes, or technology.

The Risk of Noncompliance by Utilizing External Solutions

Sarbanes-Oxley (SOX) compliance was the big buzz of the early 2000s. As with every other trend, it seems to have faded into the background and is now collecting dust on a shelf in the archives. However, as explained below, SOX legislation assesses and manages internal financial controls as a means of ensuring corporate accountability in the accuracy of financial reporting to shareholders, and SOX compliance is still mandatory. With today's shift towards the cloud, and with commercial-off-the-shelf (COTS) and software-as-a-service (SaaS) emerging with lightning speed, many businesses could be exposing themselves to risks associated with noncompliance of SOX directives, and may not even be aware of it.

How can a sponsor or stakeholder sign off and assert their company's compliance to SOX if they are not even aware of the risks associated with these products, or how these risks will impact the scope of the project? The problem is not that executives are deliberately hiding anything, but simply that they could potentially be putting their trust blindly into products without knowing the level of certification in the background in order to ensure continued SOX compliance.

Sarbanes-Oxley was brought into legislation to assess and manage internal financial controls as a means of ensuring corporate accountability in the accuracy of financial reporting to shareholders. In order to accomplish this, three primary directives were included to deal specifically with disclosure, assessments, and reporting of internal financial processes. These are Section 302: Disclosure of Controls; Section 401: Disclosure of Reports; and Section 404: Assessment of Internal Control.

What that means is that SOX legislates the controls and accountability for ensuring adequate internal control over financial processes, regardless of the mechanism for automated controls and processes. To be precise: Sarbanes-Oxley dictates that every publicly traded company in the United States is accountable for financial controls and reporting. When acquiring COTS, cloud, or SaaS solutions, those companies are turning that control over to an external vendor and trusting that they will remain compliant. However, here is what is known about these solutions, or rather, what is *not* known about how they comply with SOX.

From a business perspective, without documentation and accountability on the part of the vendor to certify and provide a guarantee, there is no real assurance that any of these solutions comply with SOX because they are external. In the case of COTS, they are externally developed, and in the cases of cloud and SaaS, they are also externally managed. That means that not only does the business not have a say in the back-end processing or controls, but it does not have purview either. At the end of the day, if the company's name is on the bottom line, it should have access to all of the detailed information that gives them the confidence in the solutions that they bring into their enterprise architecture. Unfortunately, these solutions do not just run the processing and manage the company's controls; they also store and control the data.

Companies must determine the strategy for how to manage not just SOX compliance, but also configuration management across these solutions, and how all of it impacts scope on individual projects. It can be too easy to "pass the buck" to the vendor here. The real questions are: How much responsibility actually shifts to the vendor, and is the company still accountable for what they're doing and how they're doing it?

From a technology perspective, there seems to be a dichotomy here that presents a business quandary. Every year, the Standish Group generates and distributes their Chaos Report, and it clearly shows that there are major issues with the software development process. Now, while there is no guarantee that this would be any less true with externally built and managed solutions, there is one key difference, and that is the level of ownership that the company has over the end solution. At the very least, the company executives know who put it together and that it was built to meet their specific internal processes and controls that meet SOX compliance. That alone gives some assurance that companies can be confident that they are compliant to the best of their own ability.

However, that does not mean businesses should not be implementing these solutions. In fact, there is nothing wrong with selecting any of them over building something in-house. However, the stakeholders and the project team will need to identify, understand, and mitigate the risks that these solutions pose to the company's ability to remain SOX compliant.

Mitigation Strategies

COTS, cloud solutions, and SaaS are supposed to be cheaper and easier to implement right? Wrong! All too often, businesses make the assumption that they can simply unpack the box, or click the link and install it on systems in their environment because that is basically what people do at home. The costs, risks, and complexities of SOX compliance, coupled with an enterprise network, make this a vastly different scenario than simply downloading to any personal system. There are strategies for mitigating the risks of noncompliance, which are described here.

Strategy #1: Create a strategy for COTS, cloud, and SaaS program management.

Far too many companies do not even consider the cost of maintaining or upgrading COTS, cloud, and SaaS solutions or in-house software, simply because it is considered a future project slated for another budgetary year. But the truth is, that it is a lot like owning a car: everything is manageable until the owner starts spending more on repairs than it would cost to replace it. What are the long-term benefits of the software? What is the expected life span, and how many upgrades do you expect to do over that lifetime? How much will the company spend on maintaining it? How much will all of that maintenance cost? Do those costs change and increase with COTS, cloud, and SaaS solutions over in-house solutions?

Businesses need to realize that there is still a cost associated with maintaining and supporting these solutions while they are in the environment. While the company can pay support fees or work this into the licensing fees, the reality is they are still paying more than if they were to have the talent in-house to deal with routine issues that arise.

Worse still, there are hidden costs and scope items associated with implementing these solutions into the existing architecture. These will only be discovered by conducting a proper analysis and business readiness assessment.

Strategy #2: Define strategies for COTS, cloud, and SaaS configuration management.

Another aspect that businesses may overlook in the acquisition of these solutions is configuration management. What does configuration management look like when the vendor runs and controls the applications outside of your environment? The question has to be answered on an individual program-by-program basis, but a company cannot assume that the business is off the hook for it simply because the business world is increasingly utilizing COTS, cloud, and SaaS solutions. In fact, with so much control going over the proverbial fence, companies need to start thinking in terms of: "How can we capture consistent snapshots of data and the utilities so that the company remains SOX compliant?"

Strategy #3: Engage a business consultant.

Many companies feel they can complete the research and product selection without the input of a business consultant simply because they are pretty good evaluating up-front costs. Unfortunately, they could be missing the bigger picture and select a solution based on limited criteria, such as the cost per license, for features, and for interactions with the environment. They will make this selection under the assumption it can simply be installed as-is, and they will not have to document requirements for these implementations.

However, the truth is, the only costs that companies are really saving are the costs to build from scratch. In addition to SOX compliance and configuration management issues, companies could be missing elements of scope related to business readiness, specific implementation requirements, code extensions, and overall maintenance costs, as well as program management and vendor stability.

The fact is that companies also have to consider specific questions about the overall costs as well as the benefits of implementing these types of solutions into the environment. The value in bringing on a business consultant before the all-critical decision to build or buy is made, is just as important as bringing them on before the decisions about the specific COTS, cloud, and SaaS solutions are made. In fact, by bringing a business consultant on early enough to support research and cost benefit analysis, companies would be able to expose unknown risks that may otherwise remain undiscovered until long after implementation of the solution has occurred.

Strategy #4: Define strategies for COTS, cloud, and SaaS implementations.

Every single implementation needs a plan to direct the activities, drive it forward, measure success, monitor activities, and track feedback. This is the only way to ensure that the selected product is being implemented properly, will be utilized by the user community, meets the business needs, and can be managed on an ongoing basis. Without this implementation strategy, the project team's efforts could be a big waste of time and money. Failing to plan is planning to fail.

Strategy #5: Develop requirements for COTS, cloud, and SaaS implementations.

Without requirements, companies are missing the critical details that will make their COTS, cloud, and SaaS solutions implementation a success in the long run. Requirements for code extensions, impacts to the environment, configuration management, product life cycle, program management, features, and the implementation, all still have to be documented for successful COTS, cloud, and SaaS solutions implementations.

Strategy #6: Establish disaster recovery plans for COTS, cloud, and SaaS solutions.

The upheaval in Egypt in 2011 should definitely highlight the issues of continuing to maintain in-house disaster recovery plans, even when it comes to COTS, cloud, and SaaS solutions. This planning should include negotiating control/ownership in the event that the vendor fails; recovery in the event that geopolitical forces intervene; or natural disasters occur. Many COTS, cloud, and SaaS solutions vendors do have disaster recovery built-in for natural disasters, but what about all the other things that can go wrong with this arrangement?

What happens to the software if the vendor has been paid, and they are in the process of extending code and customizing it when they go bankrupt? What if the vendor goes bankrupt and the company loses access to all of its data? What is your recourse if someone hacks into the vendor's systems, and steals, vandalizes, or jeopardizes the data it holds? What happens if the vendor's foreign government is overthrown?

At the end of the day, the company is still on the line for utilizing an external vendor to provide COTS, cloud, or SaaS solutions, and that means executives and stakeholders need to understand, recognize, and manage all

aspects of continued SOX compliance while utilizing these services. Not doing so could be financial ruin in an economy tired of hearing about corporate
mismanagement and ignorance.

In closing, here is a checklist of questions to ask about what COTS, cloud,
or SaaS solutions are really going to bring to the company, and how that solution aligns with Sarbanes-Oxley:

- To what level have these products been documented and tested for
  SOX compliance?
- If stakeholders and executives assert to shareholders that documenta-
  tion and testing for SOX compliance has been done, does the project
  team need to have copies of, or access to the documentation, or is it
  enough to get the signature of the vendor and hold them accountable?
- Can the vendor be held accountable if the company is found to be
  non-compliant?
- Without the documentation, is it possible for the business sponsors
  and stakeholders to understand the flow of transactions?
  - How deep does that understanding go?
- How do the controls of these externally developed and/or managed
  solutions align to the COSO (Committee of Sponsoring Organizations
  of the Treadway Commission) framework? COSO is a "voluntary
  … initiative dedicated to improving organizational performance and
  governance through effective internal control, enterprise risk manage-
  ment, and fraud deterrence."[1]
- What, if any, fraud risk assessment has been done by the vendor to
  ensure that the company is going to be compliant with their product?
  - Have they, or can they, prove that?
- How are fraud prevention and detection controls evaluated?
  - Have they, or can they, prove this to you?
- What is the flow of control over period-end reporting procedures?
  - How can these procedures be evaluated?
- Is data consistently and routinely backed-up?
- Are configuration management techniques and principles for COTS,
  cloud, and SaaS solutions being applied?
  - How are these governed?
- Does the product fully support initial and evolving requirements?
- Does the product fully support fixed/unchangeable operational
  requirements and procedures?

- Finally, does the product meet quality requirements for reliability, performance, usability, etc.?

BUSINESS READINESS

One of the critical planning areas of transitioning ownership of the new solution to the BAU operations is an assessment of business readiness factors. Unfortunately, this is also one of the areas where companies do not plan in as much detail as is needed in order to be successful. All of this planning is really hinged on asking one simple question: What else do we need to do to be successful?

Shiny Tool Syndrome

The Shiny Tool Syndrome is when a person with authority and a budget finds a new tool and decides "I like it," "I want it," "I bought it." The problem with the Shiny Tool Syndrome is that the person making the decision often has limited information on which to base his or her decision. They may have even been wowed by a product demonstration provided by salespeople. Too bad, the salespeople are actually trained to highlight the good aspects of the product and to minimize the bad because they are after only one thing: the sale.

Unfinished Product in an Insurance Company

A couple of years ago, an insurance company struggled with a broker portal, which had been intended to support the independent insurance brokers who sold their insurance products to the general public. The portal, as it turned out, was not quite finished being developed, and the parts that were finished did not function properly, producing numerous error messages on a daily basis.

What this meant for the company was that the support and business analysis teams were in constant fire-fighting mode. They could not work on or focus on new products or technologies to improve their business because they were hung up in reacting to this constant battle against a poorly designed and implemented system.

To make matters worse, the portal did not interact with or integrate with any of the other systems in the environment, so its administrators were tasked with pulling data from the portal in order to feed it into other systems, and vice versa, several times per day. When the portal crashed, all of the data was suddenly at risk, and often outdated by the time it was finally entered.

In this case, the business did a sum total of zero business readiness planning (among all of the other types of planning they skipped), thought they could just install the software, everything would magically work, and all of their problems would be solved. To say the least, they were surprised and increasingly angry that this did not happen.

As described in the insurance company example, Shiny Tool Syndrome is bad because what really happens is that the person who has it rarely utilizes a simple procurement strategy, and as a result, does not ask key questions about business readiness and project scope that can ultimately spell D-I-S-A-S-T-E-R for companies and implementation projects.

VirtuDocs

Many years ago, a company bought an application we will call VirtuDocs, which is a software package for creating business forms for tasks like performance management and purchase orders.

What made VirtuDocs unique is that you cannot only create and manage the forms for everyone across the company, but the data that is entered into the forms is all stored in a database at the back-end. By doing this the company could retrieve the data later, and reuse it to fill out new forms and create new records, so they did not have to reenter the details each time they needed to fill out a purchase order for office supplies.

However, this company decided not to buy access to the database because they felt that it cost too much.

Every time an employee would enter information into VirtuDocs and click "Submit," the information would disappear. It could not be recalled, viewed, edited, printed, or deleted. As a result, the employees did not want to use VirtuDocs because using the software was like using a typewriter. It was that ineffective.

In the end, it cost more money to get people to use VirtuDocs than it would have cost the company to buy access to the database from the start. This company actually doubled the cost of the database by not buying the access to it when they bought the VirtuDocs software!

The VirtuDocs example could have been very different if the company in that situation had only asked two key business readiness questions: "Do I need the database? What else do I need to do to make VirtuDocs work?" The company would not have had to initiate an entirely new project to implement the database when they finally realized that they could not get by without it.

The assessment of business readiness requires a road map. However, this road map becomes a plan for the transition because it provides many of the details about how the new solution fits into the business and enterprise architecture around it. A road map can be structured in many ways, and could include the following details:

- Physical: new IT systems integrating with the solution
- Workflows: new business processes and relevant rules
- Communication and marketing the new solution to the appropriate audiences (employees, customers, vendors, and partners)
- Agreements, such as those negotiated with unions
- Behavioral or cultural changes: those changes that must occur before the implementation and adoption of the new solution can be successful
- Training: immediate and ongoing training must be in place not only to start training existing resources, but also to ensure continuity between periods of staff attrition and growth
- Operational support: Who will service this new solution, when, and how?
- Organizational responsibility: Who will own this solution? How will they manage it and authorize changes to it?

BENEFITS AND BENEFIT REALIZATION

Benefits realization is the planning, delivery, and subsequent management of benefits across the full end-to-end product life cycle. Typically, this is related to a very specific corporate financial investment. In short, the business identifies specific benefits that it wishes to achieve, then plans how to achieve them and when those benefits will be realized. This planning includes identifying what those particular benefits mean to the company (such as how the benefits relate to or impact the top and bottom lines).

Unfortunately, too many businesses are not doing this type of planning when it comes to technology solutions. While it is likely some of the lack of benefits planning originates in mismatched expectations between the stakeholders and the project leaders, it could also be attributed to a lack of experience from the allocated resources on the business side. However, these same business resources may be relying too heavily on the consultants to provide guidance about all of the planning and steps that must occur in order to be successful in delivering and implementing a solution.

When the consultants arrive, they are often handed a predetermined solution, and then they make the assumption that the business must have already conducted the benefits realization planning during the solution definition and selection stage (i.e., the business case). However, Ahmad Al Mulla, in his article entitled "The Most Common Mistakes Made By CIO's," cites both simply overlooking the big picture and inexperience as a cause for overlooking it.

One of Al Mulla's specific criticisms of technology designed and built for the business is that the chief information officer often misses the so-called "big business picture": "This eventually results in not being able to present the justifications for investments in a convincing business context. In other words, decisions must be ably supported with business reasoning rather than limiting them to technical enhancements or features."[2]

It should be stressed that neither the business cases nor decision cases are benefits realization plans. Whereas a business case justifies the expenditure from a cost-benefit perspective within three possible scenarios (doing nothing; doing something to fix the existing; or, replacing "it" entirely), it is the benefit realization plan that details the specific benefits against milestones and tangible key performance indicators. In fact, the business case does not contain timelines, baselines, or milestones to quantify the achievement and realization of desired benefits. There are very few identified benchmarks in the business case to ensure that the benefits are actually being realized, and there is no assessment of the total cost of ownership (TCO).

The benefits realization plan, on the other hand, details the estimated return on investment; an estimated TCO; other anticipated benefits such as increased revenue, decreased costs, or decreased service times; as well as milestones for the achievement of those benefits, returns, and costs against a timeline. This plan is used to assess and analyze the progress of the solution in meeting those milestones and benefits throughout its life span within the environment.

One of the latest trends within information technology is to attempt to formalize benefits realization planning under the auspices of portfolio management (where groups of related products and/or projects are managed at a strategic level instead of merely a tactical level). It is portfolio management that provides both the business and technology sides with a greater ability to see the project or product within the context of the overall business and strategic objectives.

Within the context of scope and transitioning the solution to operations (also known as BAU), benefits realization planning enables more full and complete solution definition and includes considerations (as assumptions, constraints, or requirements) for business readiness and long-term business objectives, ultimately ensuring alignment between the planned and the implemented solution, and the architecture around it.

An estimated 40%[3] of software features are never used. Ironically, one of the reasons for the high volumes of project challenges and failures that are cited in The Standish Group's annual Chaos Report where this statistic appears, is the lack of user involvement. Where there is a general lack of user involvement, it can be assumed that there is no project-level effort to perform benefits realization planning because the planning process is heavily user-centric and the high rate of failure suggests a lack of user involvement.

The triple constraint theory of project management suggests that the budget is a major factor in what can be delivered and when. Since the ability to budget all needs into a single project will directly impact the benefits realization plan, it becomes even more critical to conduct this planning at the project or program level in order to ensure that actual benefits will be derived from the new solution.

While both the budget and the lack of benefits realization planning play a significant part in the implementation of specific features and even specific solutions, the business and project teams responsible often have an inability to correctly prioritize and categorize needed features in order to develop the solution within the budgetary limitations. This is because projects do not have or seek appropriate levels of user involvement.

The benefits realization plan contains benefit statements, baselines, and timelines for both tangible and intangible benefits. These tangible and intangible benefits include: financial, quality, service (customer experience), products development process, team competency, and emotional benefits.

There are seven basic steps to perform when conducting benefits realization planning. These are:

1. Identify the problem or need.
2. Identify the desired outcomes and results.
3. Define the benchmarks.
4. Determine priority:
   a. Plan the new or changed capabilities.
   b. Plan any additional investments.

    c. Optimize the plan.

    d. Complete a risk/impact assessment.

5. Create the plan:

    a. Design and obtain agreement with the business sponsors, stakeholders, and leaders.

6. Communicate the plan to the team.

7. Consistently review planned vs. actual realizations.

As evidenced above, benefits realization planning is not necessarily a magnanimous task, but it does force both the business and the project team to think in terms of the long-term benefits that will be derived from any investment.

OWNERSHIP, RESPONSIBILITY, AND ACCOUNTABILITY

It is imperative to identify and log key owners, responsible and accountable groups for providing ongoing support, and controlling changes to the new system/process after implementation of a new system.

    TIP: Provide functional roles in an ownership matrix vs. naming a specific individual, as the function typically changes less often and is associated with the role, not the person. A sample ownership matrix is provided in Table 11.2.

Implications of Business Ownership Roles and Responsibilities for Scope

To be completely honest, the biggest impact from business ownership on the scope of a project is the personal agenda of the stakeholder and the business sponsors. These individuals are working to meet their own business goals, and they will often translate those goals onto the scope of the project. Consequently, when ownership or sponsorship changes, so too can the entire direction of the project. The project could get sidelined and come to a screeching halt right in the middle of it.

    It is important to note, however, when the project makes its implementation, that the business owner of the application, the respective processes, and the business rules are fully aware of what has been done and why (let's just assume they were a part of this project), and they will have to sign off on the new elements that have been created as a result. Not only this, but everyone else within the business must know who owns the new solution and

Table 11.2 Sample ownership matrix

Functional Role	Business Unit	Held By	Contact Info	Responsible	Accountable	Contributes	Informed
Contracts Administrator	Finance	Betty Mann	bmann@123z.com	X		X	

its subcomponents in case it interferes with their own business areas or applications in the future, or in case they simply need to make changes as they evolve their own departmental tools.

All of this takes a formal ownership document, with formal sign off as acceptance of the product as it has been delivered, and marketing to the remainder of the company's employee, customer, and vendor population (where appropriate and applicable).

SUSTAINING THE CHANGES

Even when changes are expected to be temporary or transitional, there has to be some form of supporting and maintaining them until they are no longer necessary or needed. This means that every project should consider how to support and sustain the changes until such time as the business deems them no longer necessary and decommissions them.

As a part of the strategy for sustaining the changes, it may be necessary to identify changes that may be needed within one or more of the following areas: human resources and management systems, as well as the physical structure of the workplace itself.

Human Resources

While human resources can be impacted in terms of individual policies and procedures, the most common and most important areas to consider are for recruitment, ongoing training, ongoing performance management, and new resource onboarding.

Recruitment strategies and systems may be impacted when significant changes to technologies require prospective candidates to have skill sets that were not previously considered to be mandatory or even an asset. The rapid adoption of cloud and mobile technologies, for example, has led to a widespread surge in the search for developers with these capabilities.

In addition to initial training, the need for a consistent and regular ongoing training program becomes necessary in order to ensure that all resources perform consistently over time with the new solution. This is especially important when considering that people learn in different ways and may or may not have the opportunity to apply the knowledge gained in a onetime only crash course.

Does This Retailer Have a Methodology?

A number of years ago a mid-sized retailer realized that its project success had not increased since it had adopted and implemented a new project methodology based on the Rational Unified Process. The retail business believed that this lack of success was because the business analysts were struggling and needed training in business analysis skills.

A new consultant was brought in to train the business analysts, but before this could happen, the consultant set about understanding the full scope of the issues the company was facing, and how she could help to address them. It was determined that the consultant needed to conduct a review of all of their current project processes in order to recommend training for the business analysis team.

During this review, it became apparent that only one project manager really utilized the new project methodology because the company that had created it merely conducted a handful of training sessions over the course of a single month. No one outside of the project management office even knew they had a methodology!

In the retailer's methodology example, it was clear that the company created a solution and literally dropped it into the laps of the business. However, with no ongoing training, there was no way to refresh skills or even to ensure that everyone was trained in using it.

Quite literally, the same goes for ongoing performance management as it does for ongoing training. Where ongoing training provides the vehicle for understanding the solution, ongoing performance management provides the framework for compliance and ensures that people are performing as well as they could with the new solution.

This may mean the development of new key performance indicators (KPIs) that enable management to measure and track the performance of individuals and teams as they adopt and fully engage new technologies and processes. These KPIs are as much for the personal growth of individual resources as they are for the solution.

The final element to consider with respect to training is really about how new resources will be trained going forward. It is important to consider and plan how all new resources (contracted or full-time employees) will be trained as they come on board because the *de facto* training that they will receive supports the old workflows and technologies, and may create rifts and inconsistency in performance if the "newbies" are not all trained in the same methods and techniques.

Management Systems

One key consideration for business readiness planning is about the existing management systems, and how those systems will support and enable the maintenance of new systems within the environment.

Preparation Means Less Duplicated Effort

Several years ago, a company wanted to re-architect its entire website. As it turned out, there was no simple way to understand the website or the business rules that governed its retail transactions. All of the business rules were buried in the code. That code was so messed up that it typically produced 600-1,000 error reports every day because it did not work consistently. The effort to re-architect the website required a full-scale documentation effort in order to document the workflows, and to mine the business rules from the existing code.

However, with the existing processes being primarily undocumented, the team determined that it would be necessary to define and create a document management strategy and portal in order to prevent the situation from reoccurring, once the new processes had been authored.

In the website re-architecture situation, the project manager recognized that creating a new management system would best support the maintenance of the new work products, and would prevent a re-occurrence of scattered and spotty documentation. By implementing a new document management strategy and system before making changes to the documents themselves, the company was poised for success without a lot of duplication of effort.

However, this was not the case when a company did not prepare this same strategy and structure ahead of the project effort so that its subsidiaries also could benefit.

We Need to Extend Your Contract

A company set about documenting its processes in order to comply with SOX legislation. Over the course of two years, a team diligently prepared business process models and labeled each one according to a standard. Unfortunately, the standard was applied at each subsidiary company without regard for any other subsidiary.

The result was that each of the document sets for each of the five subsidiaries contained duplicate names. However, this wasn't discovered until the

> end of the two years when the document management system was being customized and populated.
>
> In this case, the company had to extend their project by well over six months to rename and populate the document management system. All of this extra time and effort could have been avoided if the project team had done some of the business readiness planning up front and recognized that this was going to be an issue.

Here is where it becomes especially crucial to ask the question: What else do we need to make this work? This question has been illustrated quite well with the two stories of real projects. One was successful and delivered on time and on budget because the project team asked one simple question and determined that there would be more to the project than simply creating a bunch of workflow diagrams and dropping them into the lap of the business. The other did not.

Another consideration for the business readiness of management systems is to determine how ongoing issue management will be handled. This is effectively the set of procedures for handling errors that may occur as the solution is live in the environment. In many cases, technology-based issues would be escalated to the help desk, and process-based issues would be escalated to the business owner for resolution.

The reason that ongoing management features in a discussion about scope and business readiness is that it may be necessary to include certain tasks or maintenance considerations in scope in order to deliver a solution that will be successful over the long term.

The final consideration for the business readiness of management systems is to determine the impacts to ongoing asset management. *Asset management* is effectively the way in which a company acquires, distributes, and manages its physical and software assets that will be utilized in its day-to-day operations and regular work life. Both hardware and software components are considered assets, although they may be managed with different approaches. Asset management impacts scope when it is not considered in the project and nothing is done to ensure that it has been accounted for.

A Licensing Issue When Upgrading Software

Many years ago, a company initiated a project to migrate from multiple Windows operating platforms to a Windows upgrade. In the process, the team was mandated with removing older software and replacing these products with the Microsoft Office upgrade.

Toward the end of the project, when the project manager and the business stakeholders felt that they hit the tipping point, the project manager happily announced that the company was no longer at risk of a lawsuit for violating their licensing agreements with the product vendors because enough systems no longer had the products.

In this situation, it turned out to be a lack of asset management planning within business readiness of previous initiatives. These previous initiatives had neglected to include the removal of the software from the systems when it was not needed by the new user, and they did not secure new licenses for additional copies they were distributing. Once the issue was discovered, they quickly remedied the situation and created more stringent guidelines for asset management as a means of preventing it from happening again.

Physical Structure

Another key consideration in business readiness is to identify new physical requirements for maintenance of the new system. This may include increased workspace in order to accommodate new hardware, or it may include relocating resources to accommodate new ways of working (such as colocating for the adoption of Agile practices).

Ummm... Where Are the Phones Going to Plug In?

A company had decided to expand its travel offerings to include vacation bookings as a means of extending its reach and increasing value to its customers. As a part of this expansion, they decided to build a new travel office that would be centrally located and would look like any other storefront travel business.

Everyone was excited about moving to the new location and getting a change in their work. Nothing else had really changed in decades, so this was a big deal both to customers and to staff who were anxious to try something new.

> The day came when everyone packed up their desks and the moving company came to get them. The boxes were moved to the new location, where the desks were already in place. As people began to unpack, they realized that no electrical extensions had been installed and so not a single desk had the ability to plug in phones, desk lamps, or computers.
> They spent the rest of the day repacking and moving back to the old building to wait for the work to be completed.

Sure, not noticing an obvious need like power at a new location may be a rare occurrence, but the reality is that it does happen. Business readiness really means considering everything that may need to be put into place before the team can be fully functional and the operations can be live. This may include ordering the right desks, having the right space available for offices, or access to electricity. Whatever it is, it must be planned and put in place before the project solution is implemented, or it simply cannot be called a success.

Impacts of Maintenance on Scope

Ongoing support and maintenance of the solution within the business and enterprise architecture is partially a consideration for scope because it may have specific impacts on business readiness, especially when the business cannot fully achieve readiness prior to implementation. However, that being said, some of the critical high-level scope items which directly translate into the product and absolutely must be considered before development begins, are the service expectations that will later become the SLAs for the product. It is these expectations that will become requirements and design items, and must be factored in by the project team in its development work so that the product can meet its other objectives. Some of the key factors to be included are scope and high-level nonfunctional requirements for supportability, maintainability, portability, and security.

OBSERVING AND MONITORING IMPLEMENTATION PROGRESS

One of the final tasks in the transition process is to track the success and progress of the implementation itself. This means that the project team is responsible for identifying and logging key metrics and milestones. These will be utilized for ensuring the successful transition and progress of the handover during the implementation of a new solution. By leveraging these milestones, the team is able to make corrections as needed in order to install the product correctly into the new environment.

Regression Testing

One of the techniques utilized for this purpose is regression testing. This type of testing ensures that other systems within the environment (particularly, but not exclusively, those which integrate with the new one) continue to function as they did before any changes were made.

Anytime a new solution is implemented, regression testing should be in scope as a means of ensuring that all systems still process the same number of transactions at the same rate that they did before the implementation.

ESCALATING LESSONS LEARNED AND TRANSFERRING OWNERSHIP

Lessons learned are those bumps, bruises, and successes that were encountered and learned throughout the project life cycle. These lessons are intended to make the good aspects (things that worked) repeatable for other projects, and to make the not-so-good aspects (things that did not work) an event of the past so that other projects do not have the same issues time and time again.

By not recording and internalizing these good and bad lessons, every project is doomed to repeat the same mistakes over and over again. But it is more than this. One of the biggest impediments to adopting lessons learned is ego. That ego costs companies around the world a lot of hard-earned money every year. Ego gets in the way of reporting the escalating problems and issues that occurred along the way, and how they were addressed, but it also hinders the ability to admit that resources (or whole teams) may not know everything and should be learning from the missteps of other project teams.

However, ego is not the only thing that often stands in the way of the company learning as it goes along. Sometimes, it is the nature of the company that is highly risk-averse and slow to change, and other times it is purely the inexperience of the stakeholders and the technology resources. Still other times, these resources are so anxious to adopt industry best practices, that they do not consider the past mistakes because they believe that those best practices will lead to the promised land. Yet, they do not necessarily know how to interpret them, incorporate their own experiences (lessons learned), or implement them.

A best practice is really just a label for someone else's lessons learned that have been incorporated into a repeatable process. It does not mean that those practices translate across to the company at hand or the project at stake. Instead, logic must be applied so that industry best practices can be blended with a company's own unique experiences and translated into a useful process for success within their own organization.

REFERENCES

1. Committee of Sponsoring Organizations of the Treadway Commission (COSO). 2013, June. "The 2013 COSO Framework & SOX Compliance." http://coso.org/documents/COSO%20 McNallyTransition%20Article-Final%20COSO%20Version%20 Proof_5-31-13.pdf
2. Ahmad Al Mulla, Ahmad. 2012, October 2. "The most common mistakes made by CIOs." www.linkedin.com/the-most-common -mistakes-made-by-cios
3. The Standish Group. 2011. Chaos Report.

DECOMMISSIONING AND SUN-SETTING

WHAT IS DECOMMISSIONING?

Decommissioning is the process of retiring a system once its life cycle has completed. Typically, this means it has either been replaced by another system, or the program that the original system supported has been retired altogether. While a product can be terminated at any point in its life cycle (post-implementation), decommissioning is the specific process of turning it off and finding alternate courses for the workflows managed by it.

There are two important types of applications that create implications for project scope when considering decommissioning. These are internal (employee-facing) and external (customer/vendor-facing) applications.

Each of these scenarios presents issues, challenges, and concerns that will impact scope. Where one brings a host of organizational change management considerations, the other brings considerations for long-term support.

Decommissioning Internal Applications

With internal applications, the company has more control over the decommissioning of a given application. This is because, in most cases, the company controls, maintains, and determines which tools are to be used by its employees and contractors.

The biggest concern over decommissioning of internal applications is change management. Employees and contractors will need to be set up for success early so they can move seamlessly from one application to another. The last thing a company wants or needs is resistance and sabotage of the new applications by employees who do not have buy-in.

Decommissioning External-Facing Products and Applications

On the other hand, decommissioning external applications can be more intensive and have a greater impact on the long-term planning of the company, as well as the scope for specific projects. This ultimately requires more effort on the part of the company, and much more planning within the scope for specific projects.

The biggest concern over decommissioning of external applications is maintaining and supporting customers for an extended period of time beyond the life of the actual product. Customers will not only need to be aware of changes to potential upgrades, they will also need to know how long the company intends to support their usage of the product, and what that support looks like. The last thing a company wants or needs is unhappy customers who feel abandoned after they spent their hard-earned money on the product.

IMPLICATIONS FOR SCOPE

In order to really understand and drive home the rationale behind why decommissioning should be a part of scope (or at least listed in the assumptions and constraints as a consideration), it is important to understand what happens when this is not done. An example that works well was found at an insurance company that used its best intentions.

The Best Intentions

Several years ago, an insurance company undertook the development and implementation of a new driver risk program. This program required the development of the technology system, which would automate the entire program and make it easier for the company to manage.

At the outset, this project was only supposed to last six months to build the new program that would replace the existing, outdated program. The plan and the scope of the project had been set with the new program and the existing program operating in parallel for two years so that adequate assurance could be made that the new program worked as planned.

In this story, the scope included considerations for how the old system was going to be decommissioned, even though the decommissioning itself was not going to be a part of the project. However, there were key decisions that the team needed to make in the development of the new program, which required them to have this information and to consider it. These decisions were: how to migrate the users from one system to the next seamlessly, slowly migrate functionality from one system to the next over the two years, and test the new system throughout that process.

Any given business system or application contains crucial data about how the business performs specific tasks and who they perform them for. At the end of the life cycle of any of these products, the business cannot simply turn it off and expect everything to run smoothly. The first question to be answered is: "How is the data (which often includes user profiles and profile elements) going to be moved from one system to the next, so that it is usable by the new system?"

Data migration is often encompassed within the scope of a decommissioning project itself, but in reality, the project for the new system must consider what that data looks like and how it should be prepared, and determine what the risks and limitations of that data are.

As an example, in a particular company with a driver risk program, data had been previously merged from two different databases and many of the numbers turned out to have duplicates in the other system. This error was not corrected, and it created some painful business processes for those who were impacted over the years. This situation could have been prevented if the data had been cleaned and managed in the scope of the systems merger, instead of waiting until the end, when it was too late to do anything but try to work around the problem until the licenses expired and new ones could be issued. Consider what happened next in the driver project that ran away.

Runaway Driver Project

After two years of building the application for its driver program, the team finally implemented some of the functionality. By this time, it was overdue, severely over-budget, and had been broken into phases to attempt to regain control.

Unfortunately, that first phase of functionality duplication made a big mess of all of the other systems that the driver program interacted with. The overall impact was that finance had to perform manual billing for in excess of 60,000 customers on a monthly basis.

It is critical to understand that there are risks and impacts from making decisions (and assumptions) about the end of a product's life cycle without considering some of the crucial factors. Another factor is about how to migrate specific functionality from one system to the next over the course of the decommissioning process.

Remember that the scope and the plan called for the programs in the story to run in parallel with each other over a couple of years, while the expectation was that a decommissioning project was gearing up to shut off the old system. This means that there would be some overlap between the two systems during that time, and it requires intervention and follow-up to prevent duplicate transactions from occurring.

Let's look at what really happened in order to understand why these decisions are important factors in a project, even when decommissioning is not going to be a part of the scope.

Root Cause (Analysis) Revelations, Part A

Within the driver program replacement project, there were things going on in the background that not all team members were aware of. Once implementation revealed some fundamental cracks in the application, and finance was scrambling to make the best of the situation until it could be fixed, a root cause analysis was undertaken to determine what went wrong.

The root cause analysis uncovered that two major mistakes had been made without considering the true impacts on scope (or time and budget). The first mistake made was that the design and the requirements were approved by two disparate groups on the same day without any knowledge of or even how each related to the other.

What was not considered in requirements was the fact that the old system was broken from the time it had been implemented 20 years earlier. The information systems division then decided it would break up that old system across four segregated servers. None of this was considered in the scope or requirements of the new system.

In addition to this, the scope must contain considerations for integration testing of the new system as well as regression testing throughout that process. In the previous story, one of the key issues was that the implemented changes could not be backed out, and inadequate testing had been done.

Where scope often identifies that some forms of testing must occur, it does not usually specify what types of testing will be done or are appropriate for the project. This means that scope leaves some ambiguities and assumptions about testing to the team. Instead, these decisions should be accounted for up front in the scope so that appropriate types of testing can be planned and the environment prepared, and then all testing can be effectively executed.

Remember that decommissioning is not simply about shutting something down or pulling something out of the environment; it is about extracting it from the architecture so that nothing else breaks down and so that new systems can operate as planned.

Root Cause (Analysis) Revelations, Part B

Next, after events described in Part A, the development team determined that some of the functionality required in the design of the new system already existed in the old system (despite being broken). The plan was to duplicate that functionality into the new system and then to fix it while developing the new functionality.

Instead, the development team simply built the new code into the old system and fully integrated the two. The end result was that the old system could not be decommissioned without considerable additional effort (and time and cost).

Decommissioning is a complex task, and while many projects opt to perform decommissioning as a separate project, it is imperative that some considerations be made in the immediate project for how that will happen. After all, the old system represents another integration point, albeit a short-lived one. While those decisions were indeed made, it turned out that they were not realistic nor appropriate for the real situation.

PRODUCT LIFE CYCLE

The life cycle of any given product starts with the need. It is refined from concept to fully tangible product throughout the project to define and build it, and then transitions to the application of its functionality by those who will use it at work or play. The more formal methodologies for product life cycle management (PLM) illustrate four distinct stages: introduction, growth, maturity, and decline as depicted in Figure 12.1.

What is important to understand is that throughout that life cycle, the product is often updated or enhanced to capture new features desired by the users.

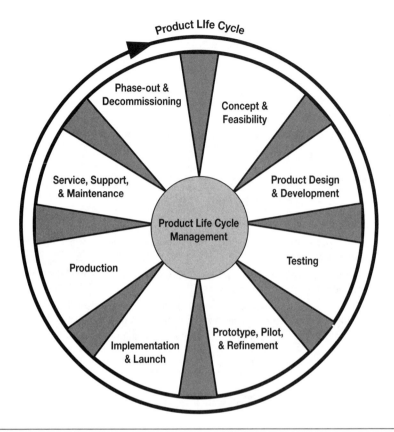

Figure 12.1   Product life cycle management (PLM)

At the end of it all, the product is no longer used, made, or sold, and eventually, it is no longer supported by its manufacturer.

Life Span of the Average Vehicle Model

Consider the average vehicle introduced to the marketplace. Every five years, the manufacturer updates the major components such as body style, seating, and overall design, while every other year in between, only minor changes are made to headlight shapes and console shapes.

While the same should be true of projects as in the average vehicle model sidebar, it is not always the case. In some cases, businesses frantically attempt to include as much functionality as possible and load up the scope of the initial project with infeasible and inappropriate features because they know it will be the only time they have a chance to get it. In other words, there will be no future iterations, enhancements, or upgrades.

Maintenance

One of the considerations for scope related to product development and planning of the overall life cycle is how the product will be maintained and sustained. Maintenance must extend right up to the decommissioning of the product, whether that product is customer- or employee-facing. That means the product must have an owner who is responsible and accountable for ensuring that it works as planned, and provides the intended value back to the company.

Maintenance is done by meeting service level agreements about downtime, scheduled outages, and upgrades. Essentially, maintenance ensures that the product is operational throughout its life. It would be like getting routine oil changes and tire rotations on a car in order to maintain it.

A key area where businesses and projects alike do not plan in appropriate detail is the scope for maintenance after the new system becomes operational and is managed by the business units. While this is a joint effort, it must be considered in scope to plan how this will occur, who will own the product, and how it fits into the maintenance of all other products.

Total Cost of Ownership

Another important factor in the overall scope should be the total cost of ownership. This is the cost to build, implement, support, and maintain the product throughout its life, but also includes the cost of decommissioning it. Understanding how much the product will cost overall enables the business to make key decisions about scope and even phasing in a new product.

Benefits and Benefit Realization

As discussed in Chapter 11, benefits realization is the planning, delivery, and subsequent management of benefits across the full end-to-end product life cycle. One of the crucial decisions that must be made in the life of any given product is when to terminate its life. This decision and the timing of making it will depend largely on that product's ability to achieve its desired benefits on or before the milestones identified in the benefits realization plan.

Return on Investment

Return on investment (ROI) is a type of performance measure that is used to evaluate a particular investment. To calculate the ROI, the return value is divided by the total cost. The ROI formula is as follows:

$$ROI = \frac{(\text{Gain from Investment} - \text{Cost of Investment})}{\text{Cost of Investment}}$$

Anticipated ROI (seen as a specific individual benefit) is an important factor in making key business decisions about initial project scope, as well as managing changes as scope evolves. Whether or not ROI is a visible factor, it must be recognized that it is certainly an underlying business consideration in the ongoing evaluation of the product. Certainly a consistently negative return would speed up the demise of both a project and a product as a business must at some point begin to realize positive investment returns.

Whether the ROI accelerates the demise of a product or not, the ROI factor must be considered in all scoping decisions about decommissioning. This is because it drives scope as a means of the business achieving its goals through development, implementation, and subsequent usage of the product.

At the end of the product life cycle, while an overall evaluation must occur to forensically study and understand the real ROI achieved, it also provides for key decisions that must be made about how to decommission and how long an expired product will be supported. Consider the off-the-market scenario.

Off-the-Market Product Support

When a company builds a software application and sells that application as a commercial-off-the-shelf product that comes in a box, the consumers purchase the application and install it on their computers. They spend many years happily enjoying the product and using it.

However, in this case, a year after the company sold the application, it did a major upgrade to the product and started selling the next version. After ten years, the application was retired and the company started selling a replacement product.

By now, the original customer had upgraded their operating system, and the application no longer worked properly. So, customers contacted the company that sold it to them. Since the company no longer sold the product, they no longer offered any support for it. The customer must now purchase a new product.

In the off-the-market product scenario, the real question is, "How long does a company provide support for a decommissioned product, which it no longer sells?" The answer to that question lies in the evaluation of the ROI. The truth is that ROI should be estimated as part of the initial benefits realization and business case, and should then be reevaluated as a part of scope throughout the project, and certainly again when scoping considerations for decommissioning.

PLANNING DECOMMISSIONING

Planning for decommissioning occurs at two points, and often across two or more projects. The first planning occurs within the original plan for the product and again once the decommissioning project begins. This means that decommission planning must be in scope for both projects. While decommissioning expiring products or products that are being replaced is an option, it is not commonly recommended because the new product functionality must be confirmed prior to removal of the existing products.

A plan for decommissioning must be started within the original plan for the product. In doing so, there is reduced risk of unforeseen issues arising out of the original build process. This plan begins with asking questions about all of the existing applications and systems within the enterprise architecture. These questions are primarily about identifying overlapping and competing functionality.

While it does not have to be a solid plan, a skeleton of what will happen and when, should be in place to guide those build decisions made on the current project that will impact the ability to decommission quickly (or at all). The more formal plan can be laid out at the start of the decommissioning project (if it is separate from the project to build the replacement application).

The basic elements of the skeleton plan include a timeline for decommissioning, how decommissioning of the application will occur, what business readiness items must be complete prior to decommissioning, how it will occur in relation to the current build project (triggers), and considerations for testing, among other factors.

Considerations for Testing

Planning the scope for decommissioning a product is a complex matter. It is important to ensure that this plan includes considerations for how the new products will be tested, as well as how testing will occur once decommissioning has been completed. This may be as simple as regression testing, but then again, it really depends on the new product and the complexity of extracting the expired product from the architecture.

Policy Renders Future Dating Functions Untestable

One of the problems that surfaced on the driver risk program at the insurance company was how the program was to impose penalties on drivers for demonstrating risky driving behaviors (like speeding or driving while intoxicated).

According to the scope of the project, the penalties would be imposed over the course of three years. In addition to the initial fine or ticket, the driver would have increased insurance rates, and would also receive an extra penalty fee annually for three years. This meant that the program application had to generate invoices over those three years for each of the drivers.

However, in discussions with the testing team, it came out that this multi-year functionality could not be tested. The testing environment was set up to test functionality based only on the current date because it was against policy to push the dates forward in the testing environment for future functionality.

In this story, the real issue was more than the fact that a functionality listed in the scope could not be tested. It became apparent that decommissioning could not occur until well after three years, instead of the planned two years, because there were elements that could not be tested until well after the target date. If decommissioning were to occur before all functions and scope could be tested, and then something broke, it would cause a serious problem for the company because they would be operating without a back-up system.

Back-up Planning

Every decommissioning effort will require back-up planning so that if something does go wrong in the extraction process, the retired application can be restored until the issues can be resolved. The driver risk program discussed in the section above had this issue.

Remember, in the driver risk program story, the new code fully integrated into the code for the expired program, which made it impossible to decommission without a significant rewrite of the new program, and a decommissioning effort for the old one. What compounded this issue was the fact that no back-up planning or efforts took place prior to the build process. There was no way to back-out the changes that crashed the program and broke everything.

In an ideal situation, the expired application and some of its nested architecture would have been duplicated in case this situation occurred and the changes needed to be reversed. This would have made life for the finance team a lot easier.

Disaster Recovery Planning

Disaster recovery planning is an area where many project teams do not spend enough time. The general exception to this rule is when the project is complex or the organization has both a deep understanding of, as well as a very low tolerance for, risk.

A Need for a Plan B

A great example of disaster recovery planning is the driver risk program. In this project, the team was tasked with implementing a driver penalty program at an insurance company. Phase 1 of the implementation was implemented with almost 400 defects and literally ground everything to a halt (both the finance and the project teams).

The root cause analysis revealed that the new code was actually developed into the old (and seriously defective) code, as a means of cutting down the work to be done. Unfortunately, what also came to light was that there were no project-level disaster recovery plan and no back-up for any of the systems. Ultimately, this meant that there was no ability to back-out the implemented changes and revert back to the old systems while the defects were traced and fixed.

As a result, the business and the project were at a standstill while the team worked to fix the defects one at a time over the course of two months, and the finance team was overwhelmed with manual billing for customers.

In the driver risk program story, the project team did not leverage any of the principles of disaster recovery in order to ensure that a Plan B could be triggered once Plan A did not implement properly. Disaster recovery in the project sense is about ensuring that the project team has a way to back-out all of the implemented changes, and has the ability to perform regression testing to prove that the changes have been fully removed and the systems restored, while the defects are identified and corrected.

Every project that is making process or system changes (ANY changes such as new systems or upgrades to existing systems) must have a plan in place to react when things do not go smoothly, and the team must have the ability to back-out (remove) all of the implemented changes put in place. First and foremost, this plan must include a way to replicate and back-up all the existing systems and architecture before the new changes are introduced.

The results of not having a plan in place, and following through on it, could be catastrophic.

A Need for a Plan B (Part 2)

In the driver risk program, the objective was to develop and implement the new program, and then have it operate alongside the existing program for two years until all impacted customers had been migrated over. At that point, the objective was to decommission and shut down the old program.

However, because of the lack of backup (among a host of other issues), coupled with the development of the new code into the existing code, decommissioning was not going to be possible without a full redevelopment of the new code as a separate entity.

In the story above, the finality of the situation that both the team and the business found themselves in, could have been avoided with a back-out plan from the start. Back-out planning demands that the project teams ask how to recover from the worst-case scenario before, during, and after implementation.

As an integral part of that planning, the project team must plan for and have the ability to perform regression testing in order to prove that the changes have been removed and the systems restored back to the original state. In other words, once those changes have been reversed, regression testing must be performed to prove that the systems have been restored. While the regression testing is occurring, the remainder of the project team is involved in identifying, tracing, and correcting the defects. All of this must be performed, without exception, every single time an implementation is done. This is because there is no guarantee that all defects have been exposed and corrected before re-implementation.

APPENDIX A

SAMPLE DOCUMENT TEMPLATES

The sample templates in this book can be used to support the management of scope across the life span of a variety of projects. They are designed to be flexible and adaptable to the uniqueness of projects while still providing a common framework to draw from.

AMBIGUITY LOG CONTENT SAMPLE

Table A-1 Ambiguity log

AID #	Code	Requirement & Location	Ambiguity Description	Entered By	Entered On	Resolution	By	Resolved On	Source Updated
1									
2									
3									
4									
5									

CHANGE CONTROL LOG DOCUMENT CONTENT SAMPLE

Table A.2 Sample change control log

ID#	Requirement ID	Requirement Name	Change Description	Date Submitted	Approved Y/N	Business Criticality	Priority	Assigned To

CURRENT STATE DOCUMENT CONTENT SAMPLE

Business Problem Statement

Business Processes Affected

The following business processes are affected by this problem:

- List business processes.

The following business processes are in scope, and will directly or indirectly be addressed by this project:

- List in-scope business processes.

The following business processes are out of scope, and will not be addressed by this project:

- List out-of-scope business processes.

Systems/Applications Affected

The following systems and/or applications are affected by this problem:

- List systems/applications.

The following systems and/or applications are in scope, and will directly or indirectly be addressed by this project:

- List in-scope systems/applications.

The following systems and/or applications are out of scope and will not be addressed by this project:

- List out-of-scope systems/applications.

Assumptions/Constraints

- List assumptions/constraints.

Risks

- List risks.

Related Documents

- Project Plan
- Project Scope
- Project Charter
- Cost Benefit Analysis
- Statement of Work
- Existing System Architecture Document
- Existing Technical Design Document

Business Process Flows

- Business Process Name

Current State Process Flow

- Insert high-level diagrams or process descriptions.

DECISION CASE CONTENT SAMPLE

Section 1, Executive Summary

1.1 Issue

- Consulting perspective: describe the consulting firm's perspective.
- Client perspective: describe the client or business perspective.

1.2 Anticipated Outcomes

- Describe the anticipated outcomes of this project.

1.3 Recommendation

- Describe the recommendations for going forward.

1.4 Justification

- Describe the justification utilized to support this project.

Section 2, Problem Definition

2.1 Problem Statement

- Describe the problem statement in clear and specific detail.

2.2 Alternatives Analysis

- Identify the alternatives considered for resolving the problem.
  - Do nothing.
  - Alternative 2.
  - Alternative 3.
  - Alternative *n*...
  - Recommended solution.
- Define the alternatives considered for resolving the problem.
  - Do nothing: describe this alternative.
  - Alternative 2: describe this alternative.
  - Alternative 3: describe this alternative.
  - Alternative *n*: describe this alternative.
  - Recommended solution: describe this recommendation.

2.3 Outstanding Issues

- Describe any outstanding issues to be addressed before this resolution could be successfully implemented.

Section 3, Project Overview

3.1 Project Description

Table A-3   Description of project

Description of Project
Describe the project.

3.2 Goals and Objectives

Table A-4   Project goals and objectives

Business Goal/Objective	Description
Goal/objective	Describe the goal/objective.
Goal/objective	Describe the goal/objective.
Goal/objective	Describe the goal/objective.
Goal/objective	Describe the goal/objective.
Goal/objective	Describe the goal/objective.

3.3 Performance Measures

Table A-5   Performance measures

Key Process/Services	Performance Measure
Process/service	Describe the performance measure(s).
Process/service	Describe the performance measure(s).
Process/service	Describe the performance measure(s).

3.4 Major Project Milestones

Table A-6   Project milestones

Milestones/Deliverables	Target Date
Identify milestones and key deliverables.	Set date.
Identify milestones and key deliverables.	Set date.
Identify milestones and key deliverables.	Set date.

3.5 Consulting Firm and Client Environments

Table A-7   Consulting Firm and Client Environments

Stakeholders/Customers	Description
Client	• Owner of the environment wherein the systems & business processes operate
Consulting Firm	• Owner of the tools & methodologies used to integrate & develop solutions within the context of the client's environment • Manager of the resources using the tools & methodologies within the context of the client's environment
Strategic Consultant/ Practice Area Manager	• Creator of the workflow, tools & methodologies, competencies, resource filtering & pipelining activities, and originator of the training curriculum • Manager of the workflow, tools & methodologies, competencies, resource filtering criteria & pipelining activities, and owner/manager of the training curriculum
Employee/User	• User of the ongoing workflow, tools & methodologies for application within the context of the client's environment to define the end-to-end integration & development of the multi-tiered, decision management business solution
LCD—Learning & Competency Division	• Manager of the ongoing training tools used in all training sessions
Trainer	• Delivery of the specified training curriculum
RMG—Resource Management Group	• Manager of the ongoing resource filtering & pipelining processes

Table A-8   Impacted Processes

Processes/Services	Description of Modifications/Automation
Impacted process	Describe impacts to process.
Impacted process	Describe impacts to process.
Impacted process	Describe impacts to process.

3.6 Project Assumptions

• Identify and describe project assumptions.

3.7 Project Constraints

• Identify and describe project constraints.

Section 4, Project Evaluation

4.1 Statutory Fulfillment

Table A-9   Statutory fulfillment

Mandates Related to Project	Statutory Citations	Penalties/Funding Losses
Identify and describe project mandates.		
Identify and describe project mandates.		
Identify and describe project mandates.		

4.2 Strategic Alignment

Table A-10   Strategic alignment

Plan	Goals/Objectives	Relationship to Project
Identify strategic plan.	Goal/objective	Describe relationship to project.
Identify strategic plan.	Goal/objective	Describe relationship to project.
Identify strategic plan.	Goal/objective	Describe relationship to project.

4.3 Financial Analysis

Table A-11   Financial analysis

Methods: Project Cost Estimates	Estimate Factors/Underlying Assumptions

• Est. Loaded Cost of Practice Manager salary
  o $TBD / yr
• Est. Loaded Cost of Resources
  o $TBD / yr
• Est. Cost of maintenance & support
  o $TBD / yr
	• List estimation factors/underlying assumptions.
	• List estimation factors/underlying assumptions.
	• List estimation factors/underlying assumptions.
	• List estimation factors/underlying assumptions.

Methods: Agency and Constituent Quantitative Project Benefits	**Estimate Factors/Underlying Assumptions**
• Describe project benefits. • Describe project benefits. • Describe project benefits.	• List estimation factors/underlying assumptions. • List estimation factors/underlying assumptions. • List estimation factors/underlying assumptions.

4.4 Initial Risk Consideration

Table A.12   Initial risk consideration

Risk	Rating*
Identify risk.	Rate from 1-5.
Identify risk.	Rate from 1-5.
Identify risk.	Rate from 1-5.

*The rating scale is a 1 to 5 rating, with 1 being high risk and 5 being optimal low risk.

Section 5, Project Selection

5.1 Methodology

- Describe the methodology to be used.

5.2 Results

- Describe the target results.

5.3 Project Selection Criteria

The criteria for project selection are based on the following weighted factors:

- SF, Statutory Fulfillment: Does this project align with commonly accepted US fair business practices and company policy?
- SA, Strategic Alignment: How well does this project align with business strategic plans?
- FA, Financial Analysis—Consulting Firm/Client: Does the cost benefit analysis support the project outcomes despite any perceived initial risks?

Table A.13   Summary of project evaluation factors

Summary: All Project Evaluation Factors			
Line	Factor	Maximum Rating Possible	Rating
SF	Statutory Fulfillment	35	33
SA	Strategic Alignment	45	43
FA	Financial Analysis—Consulting Firm/Client	60	57
RC	Initial Risk Consideration	45	34.5
AA	Alternatives Analysis	30	28
	Total, All Project Factors	215	195.5

- RC, Initial Risk Consideration: What are the initial perceived risks and weighting criteria for consideration?
- AA, Alternatives Analysis: What other resolution options have been presented, and how does this solution compare to these other options?

Table A.14 Summary of cost-benefit analysis

Line	Measure	Year 1	Year 2	Year 3	Total
RA1	Agency Benefits (Cash Inflow)	$	$	$	$
RA2	Ongoing Costs (Cash Outflow)	$	$	$	$
RA3	Cost-Benefit Variance (Net Cash Flow)	$	$	$	$
RA4	Cumulative Net Benefits (Cumulative Net Cash Flow)	$	$	$	$
RA7	Breakeven Point (Years 1 to 10)			Profit is approx....? X cost	

5.4 Financial Assumptions

These assumptions were used to generate the estimates for this business case:

- Financial assumption 1.
- Financial assumption 2.
- Financial assumption 3.
- Financial assumption n…

FUTURE STATE DEFINITION DOCUMENT CONTENT SAMPLE

Project Overview

- Discuss project overview here.
- Include high-level problem statement, project goals, and objectives.

Business Problem Statement

- Describe the business problem.

Business Process Changes

The following business processes will be changed during this project:

- List business processes.

The following business processes will be added by this project:

- List business processes.

System/Application Changes

The following systems and/or applications will be changed during this project:

- List systems/applications.

The following systems and/or applications will be added by this project:

- List systems/applications.

Assumptions/Constraints

- List assumptions/constraints.

Risks

- List risks.

Related Documents

- Current state document name
- Business process models name
- High-level requirements name
- Gap analyses and assessment name
- Change and implementation plan name
- Existing system architecture document name
- Existing technical design document name

Business Process Flows

- Business process name

Future State Process Flow

- Insert high-level diagrams or process descriptions, highlighting changes in red or yellow.

HIGH-LEVEL REQUIREMENTS DOCUMENT CONTENT SAMPLE

Table A.15 Sample high-level requirements

Business Requirement Description	Priority **M:** Must Have **N:** Need to Have **L:** Like to Have
Functional Requirements	
Input and Output Requirements	
The system or app has to take Data X and process it into information for System or App Z.	
Nonfunctional Requirements	
Security Requirements	
The system or app has to meet standard security protocol. List any potential questionable areas of concern.	
Portability Requirements	
The system or app has to be available on or off the network.	
Operational Requirements	
The system or app has to be used by Department X to manage stored data for X-Y-Z processes.	
Technical Requirements	
Architectural Requirements	
The system or app has to interact with X-Y-Z systems and environment to function.	

IMPLEMENTATION PLAN CONTENT SAMPLE

Introduction

Intended Audience

The intended audience for this document is...

How to Use This Document

It is intended that this document will serve as a point of reference and provide...

Assumptions

- Assumption 1
- Assumption 2

Constraints

- Constraint 1
- Constraint 2

Inform

Vision Statement

- Vision Statement

Project Contacts

Project Contacts:

1. Main Point of Contact
   - Phone
   - E-mail
   - SkypeID or other instant messaging (IM) account details
2. Project Website URL
   Site contents specifically include:
   - Vision Statement
   - Point of Contact
   - Escalation Procedure
   - Project Communiqués
   - Schedules
   - Online Training Resources
   - FAQ's about the new processes

Communication Plan

Table A.16 Sample communication matrix

Communication Type	Communication Purpose	Delivered By	Audience	Communication Format	Frequency
Identify the general descriptive title of the communication. See examples below.	Describe the purpose of the communication.	Who on the team is responsible for delivering the communication?	Who will be receiving the communication?	What format type is the communication delivered in? (There may be more than one type.) Use the Project Documentation checklist to identify if a specific template should be used.	How frequently is this type of communication required? List any specific days/times if known.
Examples:					
Status Updates	Inform status of project activities.	Project Team	Project Manager	E-mail, Use the Weekly Status Report Template	Weekly, Friday, 12:00 P.M.
Review	Discuss current progress and set weekly goals.	Project Manager	Project Team	Meeting	Weekly, Monday, 9:00 A.M.
Status Reports	Inform status of project activities.	Project Manager	Client Project Manager, Project Sponsors	E-mail, Report	Weekly, Monday, 12:00 P.M.
In-Process Reviews (IPRs)	Inform status of project activities, provide updates to work plan, and provide performance reports.	Project Manager	Steering Committee	PowerPoint presentation, Report	Monthly, First Tuesday of the month, 10:00 A.M.
Steering Committee Meetings	Discuss issues and changes affecting project outcomes.	Project Manager and selected Team Members	All	PowerPoint presentation, Report	Semi-Monthly, Second and Fourth Tuesday, 10:00 A.M.
Quality Review(s)	Provide objective review of projects to ensure adherence to policies, processes, standards, and plans	QA Mgr	Project Manager	Report, Meeting, 1-on-1	Quarterly

Involving The Stakeholders and Teams

Phase I

Planning for the preliminary meetings and information sessions.

- Goal

    To involve stakeholders and achieve a level of buy-in that will support the activities and transition of the project from a leadership perspective. (Workshops within this session are appropriate, if applicable.)

- Audience

    Program managers, project managers, and team leads responsible for ensuring the buy-in, adoption, and ongoing compliance of their functional and project teams.

- Invited Attendees

    The following people will be invited to attend these initial rounds of training to support early adoption and evaluation of the training material. This will ensure that once sessions are run with the team members, the material is complete, easily digestible, and presented in a manner that renders it readily acceptable to the audience and participants.

- Location
    o TBD
- Equipment
    o List any equipment, such as projectors, laptops, or project give-away items for this session.
- Content
    o Information for session
    o Timeline/Project schedule
- Expected Participation

    Participants will be asked to contribute to the discussions, review the training materials and content, and make recommendations for improvements to the materials and content prior to the training sessions with other groups and team members.

- Session Task

Identify people within this group who seem obstinate or against the change, as well as those with additional questions, and seek to spend time with them in small groups or as individuals.

Phase II

Planning for the secondary set of meetings and information sessions.

Transitioning to the New Processes/Systems

Goal

To involve mainstream acceptance and achieve a base level of buy-in that will support the activities and transition of the project. (Workshops within this session are appropriate, if applicable.)

Training

Training Package

Each training session will utilize elements and delivery mechanisms that appeal to multiple learning styles including tactile, auditory, and visual. As a continuation of this training, the sessions will provide packages for each participant that includes PowerPoint or other dynamic presentations, round table discussions, hands-on exercises, handouts, and job aids.

Training Plan

- Invited Attendees

  The invited attendees for these sessions include...
- Location

  The training facility is to be...
- Equipment
  - List any special equipment and access requirements.
- Content and Scheduling
  - List schedules and training.
- Session Task

  Identify people within this group who seem obstinate or against the change, as well as those with additional questions, and seek to spend time with them in small groups.

Observing and Monitoring Implementation Progress

- Identify and log key metrics and milestones for success and progress during the development and implementation of a new system.

Ownership, Responsibility and Accountability

- Identify and log key owners, responsible and accountable groups for providing ongoing support, and controlling changes to the new system/process after implementation of a new system. **TIP**: Provide functional role vs. naming a specific individual as this typically changes less often and is associated to the role, not the person.

Table A.17 Owner matrix

Functional Role	Business Unit	Held By	Contact Info	Responsible	Accountable	Contributes	Informed

RESPONDING TO REQUESTS FOR INFORMATION

Project Communication Policy

The following list represents the basic project communication policy for managing communications with the various teams.

1. Main Contact Person:
2. Response times. The standard response times will be as follows:
   - o Acknowledgement—
   - o Provision of the requested information—
   - o Closure of request—
3. Response formats: Response formats will be the same as the incoming formats, with follow-up via e-mail to confirm details or report requested information.

Automatic Response E-mails

Automatic response e-mails [will/will not] be utilized for this initiative.

Project E-mail Account

A generic, open project e-mail account for people to submit general comments and concerns to the project team [will/will not] be utilized for this initiative.

Sustaining the Changes

Human Resources

- Recruitment strategies and systems, if applicable
- Ongoing training
- New resource orientation, if applicable

Management Systems

- How do management systems reflect the new culture?

Physical Structure

- Identify new physical requirements for maintenance of the new system (e.g., increased workspace).
- Ongoing Issue Management
- Ongoing Asset Management

References to Other Documents

- Identify other documents that were used as reference materials for this one

RASCI MATRIX SAMPLE

Table A.18   Sample RASCI matrix

Name	Position	R	A	S	C	I
Sally Smith	Project Manager		X			
Antonio Johnson	Testing SME				X	
John Doe	Interface SME				X	
Jane Doe	Resource Center			X		
Barbara Davis	Business Analyst Team Lead	X				
Raj Smith	Forecasting/Bidding				X	
Vic Tran	Call Center CSR Mgmt		X			
Skippy Jackson	Call Center QA				X	
Allie Melon	Call Center IT					X

REQUIREMENTS RISK ASSESSMENT DOCUMENT CONTENT SAMPLE

Client Name

Project Name

Table A.19   Risk assessment document details

Document Title:	Requirements Risk Assessment	File Name:	
Prepared by:		Create Date:	
Status:	Version	Status Date:	
Test ID:		Due Date:	

Impact Table

Table A.20   Impact definitions

	Impact
High	• Will have severe impact on the delivery schedule, environment, number of known defects, testability break and fix volume, and service level agreements of delivered product, and could result in scrapping application, lost return on investment, and greater than 25% application downtime.
Moderate	• Will have moderate impact on the delivery schedule, environment, number of known defects, testability break and fix volume, and service level agreements of delivered product, and could result in lost return on investment and 10 to 25% application downtime.
Low	• Will have low impact on the delivery schedule, environment, number of known defects, testability break and fix volume, and service level agreements of delivered product, and could result in minimal return on investment loss and 0 to 10% application downtime.

Probability Legend

Table A.21   Probability of occurrence

Probability of Occurrence	
High	70–100% chance of occurrence
Moderate	30–70% chance of occurrence
Low	0–30% chance of occurrence

Test Priority Legend

Table A.22 Testing priority legend

Testing Priority	
1	• High probability of occurrence + High impact
2	• Moderate probability of occurrence + High impact • High probability of occurrence + Moderate impact • Low probability of occurrence + High impact
3	• Moderate probability of occurrence + Moderate impact • Low probability of occurrence + Moderate impact
4	• Moderate probability of occurrence + Low impact
5	• Low probability of occurrence + Low impact

1. Requirement:
   1.1. Risk Event Table:

Table A.23 Risk event

Risk Event/User Scenario	Probability	Impact	Risk Strategy

   1.2. Requirement Test Priority:

Table A.24 Testing priority

Testing Priority
assigned value

INDEX